TALES FROM T
TILLERMAN

TALES FROM THE TILLERMAN

A Life-long Love Affair with Britain's Waterways

Steve Haywood

ADLARD COLES

LONDON • OXFORD • NEW YORK • NEW DELHI • SYDNEY

Thanks to my old friend Miles Hedley whose care and attention correcting the first draft of my books propagates the fallacy that I can actually write, let alone spell.

And to my grandfather Arthur Hoden without whom none of this would have been possible…

ADLARD COLES
Bloomsbury Publishing Plc
50 Bedford Square, London, WC1B 3DP, UK
29 Earlsfort Terrace, Dublin 2, Ireland

BLOOMSBURY, ADLARD COLES and the Adlard Coles logo are trademarks of Bloomsbury Publishing Plc

First published 2021

A catalogue record for this book is available from the British Library

Library of Congress Cataloguing-in-Publication data has been applied for

ISBN: PB: 978-1-4729-7700-7; ePub: 978-1-4729-7701-4; ePDF: 978-1-4729-7698-7

2 4 6 8 10 9 7 5 3 1

Typeset by Deanta Global Publishing Services, Chennai, India
Printed and bound in Great Britain by CPI Group (UK) Ltd., Croydon, CR0 4YY

MIX
Paper from
responsible sources
FSC® C020471

To find out more about our authors and books visit www.bloomsbury.com and sign up for our newsletters

CONTENTS

Prologue

At my age, you never know when it's all going to end. But I certainly know when it all began: in Banbury, the very afternoon we set off on what turned out to be a four-year trip travelling about on our 57ft (17.4m) narrowboat *Justice*, a trip we'd promised ourselves we'd do someday when work allowed. My wife Em went off to do some last-minute errands in the shopping centre and I was left the job of filling up our water tank. I jammed the end of the hose into the water inlet on the boat and turned the tap on fully while I pottered around doing a few other jobs. It was OK for a while but then suddenly the hose broke loose under the pressure. It went flying into the air like a rocket before hitting the ground, snaking about, spraying water everywhere.

I dodged to get out of the way but I must have pulled something. An agonising jolt of pain shot up my leg and I collapsed on the towpath in excruciating agony. It wasn't a good way to start an expedition like this, but hey, what could we do? We'd only just given up our home. We'd rented it out to tenants. We'd got nowhere else to go.

Life can be a bitch sometimes.

Actually, it can be a bitch quite a lot of the time.

I just had to grit my teeth and get on with it.

I

The Ribble Link: gateway to the Lancaster Canal

It wasn't until Harry, the lock keeper, opened the gates and the flow of the river hit us, exploding against our bows with the force of a mortar shell, that I understood why people are so terrified of this stretch of water.

The boat immediately lifted and pitched to one side, stopping dead for a moment in the surge. Then the flow of the river swept the boat towards one bank and almost immediately afterwards spun it awkwardly towards the other until it stopped again, trembling against the current. Now it was trapped, going nowhere. I wound up the speed wheel, but to no effect. I wound it up more with added urgency, increasing the engine revs until the exhaust pipe in the roof was discharging a thick plume of smoke as black as the chimney of a Victorian factory. Yet still the boat made no progress against the tide, which was ripping down the River Douglas at a terrifying rate. It was a high tide, the very highest on which they'll let a boat out, we learned later. Cascading down with it were clusters of sodden wood: branches, trunks of trees and discarded timber, known in these parts as 'crocodiles'. Any one of these could jam our propeller, stopping it dead in its tracks and leaving us without any means of steering.

The most important thing now was to stay calm and in the centre of the river. If we touched the muddy bank, however briefly, it would throw us off course and we'd lose control completely.

We might spin around until we dammed the narrow tributary and were swamped by the oncoming water. Or we might be flushed backwards, past the lock mouth we'd just exited, where we could encounter shallows. Either way, it would end in tears.

I'd only felt as frightened as this once before on a boat. It was when I was with a friend on his Dutch sailing barge and we were coming out of the lock at Vlissingen in the Netherlands to cross the wide estuary of the Western Scheldt, the main shipping route from the North Sea to Antwerp. The weather had started getting blowy the previous night and by the morning it had developed into a raging gale. We should never have gone out in those conditions. My boating expertise had been acquired exclusively on the meandering byways of England's placid canals. My friend hadn't even got that much experience. He'd only recently bought the barge, his first boat, and he'd conscripted me as crew to help him take it to London, where he was planning to live on it.

Once clear of the lock and in open water the wind intensified and the waves became more powerful. The first we hit picked the boat up 5–6ft (1.5–1.8m) and dropped it in a crashing welter of spray that I was convinced would overwhelm us. I remember thinking, ridiculously, that at least we were close to the shore and that it wouldn't take a lifeboat long to get to us. I was on the tiller. It was one of those tillers you get on traditional Dutch barges: a huge block of wood operated through pulleys by ropes that you have to wind around your hands to secure. It's a cumbersome arrangement and I was unfamiliar with it. Every movement of the boat stretched the ropes taut until they gouged into my flesh, leaving raw weals across my fingers. Each wave we hit wrenched my shoulders as if to pull my arms from their sockets. I wasn't confident I could handle the boat with this set-up. It was virtually flat-bottomed and I couldn't see how I could keep it upright in these conditions. Soon it began rolling as well as pitching, its gunnels slicing through the water on the port side, flooding the deck, and then lurching over to starboard to do the same, its mast like some huge metronome oscillating across the dark and threatening sky...

But that was then and this was now.

Then, the storm had blown my friend and me to calmer waters, and the rest of our trip was uneventful – fodder for one of those tales old salts tell, peppered with what-ifs and might-have-beens. Now, however, on a narrowboat on the River Douglas fighting against the tide to get to the River Ribble, Em and I couldn't depend on anything except our own experience to get us out of trouble. We were alone, reliant on nothing and no one but ourselves. I handed the tiller to her and disappeared below deck into the engine room. There, against the furious and deafening roar of our vintage three-cylinder Lister, I managed to reconfigure the controls of the boat in order to tease more power out of the throttle. After a heart-stopping interval that seemed an hour long, a jubilant shout from Em outside seemed to be a sign I'd been successful and with some relief I hurried back on deck.

The boat was moving forwards more confidently now, not fast, but at least faster than before. It wasn't hard to see why. The engine was burning much cleaner and the black smoke from the exhaust had all but disappeared. It seemed that by revving up the engine I'd effectively de-coked its cylinders. The crud this had displaced was scattered across the top of the boat: flakes of soft soot and oily fragments of carbon, like the residue from a greasy volcanic beach. A great deal of the discharge seemed to have found its way on to Em's face, where it looked as if she'd closed her eyes and started experimenting with mascara. My own face wasn't much better. I was like a Celtic warrior decorated by someone with double vision.

Once we logged that the immediate danger was past we broke down in a fit of the giggles. Before long, we were laughing uncontrollably in a way that was perhaps a tad too hysterical to be normal. With the benefit of hindsight, I can see what made us act like that. It was relief – pure, unadulterated relief. A release from the tension we'd both been feeling since leaving Tarleton Lock. The fact is, there'd been an ugly moment or two when we'd both been convinced that the boat was going to sink and take us down with it.

The only way to get to the Lancaster Canal without going around the coast is to take this route along the River Douglas and on to the River Ribble, but the hazardous journey this involves is the main reason narrowboaters are so reluctant to explore what is the very northernmost outpost of England's canal system, a waterway that stretches virtually up to the Lake District. Crossing the 'Ribble Link', as it's known, is not like cruising the placid waterways of the Midlands, the bits of the system you see in innumerable celebrity TV programmes; and it's certainly not the sort of waterway you can navigate after a ten-minute seminar from a boatyard at the start of a family holiday. As you battle down the Douglas punching the tide, the force of it mercifully abates as the river widens, until at length it joins the estuary of the Ribble, which at this stage is so close to the Irish Sea, it *is* the Irish Sea. The waters here broaden spectacularly into one huge and shimmering expanse of water so wide that even in clear weather you can hardly make out the far bank. The winds become more forceful, too, the waves increase in size and the sky seems to expand suddenly as if it's just exploded above the world. At this point you have to round a beacon, there to warn you that you're getting close to dangerous shallows which could ground you. So imbued in the consciousness of ocean-going sailors and inland skippers alike is this beacon – the Astland Lamp – that it has become notorious in a way that scarcely seems warranted given that it's only a frail-looking wooden stanchion sunk into the bed of the river with a ladder propped up to it and a few brackets to buttress it against the weather.

Even so, overhyped or not, we'd been warned not to be tempted to cut the corner on the wrong side of it, since boats doing this invariably get into the sort of difficulties that entail calling out lifeboats. We'd followed another boat out of the lock at Tarleton, a river cruiser with a powerful engine towing a narrowboat similar to ours, whose crew didn't trust its own engine to do the trip. The cruiser captain must have been familiar with the waters because as soon as he reached the Astland Lamp, he did precisely what we'd been told not to do and headed straight over the shallows, the narrowboat still in tow. We watched puzzled as both disappeared from view, but we resisted any attempt to tag along behind, dutifully following the advice we'd been given and taking a much longer route round.

Once past the Astland Lamp, heading inland towards Preston, there's a danger in thinking the worst is behind you. But we didn't relax. We knew one of the biggest challenges of the trip lay ahead as we prepared to turn into the concealed entrance to Savick Brook, which leads directly to the Lancaster Canal. 'Brook' is the wrong word altogether to describe this cutting, which was only opened in 2007. 'Ditch' is a much better one. Or maybe even 'drain'. It is muddy and narrow and overgrown with vegetation on both sides of its high, twisting banks, a channel so constricted that reeds sweep along both sides of your hull as you pass with the whisper of some water nymph threatening to embrace you and drag you down to the bed of the channel itself. You can easily miss the turning into Savick Brook from the Ribble. It's barely visible from the river, masked by tree cover. We'd certainly have missed it except that the cruiser we'd followed out of Tarleton now reappeared. It had dropped off the boat it was towing and was now accelerating and reversing across the width of the river, using its bow as a finger to point at the featureless bank where our route lay.

Em and I had travelled to the Ribble Link by way of the Leeds and Liverpool Canal, which crosses the Pennines, and which, at 127 miles (204km), is Britain's longest artificial waterway. We'd been travelling for a couple of years. At first, we'd pottered down the River Thames to London, and afterwards we had headed north along the Grand Union Canal to Birmingham. From there, we'd made our way into Shropshire, detouring over Christmas to Wales and the charming Welsh town of Llangollen, where the crashing winter waters of the River Dee are a soundtrack to the surrounding hills. It wasn't unfamiliar territory for us. We'd been messing about on narrowboats for more than 40 years, and we'd travelled to these parts of the canal system more than once. This time, though, we weren't just holidaying around those better-known pretty bits of the canal network that people recognise from the telly. Now we were actually living on our boat *Justice*. We were on an extended journey around some of the outlying and newly opened sections of the system that we hadn't visited before, either because they were too far away and we'd not had time, or because they had been derelict and had only recently been restored. Some were brand-new canals. Others, like the Ribble Link, were connecting sections, which allowed you to get to waterways that had previously been inaccessible.

We could do this because we'd only recently retired. We'd rented out the house in London for a year-long trip we'd always intended to make at some stage in our lives. Except that the planned year became two, and two somehow become three. Eventually, it was to be four years before we – and our cat Kit, who we'd taken along with us – got back home.

There are almost 3,000 miles (4,828km) of navigable canals and rivers in Britain, and although over the decades we'd had various boats in which we'd explored most of this system, we'd only ever travelled piecemeal, in disjointed sections, and never as a continuous journey with unlimited time at our disposal. Canals themselves might not have been a novelty to us, but to be away without the constant, niggling worry that we had to be back at work in a couple of weeks most certainly was.

The first time we travelled the Leeds and Liverpool Canal was in the early 1980s in the first narrowboat we ever owned, called *Pelikas* – an idiosyncratic home-built craft in which we studied for our 'O-levels' in boating. We'd had it for five or six years by that time, cruising it around the Midlands canals, so of course by then we thought we knew everything there was to know about inland waterways. We were at that stage when we were on the lookout for something a bit different. Thinking we might save time and have a bit of an adventure along the way, we decided to go north, not by the easier and slower canals, but via a much faster route down the River Trent from Nottingham, where we could rejoin the canal system at Keadby in Lincolnshire, just upriver from the Humber, and make our way to Leeds before crossing the Pennines.

The River Trent wasn't a normal haunt of narrowboats at this time. The river was still heavily industrialised and huge barges still plied their trade carrying steel and grain to and from Hull and the North Sea. They weren't best pleased at tin cans like ours getting in their way. They tended to pretend you weren't there and continue their course regardless, so you had to go scuttling to the bank to avoid them. The river itself is dangerous for any small craft, especially after rain when water levels can rise perilously and there's flooding, fierce currents and savage tides. Even so, our friend Keith from the boatyard where we moored, who'd done the trip himself a couple of years before, threatened not to talk to us if we bottled out. 'You won't exactly enjoy doing it,' added John, another friend from the yard, a former working boatman, 'but afterwards you'll be pleased you did...'

Strictly speaking, I suppose he was right: ultimately, we *were* pleased, though that's not to say that there weren't points as things began to go pear-shaped that we bitterly regretted it. At times like that you couldn't call it pleasure cruising because there wasn't a lot of pleasure in it.

That year was a particularly hot summer, with so many weeks of relentless sunshine that eventually there was a drought, with hosepipe bans and nutty government ministers advising us to take baths together to save water. Whatever anxieties we harboured about the river vanished as soon as we saw it. Rather than the torrential waters we'd been led to expect, it had turned into a grubby mudflat, and what little water was flowing along it was reduced to an apologetic trickle. It wasn't at all what we'd anticipated. We'd imagined a lion and found a pussycat. It was so sluggish and unthreatening that just beyond Radcliffe-on-Trent where the riverbank towers above the water's edge, it was so unbearably hot that one sweltering Sunday afternoon we dropped anchor and swam from the boat, diving off the roof while a throng of waterskiers towed by a high-powered dinghy played chicken around our hull, seeing how close they dared get to it.

It was idyllic and all very relaxed. Even when we went through Cromwell Lock on to the tidal section of the river – the section we'd most dreaded, the section we'd been most-warned about – it seemed sedate and benign. I was on the tiller and Em volunteered to go down below to fetch beer. It was about 8.30 pm. Conditions were perfect, pale sunshine still glazing the sky and the merest hint of a cooling breeze in the air. I was steering a course to the outside of mid-channel on a gentle, gradual bend to nowhere when...

Suddenly, as some sort of salutation to the calm evening, the boat decided to take to the air. Or at least that's the way it seemed to us. The bow rose alarmingly skywards as if it was about to fly. The stern followed, and before I could react on the tiller we slewed across the river. Em screamed and clutched our deck railings. Inside the cabin there was the sickening sound of cupboards slamming open and plates and glasses crashing to the floor. And then, just as unexpectedly, we levelled off and stopped dead. We were in the middle of the river. The engine was still running as it had been before, except that now it wasn't taking us anywhere. Its uselessness was a mockery. I turned it off and an eerie silence descended as we took stock of the situation. As far as we could make out, we were in the middle of nowhere, trapped between high riverbanks and flat fields that stretched away as far as the eye could see. The quietness enveloping us was painful. In just the space of a moment, it seemed, we'd been extracted from the water, lifted, tilted and corkscrewed to somehow become inextricably a part of the riverbed.

What was clear from the outset was that we were well and truly stuck and that nothing we could do was going to get us out of this situation. Nevertheless, we went through the motions. We pushed on our bargepole until we were in danger of giving ourselves hernias, then we dropped anchor and pulled against that until our backs seized up with the strain of it. Finally, we tried rocking the boat from side to side, which can sometimes be useful in loosening the hull from the suction on the bottom. Not this time, though. All this effort didn't shift the boat an inch. An hour later, dark now, we retired to bed exhausted.

The following day the enormity of our predicament became clear. In those days, the canals were shallower than now and you got used to getting grounded. But there are groundings and groundings. This was on a different scale to anything we'd experienced before. We'd travelled on a high tide.

The next day, after it dropped, it was apparent that we weren't so much grounded as dry-docked. Our poor boat was perched like a beached whale on a mud spit about 80–90ft (24–27m) long, its propeller totally clear of the water. You didn't need to be a forensics expert to work out what had happened: a great gouge across the spit told its own story. With so little water in the river, we'd run aground on a submerged island that was marked clearly on charts, so we'd have known about if only we'd not been such a couple of lamebrains that we'd gone on to the river without one.

We came to know Normanton Island intimately. How could we not? After all, we were quite attached to the place. Every morning, we'd clamber off the boat and take a constitutional along its shoreline. When you get bored, it's astonishing what you'll revert to in order to relieve the tedium. I could lose track of time examining river pebbles, and a freshwater mussel could hold me transfixed for hours. In the afternoons, when the river was at its lowest, we'd pass the time shovelling under the boat in the vain hope that we could somehow dig ourselves off the island. What else could we do? This was before the age of mobile phones. We simply had to be patient and wait to be rescued. It was just a shame I hadn't got any brushes with me or I could have blacked the hull.

We tried to make the best of things but after a few days we were going round the bend. One afternoon, in frustration, I tentatively waded out towards the nearest bank to see if it was possible to reach it. The water was lapping at my hips, pulling my legs from under me, before I realised the danger I was in. The Trent might have been reduced to a trickle compared to its normal flow, but even at this rate, there was enough water coming down to have flushed me to the North Sea in an hour.

'Well, at least it's not raining,' Em said brightly at one point, in an attempt to cheer me up.

'If it were raining we wouldn't be stuck here,' I said dryly.

At times like this you realise who your friends are. A single narrowboat passed while we were there, but it kept its distance, its skipper shouting something to us that we couldn't hear. He might have been encouraging us to keep our spirits up. On the other hand, he might have been telling us what a pair of wazzocks we were to get ourselves into this mess. Small cruisers were better for keeping up morale. We only saw a couple of them but both waved to us in an encouraging way. Bigger boats just ignored us. One large seagoing cruiser with decks as high as a block of flats passed us – a boat that would have been more at home in Cannes than Keadby – giving us such a wide berth it was in danger of coming to grief on the opposite bank. The regular commercial barges were even worse. They treated us like a warning buoy. Once they'd spotted us, they swung to the opposite side of the river with such resolve it looked as if they were intending to take to the roads.

Eventually, a small rowing boat with an outboard engine – a craft so flimsy it shouldn't have been on the river at all – got close enough to allow us to wade across and get on board; and – bless him – the skipper took us down to nearby Torksey and brought us back with a dinghy that the lock keeper lent us. Now, by tying together every rope we had we could attach a line to the nearest shore and haul ourselves to dry land. From there, we were able to walk the 3 miles (4.8km) or so across the fields to the village of South Clifton, where there was a small shop where we could buy food. Water was more problematic. We were down to our last couple of kettlefuls when we found a farm on the outskirts of the village where the owner let us fill a container we kept on the boat for just such an emergency. It was big enough to keep us going for two or three days but it weighed a ton. Struggling back up the riverbank with it in the heat of the day, we heard someone shouting to us. At first, we couldn't identify where the voice was coming from; it seemed to be the voice of the river itself. Finally, once we'd located it, it turned out to be emanating from a hidden cleft in the bank where a weather-beaten bloke in a rowing skiff had spotted us and pulled up to offer us a lift. He'd seen the beached boat and guessed it was ours.

We clambered on board, but only after we'd settled down on a scaffolding plank that served as a seat did we become aware that the bilge of the boat was seething with eels, squirming around in a way that made it seem as if the bottom was alive. It turned out we'd been picked up by a professional eel fisherman who worked this length of the river to supply Billingsgate in London. I was grateful for the kindness he showed us that day, but more grateful yet that as a result of it I had the opportunity to meet and talk to someone who must surely have been one of the last, if not *the* last, eel-fishers on the Trent, an occupation that must have stretched back at least to the 12th century when, if I remember my history right, King Henry I died after eating too many of them.

When we got back to our boat, the tide was up again. He helped us unload our water before spending ten minutes or so with a pole prodding around the spit on which we were trapped. 'Ay,' he purred in an odd accent with a Dutch overtone that I couldn't place. 'It'll make a good netting place when you've gone.'

This was reassuring because as far as I could see, this was the one and only positive thing that could be said about the position we were in. The days were passing and along with them our holiday. An exploratory visit by a rescue tug that had been alerted to our situation by the Torksey lock keeper had confirmed our worst fears: this was going to be as much a matter of waiting as anything. Yet successively higher tides showed no signs of liberating us, and one attempt to haul us off almost killed us when a weld on a deck cleat, to which the tug had tied a tow rope, ruptured under the strain and exploded in our direction with the sound and speed of a bullet.

Eventually another rescue date was set but no one, least of all us, was hopeful. 'We'll try again with a second tug next time but if we can't budge you then it won't be worth trying again until we've had some serious rain,' said the skipper.

'And what do you reckon the chances are of that?' I asked.

'I reckon booking this late you might be able to get yourself a good deal on a week's package to Spain.'

The morning of the rescue attempt dawned damp and unpleasant, a seeping mist rising from the river in clouds of claggy vapour. We'd been up since before dawn and had already hauled ourselves across the river in the skiff and walked in darkness to South Clifton and back, where we'd had to meet an insurance assessor; our insurance company had insisted on his presence upon realising that getting us off the mudbank could cause more damage to the boat than just a fractured cleat. At a little after 5am, a couple of rescue tugs appeared around the bend in the river, fracturing the silence of the sunrise with their noisy engines and sending flocks of mallards and Canada geese soaring skywards.

At this point – when Em and I were feeling most tense about what was about to happen, dogged by lack of sleep from our early start, our stomachs churning in turmoil and our nerves as taut as bow strings – at this precise moment, because don't these things always happen at these sorts of moments, Em chose to fall in. Well, strictly speaking she didn't *choose* to fall in, but she fell in all the same, and with such graceful style, stepping off the boat into mid-air with such a nonchalant lack of concern it was almost as if she'd purposely intended to reduce the moment to farce.

When she'd picked herself up out of the river and I'd picked myself up off the deck where I'd collapsed in laughter, the crew of the rescue boats – who I don't believe had noticed a thing – began to reverse cautiously towards us, testing their own depth every 6in (15cm) or so. Eventually they moved close enough to girth us with a couple of enormous ropes the thickness of your wrist. Then they engaged the tugs' powerful engines and pulled with much ostentatious surging and thrashing of water.

Pelikas remained unimpressed with the whole display. Frankly, if she'd been a donkey on Blackpool beach she couldn't have been more obstinate about not moving. The rescue tugs edged even closer until the three boats were almost touching. The crews stood on the decks watching the water. They were waiting. Waiting for the morning tide to rise to its highest. Waiting for just that right moment to attempt to pull us for a second time. Suddenly, without warning, the tug engines exploded into life again with a mighty roar, straining against the ropes encircling us until they began to quiver. Yet still our boat held firm. Apart from the occasional, alarming groan from its welds it seemed completely disinterested in all the effort being expended on its behalf.

Finally, with the threat of a week in Marbella looming terrifyingly close, the rescue tugs prepared for what we were told would be their final attempt. The skippers adjusted position slightly towards the near bank and opened their engines again, this time more forcibly than they'd done before, water churning fiercely from their propellers, black smoke pluming from their exhausts. For a moment *Pelikas* remained stubbornly rigid, but then she started shuddering like a reed in a stream. It was as if she was weighing the pros and cons of moving. At last, abruptly, as if she had given up the struggle, she vibrated, jarred and then slipped back into the water again with all the ease of an ocean liner at its launch.

2

The Lancaster Canal

White-water, adventure-type narrowboating is all well and good, but you'd be wrong to think that it's typical of cruising the English waterways. That's a far more sedate affair that usually involves pottering through the undulating Midland shires for hours on end at speeds so slow a five-year-old could walk faster. It's about experiencing the gradually changing topography of Britain, the diminutive differences of scenery that the placid pace allows you to gaze upon and ponder. The way plants in the hedgerows alter, for instance; the way the patterns of fields change; the way the terrain transforms before your eyes – vista melting into vista – until, with something of a shock, you realise that the whole geography of the landscape has changed without you noticing.

And the wondrous thing is that if you travel in the opposite direction, the same thing happens, but it occurs so differently that what you see is hardly recognisable as the same canal. It's not just that the perspective changes, it's that the canal – magically – transforms entirely. The same happens if you cruise it in different seasons. In that green explosion that is spring, for instance, when the countryside seems peppered with buds. Or in the lushness of high summer when the greens darken, or in misty autumn when the countryside yellows, or in winter when the boughs of trees silhouette the horizon like black lace and, on frosty mornings, the whole world seems to have crystallised, each damp twig on every hedge and tree recast as a shard of ice. But it's not only the seasons that transform England. England can change just as radically over the period of a month, or a day, or even an hour, depending on the configuration of a cloud, the strength of the sun or the direction of the wind.

It's peculiar, this country of ours, where, within a short time and a trifling distance, things can alter so fundamentally. And it's not just the topography. Not just the flora and fauna or the weather. The whole culture can transform in the blink of an eye: the way people speak, the accents they use, the manner in which they build their houses, the beer they drink in their pubs. Despite the shrinking world that is becoming increasingly homogenous, Britain is still a tightly woven tapestry of difference; and the canals let us explore the warps and weaves of the patterning. Narrowboats give you the means to do this. They take you to places you'd never visit otherwise, by routes that are unique. They let you go on long country walks without the inconvenient necessity of actually having to walk. But it's the painstakingly unhurried speed at which you are compelled to travel that makes them so distinctive, that delightfully slow pace which forces you to focus on the moment. The official speed limit on Britain's canals is 4mph, a bit over 6km/h. Most of the time though, if you're travelling at that lick, you're going too fast and increasing your engine speed won't allow you to go any faster. That's because of the physics of your propeller. The more you increase your engine revs, the more it has to draw water from the canal to feed it, but on shallow canals there just isn't enough water, and this acts as a brake to slow you down. Your stern drops in the water. Your propeller begins to drag through the mud. Sometimes it seems as if what happens is self-regulatory, as if narrowboats were preordained to travel this pace because it's the pace at which the human psyche can accommodate movement, the pace at which it can absorb a barely changing panoply of detail, configuring what is a series of almost fixed images into the experience of motion. It's like a film in which each still frame passing through a projector creates the sense of movement. On a canal boat though, this isn't a series of images flickering on a screen: it's reality unfolding before you in a perfect continuum of time and space.

After the challenges we'd had to face crossing the Ribble Link, Em and I couldn't wait to get away from rivers and back to something more restful. Unfortunately, to get to the Lancaster Canal you have to navigate Savick Brook. This tributary of the Ribble – as its name suggests – is essentially a ditch, no wider than a stream, which has been excavated and widened for boats in order to connect the rest of the waterway network to the once-isolated Lancaster Canal. But it is far from restful: with its ferocious bends, you can't relax on it at all. Unlike most canals, where you have a certain leeway steering, when going up Savick Brook you can't afford to lose concentration for a moment or you'll find yourself in trouble. With foliage trailing across your boat, and without a comforting towpath at the side of you, it looks different and feels claustrophobic, totally unlike a normal canal. That's because strictly speaking it isn't a canal at all. It's a 'navigation', a definition it warrants because passage is restricted, limited in each direction to alternate days. Even so, when it was opened in the summer of 2002 it was heralded as Britain's first inland waterway to be opened for nearly 100 years – unique in that it was the first created entirely for leisure purposes rather than industrial use.

OK, it's not the most beautiful stretch of water you'll ever cruise, but I've no truck with those who constantly bleat on about how shallow it is, and how narrow, and how overgrown with vegetation. Blimey, I do enough of that sort of carping myself without needing other people to do it for me.

The criticisms may be justified, but rather than complaining, we should be celebrating that Savick Brook was built at all at a time when so few public projects were. True, part of its charm is that its eight, somewhat ugly, locks are cussed, and you have to go up the final three backwards because there's no room for any except the shortest boat to turn a bend to go up the right way; but on the plus side you get shepherded along the whole length by waterways staff who do all the grunt work for you. And they don't hang around either, believe me. You don't spend a moment longer on Savick Brook than you have to.

Even so, when we finally arrived at the basin at the top, we were completely whacked. What with the psychological stress of the crossing, not to mention the physical demands of it, we'd had enough for one day and were just relieved we'd managed to get to our destination safely. At the top lock there's a stainless-steel sculpture welcoming you to the Lancaster Canal. It sits on a high plinth projecting over the lock, and it depicts a man steering a narrowboat, which is carrying an upended row of traditional digging tools in its hold. To me it looks disjointed because the two elements, boat and tools, are totally out of scale with each other. In fact, the tools are a lot bigger than the man, which is peculiar since the statue's supposed to be a celebration of the navvies who built the waterways, not the implements they used to do it.

It replaced an earlier sculpture called *Gauging the Ripple*, a 16ft (4.9m)-high male nude carved of oak standing on a pedestal surveying the water. I never saw this in situ because it was taken down in 2008, five years after it was erected, ostensibly because it suffered water damage. This was something I could never fathom because oak's a durable wood. For heaven's sake, the British Navy used to be built from the stuff. Then I saw some photographs of the sculpture and I was struck by one feature that made me wonder if that was the real reason for its removal.

You see, from whichever angle you viewed it, and from whatever position, the bloke gauging the Ripple looked more like he was adding to its depth. Or to put it bluntly, he looked like he was having a pee. And that's not just me saying that either. Local people who lived with the statue before it was taken down christened it 'The Ribble Piddler', which suggests a certain consensus on the matter.

Apparently the statue's still in storage and it's said it would cost £60,000 to restore. I wouldn't hold your breath. It doesn't take a lot to offend people in this snowflake world of ours and my guess is this statue might have managed to do it.

What we most wanted after the sort of day we'd had was to moor up in an idyllic spot far away from anywhere so we could recuperate at leisure. It didn't take long to find somewhere. About an hour or so northwards we tied up on a deserted stretch of water opposite an undulating field where a flock of sheep grazed placidly in the high summer sunshine. We had showers and sat on deck drinking tea, watching as a lone mallard preened itself in the stillness of a canal that was so glassy and unrippled you could see every detail of the sky above reflected on its surface.

Later, we walked up the towpath to the Hand and Dagger, a picturesque canalside pub, so far away from anywhere we wondered how anyone could make a living from it. It was one of those places you dream about being when you're sweating at work on a hot day with an hour or two to go before knocking-off time. We sat over ice-cold lagers in the garden surrounded by a flock of hens scratching around our feet. Afterwards, we had a meal of potted shrimps from nearby Lytham, and home-made black pudding with poached eggs laid by the very birds around us.

It's rare, even on the canals, for life to fall so blissfully into place, but that night walking along the towpath by torchlight back to the boat – as tipsy from the balmy night air as from the beer we'd drunk – it would have been hard to imagine a more perfect place to be. The night sky domed above us, myriad stars wherever you looked, flickering and glinting at each other in the blackness as if involved in some cosmic conversation. A copse on the other side of the cut stood black and blocklike, its outline like the shadowy hull of a sailing ship moored against a dock wall, trees like masts stretching to the sky and leaves a mesh of rigging swelling softly in the gentlest of evening breezes. The countryside has a fragrance of its own at times like this. Everything is intensified: the dampness in the fields, the aroma of the bruised towpath grass, and the canal itself, its odour hanging in the air, like the scents of rich garden soil after rainfall.

We were entranced by the whole setting. Embraced in the protective bosom of deepest England, we felt safe and out of harm's way, as sheltered from the vicious tides and malicious currents of the Ribble Link as we were from other greater madnesses of the world. From war and violence, from selfishness and greed, from oppression and tyranny.

Then Em said, 'What on earth was that?'

'That? What?'

'There was something there in the hedge, did you see it?' she said. 'It looked like a sign...'

'A sign? Whaddya mean, a sign? Whose benefit do you think that would be for then? The ducks?'

But she wasn't listening. She'd grabbed the torch from my hand and was sweeping its beam across the top of the towpath hedge along which we'd been walking. As she moved it around, the shadows of the hedge moved too, distorting with the motion in a way that made the commonplace seem surreal and sinister.

'There!' she announced at length jubilantly, as if I'd ever doubted her. 'Over there.'

The sign was headed 'Important Information for Canal Users' and I reproduce it as it appeared:

The Lancaster Canal between Quakers Bridge at Darkinson Lane (Bridge 19) and Saltwick Wharf moorings (Bridge 25) is within the Westinghouse Springfields Emergency Planning Zone.
If you hear a loud continuous siren (like an air raid siren) you should take the action outlined below:
- **Go inside your boat and stay inside until instructed otherwise**
- **Close all doors and windows**
- **Switch off all heating, ventilation and air conditioning systems**
- **Tune to the local radio station and listen for announcements telling you what to do**

Westinghouse is an American company that produces technology for the nuclear industry. 'WE ARE NUCLEAR ENERGY' it announces proudly on its website. Westinghouse's Springfield plant was over the hedge and just about visible by its lights in the distance. It makes fuel rods for nuclear reactors.

What was all that about 'feeling safe in the bosom of mother England'?

It was Em who first introduced me to canals. One year I had a couple of weeks of holiday that I hadn't taken and it was a case of use it or lose it. She suggested I hire a narrowboat. She'd hired one a few years before with some friends from uni and they'd had a whale of a time.

'Canals take you through some beautiful countryside,' she said.

'There are some lovely canalside pubs too, aren't there,' I commented.

'Boats are self-contained,' she went on. 'Everything you can possibly need is on them. They've got beds, loos and a kitchen.'

'Why do you need a kitchen? Haven't canal pubs latched on to serving food yet?'

'It's relaxing,' Em went on. 'You can't go very fast. It gives you time to unwind.'

'I'm beginning to warm to this idea,' I said 'I've got this image of relaxing in the evenings in front of a huge open fire with a rosy-faced barman pulling foaming pints of bitter...'

'Oh, for the love of God!' she exploded. 'You're obsessed with pubs and beer.'

'What? No. Oh, I'm sorry,' I said. 'You're right. But it's true though, isn't it? There aren't any drink and drive regulations on the canals, are there?'

Coming from Leicestershire, I wasn't as unfamiliar with canals as I was implying. Anyone from the Midlands tends to take them for granted as part of the landscape, and you never really notice them until they're not there. I was brought up in a village near the River Soar, which is part of the Grand Union Canal – the sort of M1 of the system that links to London. I was born in Loughborough where in 1778 the opening of the Loughborough Canal completed a connection to the River Trent and the coalfields of Nottinghamshire. So I knew a bit about the cut. They taught kids about it in my day, although we knew about it away from the classroom because we played around canals and rivers all the time, despite the warnings from our parents and the sure knowledge they'd clip us around the ear if they ever found out what we'd been up to. They were worried we'd drown, you see. And they weren't wrong to be anxious given some of the tricks we got up to. One year, some mates and I nicked a rowing boat laid up for the winter at Proctors Pleasure Park at Barrow and we went surfing over the weir in a flood until we overturned it. It was a wonder the lot of us didn't drown. We were always making rafts from old pallets and oil drums, reproducing great naval battles by throwing half bricks at each other and any other boat that happened to be passing, too.

After Em's suggestion I became quite keen on a canal holiday and I ended up hiring a boat just over the fields from the village where I used to live: a beat-up old 30-footer with no insulation and a plastic top that produced so much condensation it rained inside even when it was fine outdoors. My first day on the cut was not a great success. I'd rented the boat for a fortnight on the understanding my mate Dave would go away with me for the first week, and Em join me for the second. But when Dave and I picked up the boat, cruising was the last thing on our mind. We were both suffering from monumental hangovers, the result of a bender we'd been on the previous day that had begun modestly at lunchtime, and finished up in the early hours of the morning with copious amounts of lager in one of those dodgy curry houses where you couldn't be sure the meat on your plate hadn't been running at Kempton Park the week before.

The kindest thing to say about us is that we were not at our best. We were fractious and bad-tempered. We'd rather have been in bed. Or back in the pub. Or, to be honest, anywhere else in the world but on a boat. The rain didn't help, either. It had started as soon as we woke and it didn't let up the whole day. The bloke we'd rented the boat from wasn't a bundle of fun either. For some reason, he seemed to resent the fact he'd hired it to us at all, and he was singularly unhelpful about what we did with it. Neither Dave nor I had ever been on a boat before – or at least not one as big as this, one with an engine and places to sleep. He shrugged off all our questions about how to handle it with a catch-all answer, presumably the same answer he gave to every idiot who was stupid enough to pay what we had for renting such a heap of junk.

'You'll be all right,' he kept repeating, right up until the moment he waved us off from the quay of the boatyard. 'You'll get used to it.'

The first thing we got used to was people shouting at us. Well, yelling, actually. This is my most enduring memory of my canal debut. Knowing what I do now, I presume it must have been because we were going too fast and leaving a wash behind us, probably swamping the banks and moored boats alike. But the man at the boatyard hadn't said much about all this. How were we to know? We'd got no concept of wash. Insomuch as I was aware of the notion at all, I thought it was the thing you did when you got dirty. Then there were locks, those extraordinary contraptions to make water travel up and downhill, taking boats with it. That mystery of beams and ratchets and paddles and gates that you had to open and close in exactly the right order, and at exactly the right time, in order to prevent draining half the canal of water on one side or flooding the towpath on the other. The boatyard man hadn't said a word about them.

At the first lock we encountered we only narrowly avoided sinking the boat when I opened the wrong paddle and sent a torrent of water slamming into the bow doors and deluging the front cabin. Paddles are the mechanism by which you control the flow of water into a lock. You raise and lower them by operating a ratchet using a handle called a windlass, or lock key. You are supposed to do this gently, but it took me a while to latch on to this. At the second lock, I lifted them so quickly the boat ricocheted around the chamber like a pinball, taking shards off the brickwork as it rebounded from wall to wall. Poor Dave was left clinging on for dear life. He'd gone a ghastly white.

By the third lock, we'd got the hang of this boating lark. Or at least we thought we had. Dave had steered the boat into the chamber without any obvious evidence of major damage to either the lock gate or the boat hull; and by now I'd roughly managed to work out the principles of the mechanism, so I was able to get him out of the lock safely after the boat had fallen to a lower level. It was with some satisfaction that I dropped the final paddle and started to walk off. It fell behind me, ringing with the pleasing finality of a lump hammer striking an anvil.

It was at that point – the point when I was undoubtedly feeling pretty smug about the whole business – that an aged hobbit with a dog like a pet rat appeared from some hole in the towpath. He started waving a walking stick at me and ranting at me for breaching a set of rules I wasn't even aware existed. I can't remember much about him except he seemed to be fashioned out of clay that hadn't yet been fired, so the skin of his face looked as if it was dripping off him in folds. Apparently, we had to CLOSE gates behind us when we left a lock, not leave them OPEN as I was doing. AND – he was still shouting a lot – you don't DROP paddles, you LOWER THEM GENTLY.

The problem was, apparently, that these paddles were made of cast iron and by letting them fall in the way I did, they could have easily fractured. Paddles, I learned that day, had to be treated with a gentleness that belied their robust manufacture. Like so much else on the canals in that era – the tunnels, the bridges, the very fabric of the waterway itself – everything was worn-out, and there just wasn't the money or the will to repair it.

It was a steep learning curve, and it was only after we'd moored that evening that it began to dawn on us by degrees that somehow, by just hiring a boat, we'd crossed to a different continuum of existence. The rain had eased off and our morning hangovers had abated, so we sat on deck with our feet up, drinking a couple of the cans of beer we'd brought with us. We'd tied up along a stretch of river meadow a long way from anywhere, and as we watched the evening darkening, a pale mist lit by the moon began to form across the water. On the far bank, a couple of nervous coots scratched about on the shoreline scavenging for food, their legs so absurdly thin you'd think they wouldn't bear their weight. Around us, swallows cavorted in the air, plunging to the water in a kamikaze trajectory that they only pulled out from at the last moment, to go skimming across the surface of the river with such delicacy they seemed to have no substance but were simply flashes of reflected light.

It was magical, unreal. It was of this world but it somehow didn't seem part of the world at all. We were just a mile away from a village and yet we could have been on a different continent, so distinct was the atmosphere to anything either of us had experienced before. The silence was deafening, a turn of phrase I'd never understood until then, seeing it as just that, a turn of phrase. But on the deck that evening the silence seemed to shroud us completely, so much so that when there was any sudden noise, such as an owl screeching or a train passing in the far distance, I experienced it physically, almost as a bodily sensation that briefly broke whatever spell it was I was under.

It was as if I were on some drug. As if I'd imbibed a potion, which had delivered me to an *Alice's Adventures in Wonderland* dream. Before night finally fell, I was hooked on the waterways, totally hooked. I suppose what had happened was that I'd fallen in love, although at the time I didn't know that love could work like that. I was naïve, you see. At that stage in my life, I thought that it was only people who could touch your heart and make you ache with longing. I suddenly felt this gnawing, persistent need to be close to the water; and after the holiday was over and I returned to London, nothing was more certain in my mind than that canals would play an important part in my life.

They've got some funny ways on the Lancaster Canal, but then you'd expect folk to have funny ways in Lancashire, wouldn't you? They're like people from Yorkshire in that respect: they have their idiosyncrasies. Mind you, to a Leicestershire lad like me, most people from anywhere in the north are a bit idiosyncratic. Don't get me wrong though, it's not that I've got anything against the north. In fact, if I'm being candid, when you come from Leicestershire most people from the south strike you as a bit peculiar as well. We're not keen on them – though I grant you, we East Midlanders aren't that keen on people from the West Midlands either, especially people from Birmingham. But then, if I'm being honest, we're not overly fond of people from other parts of the East Midlands either, particularly Nottingham. In fact, to be perfectly frank, when you come from the county of Leicestershire, you don't much care for folk in the city of Leicester either.

Anyway, Lancashire people have got some funny ways about them. I was in Uppermill once, moored on the Huddersfield Narrow Canal. One day, I walked up to Saddleworth Moor. It was vile weather, the wind blowing a gale and rain like stair rods. I'd put on a pair of walking boots, long johns under army trousers, a base layer, a shirt, a fleece, a heavy sweater and an Arctic-style anorak. Yet when I got up to the top, to a local beauty spot called Pots and Pans, there were locals there wearing coats no thicker than supermarket carrier bags. In fact, they might have been supermarket carrier bags for all I know. One woman was even wearing a pair of mules. Not fluffy pink mules, I grant you, but mules all the same. Raised-heel slip-ons with a swag of imitation fur around the toes.

No one seemed in the least discomfited by their attire. Except me, that is. I felt somewhat overdressed and a bit of a prune. To be honest, the word 'namby-pamby' springs to mind when I think back to it. It was only when I was in the pub that night, however, that I learned all my contemplative musing on the sartorial idiosyncrasies of Lancashire dress codes was a waste of time since Uppermill wasn't actually in Lancashire. Apparently it was a part of Oldham now, which itself *did* used to be in Lancashire until it was absorbed into Greater Manchester in 1974. That must have been confusing for people living in a rural retreat like Uppermill: to suddenly wake up one morning to find themselves living in one of the biggest conurbations in the country.

But then, to confuse things even further, I discovered that once upon a time Uppermill had been in Yorkshire. With all this muddle about the geography of the place, you can understand why folk in these parts don't get too troubled about the relatively simple matter of what clothes to wear on the hills.

Continuing up the Lancaster Canal, Em and I moored up a couple of days later in Bilsborrow, where we tied up by a row of cottages opposite an odd development of thatched chalets with its own pizzeria and a canalside 'tavern', its own hotel and craft shops, and a sports complex featuring cricket and crown bowling. It was like a holiday camp, except it wasn't a holiday camp. Neither was it an amusement park. Nor a theme park. Indeed, it was hard to say what it was, except that it was all a bit strange. The next morning, we began to realise just how strange some of the other Lancastrian ways could be. Someone left us half a dozen freshly baked scones on the top of the boat, still warm from the oven. They turned out to be a gift from a woman in one of the cottages who included a postcard welcoming us to what we learned for the first time was referred to locally as 'the Lanky'. Now, if that sort of generosity isn't strange these days, what is? She told us about a local fish and chip shop with a great reputation, but when we walked to it later that day it was closed. At 7.30pm! On a Friday night! What sort of chippie shuts up shop before closing time on Fridays? It added to our sense of being in a place with its own way of doing things, its own set of customs and traditions.

We were to learn more about these when we moved on to the fine old market town of Garstang a few days later. Mooring had been a problem for us all the way up the canal. *Justice* is a deep-draughted boat and the Lancaster is a shallow canal. Its bottom, as the old boatmen used to say, was too near the top. This is a legacy of the canal being cut off from the rest of the system, as it was until relatively recently. As a result, the canal had been colonised by shallow-draughted plastic cruisers that bob along like motorised corks and don't need much water to do it in. This meant regular dredging became a thing of the past, which to some extent it still is. It makes it difficult for craft like ours. We are a heavy steel boat that weighs 20 tons or thereabouts. We were constantly grounding – suddenly stopping in the middle of the channel because of lack of water, or because we'd hit a mudbank. Tying up some evenings was a nightmare because we couldn't get close enough to the bank to get off the boat to hammer in mooring stakes. Eventually, we perfected a technique whereby we'd rev up our engine to full power and ram the bank with everything we'd got. We sometimes had to do this three or four times before we got sufficiently close for one or other of us to jump off the bow and secure us.

However, once we'd crossed the aqueduct over the River Wyre on the approach to Garstang, conditions changed significantly for the better. The sandstone structure was built in 1797 by the engineer John Rennie, and its single egg-shaped span carries the canal 34ft (10.4m) above the river on an elegant bowed bridge with a stylish cornice. It's a wonderful old thing, one of a number of monumental aqueducts built to facilitate the canal; and at Garstang it marks a boundary of where the canal's been dredged and, mercifully, where it becomes deep enough to moor easily.

Except we couldn't moor easily. There might have been enough depth, but there wasn't the space. It was all taken up by plastic cruisers, which weren't so much moored as abandoned with price tags in their windows. This was because they were up for sale. Garstang has become a boat brokerage yard. People wanting to sell boats leave their craft there and buyers amble up and down the towpath doing the canal equivalent of window-shopping. The Canal and River Trust (CART), who run the

Lancaster and most of the other waterways in England and Wales, obviously realised this was a problem, because a day or two later, when we finally managed to get a mooring at Garstang close to Th'Owd Tithe Barn pub, we tied up on a mooring next to a sign authorising us to stay for a week. The next morning, we woke to discover that overnight some zealous official had changed the sign. Now, apparently, we could only stay for 48 hours.

Now, tell me that ain't a strange thing to happen.

3

To Lancaster and the
Northern Reaches

Without the intervention of my grandfather – my mother's father – I doubt Em and I would ever have been drawn into the culture of canals the way we were. This was extraordinary since he was the last man in the world whose temperament you'd have thought consistent with the concepts of tranquility and Englishness that canals have since come to represent. He was a loud and blustering man, short-statured but thickset, an alcoholic who was sober most of the time, but who regularly disappeared on benders for weeks on end until eventually some drinking buddy would dump him like a sack of coal on the doorstep of the two-up two-down terrace in the Loughborough backstreets where he lived with my grandmother. Or else the police would visit to get someone to collect him from the cells after he'd been arrested, normally for fighting. He was usually blind drunk and once my grandmother had him home she'd give him a good hiding with a rolling pin while he was too comatose to know where his injuries had come from. She was a fearsome woman. With her ever-present hairnet and a fag always on the go, she was a dead ringer for the belligerent Florrie from the Andy Capp cartoons in the *Daily Mirror*.

The two of them were influential figures in my childhood, my grandfather especially. He was a bricklayer who'd made himself a bob or two working for the National Coal Board lining pit ventilation shafts. It was the sort of job for which you got paid generous money, for the simple reason that it was highly dangerous work. The shafts could collapse; the platforms on which he worked could give way; he could be hit by falling detritus loosened from the walls. Eventually, after some accident or another that laid him up for months and left him limping for the rest of his life, he took a job as gang foreman for a company in Loughborough that erected marquees for exhibitions. It was in this guise that he visited Moscow in 1961 at the height of the Cold War, putting up tents for a British trade fair. This was shortly after the Soviet cosmonaut Yuri Gagarin had become the first man in space and my grandfather, impressed by what he saw as the technical progressiveness of the USSR, came back with a suitcaseful of Sputnik souvenirs and a headful of ideas muddled by too much vodka. After that, he claimed to be a Communist, although you'd be wrong to read too much into this. When Margaret Thatcher became prime minister 20 years or so later he was one of her most passionate supporters. I think he just liked strong leadership.

Knowing him as well as I did, I can't understand why I wasn't more cautious about asking him to do any sort of favour for me. But since introducing me to canals, Em had taken me on a few more holidays on hire boats, so I was just as hooked on them as she was and the two of us couldn't get the idea of owning a boat out of our minds. The trouble was they were all well out of our price range, until one day, browsing through a waterways magazine, we saw one advertised for sale at an old gravel pit in Shardlow in Derbyshire, not far from where my grandfather lived. At £2,000 – about half what you'd pay for a new car at the time – it wasn't cheap, but we figured that one way or another we could just about find the money for it. We wanted to move fast though, so I called my grandfather to ask if he'd check it out for us and see if it was worth us coming up from London to look at.

The next day, I called him again to see what he thought of it. From the outset he sounded sheepish. All I could get out of him was that it was 'OK'. OK? Just OK? Is that all you've got to say about it? 'Well, not everything,' he admitted finally. 'I bought it for you.'

The shock Em and I felt at this was bad enough, but it was nothing compared to how we felt when we actually saw the thing. It was a wreck, a badly built amateur botch that had been knocked together from the steel of an old gas holder and lined with poor-quality tongue-and-groove that was already warping. Apparently, the guy who built it was a welder who worked on Saudi oil pipelines. I don't know whether he was a good welder or not. What I do know is that he wasn't a good boatbuilder. In fact, I don't think he'd even looked at a boat properly before he built this one. The hull was warped its whole length, as if it had been in a fire. You've heard of a dog's leg, haven't you? Well, this was a dog's dinner. It was 100 per cent Winalot. The bow of the boat was even worse. On proper boats, the bows are long and sleek so that they cut through the water like a knife. You only had to look at the bows of this boat to know that it wouldn't so much cut through the water as plough through it. It was as if, once he'd completed the hull sides, the guy who built the thing was faced with the intractable problem of what to do with the ends. His solution at the front was to bend the hull sides round and weld them together, so that the bow resembled nothing so much as one of those military landing craft used at the D-Day landings. You just knew that once you got the boat going, it would leave behind it a heaving swell you'd be able to surf on. Except we weren't able to get it going. We weren't going to get it going because it hadn't got an engine. This was another minor detail my grandfather seemed to have missed during his scrutiny of the boat.

It was a bright, sunny weekend when we first visited our new acquisition, but the weather didn't make us feel any better about the situation in which we found ourselves. We sat in the main cabin on a sort of banquette that had been made out of coarsely cut foam rubber and covered with what you could have identified as old house curtains, even if what was left of them hadn't still been hanging at the boat windows, giving the game away. They were a garish shade of orange that matched the varnished walls of the boat but they weren't as big as they should have been and didn't quite cover the glass. Blades of sunlight cut around them, creating shafts of light in which motes of dust danced madly, reflecting the confusion in our minds as to how we were going to deal with this expensive heap of junk we now owned.

We talked ourselves into the ground that afternoon examining our options. Em wanted to see if we could get our money back from the vendors, which I thought was about as likely as getting your money back on the horses after the race had finished. I wondered whether we might be able to cut our losses by putting it on the market again at half what we'd paid and seeing if we could offload it on to some other poor sucker. Except even at that price, what chance was there that we'd locate any buyer as stupid as we'd been? Eventually, we found ourselves totting up what we might get for the thing if we gutted it of anything valuable and sold the rest as scrap. But the sad truth was there wasn't anything valuable to gut. Whichever way you looked at it, it was *all* scrap.

My grandfather had quit drinking by this stage in his life, so you can't blame the booze for his decision to saddle us with this junkyard debris posing as a boat. I don't know what he could have been thinking of to buy it; I still don't. Even so, it turned out to be one of the best decisions he ever made in his life, and although we could never have known it at the time, the boat was to prove the best buy we ever made in ours because it was our initiation to life on the waterways.

The Lancaster Canal is practically lock-free, which is to say you can travel along it from one end to the other without having to go through a single one. However, there is a short arm that leads off the main line and cascades down through a flight of six locks to a substantial dock at the bottom where the small settlement of Glasson nestles close to the estuary of the River Lune. It was built in the 1780s to get around the problem of craft that couldn't navigate further up the Lune to Lancaster. At Glasson Dock, they could unload and transfer their cargoes to barges using the more reliable canal route, which avoided vicissitudes of weather, tides and shifting sandbanks.

It's a fascinating place; these coastal junctions always are. They give you a different perspective on the inland waterways. From being constrained, linear channels, restrictive and claustrophobic, the canals suddenly converge on wide estuaries, or the sea itself, confronting them with their smallness like a yappy lapdog snapping at a Rottweiler. At Glasson, canal boats mix with small ships, coastal trawlers and seagoing yachts, which nestle together, bobbing about in a small marina, their halyards slapping noisily against their masts in the breeze. There's a pub there and a smoke house where you can buy kippers and shrimps, and a swing bridge over a sea lock that leads to the estuary. The dock basin is huge, and I mean HUGE. We moored there one day during a storm and we stood inside *Justice*, looking out through a porthole into the wind, watching as a swell on the far side built to become a series of great waves topped by white horses, thundering towards us and sending us crashing against the dock wall. We're a flat-bottomed boat and we sit low in the water. We were honestly scared of being sunk. The waves broke over us and the scuppers on our front deck – the holes that allow water to drain – could barely cope. We'd have been safer moving out of the dock completely, or at least moving to a more sheltered part of it, except the short journey of a couple of hundred yards that this would have entailed was too treacherous to risk, so we had to drop our fenders and sit it out.

It was worth it, though. The next morning, we woke to sunshine as bright as crystal streaming into the boat. The dock was like a garden pond, and on the seaward side of the basin the mossy beach to the estuary, slashed by the black scars of drainage rivulets, looked like a luxuriant lawn. It was speckled with swags of yellow ragwort, purple salvias and blousy crimson poppies, larger than anything I'd ever seen before, their petals flapping on their stalks like washing on a clothes line, the whole scene so vividly colourful it seemed illusory.

After a few days at Glasson Dock, we went back up the locks and cruised to Lancaster, where the canal skirts the city centre. We kept returning there at intervals while we were on the canal, so imposing a place is it, and so unlike anywhere else in the country in that it seems to have emerged organically out of the ground itself: cobbled squares, blackened stone pavements, and sandstone buildings working themselves to the surface as if by some seismic movement of the earth. There's a castle, of course, and the lovely Priory Church behind it, although for pure arresting presence, the Town Hall takes some beating. It's a fabulous confection with a huge columned portico and a pediment above it, like a museum. It's made of conventional sandstone, but inside it's all high-end varieties of marble: red, white and green. You can get married there if you're willing to risk the bride being upstaged by the walls.

The tab for this expensive architectural eye candy was picked up by James Williamson, later 1st Baron Ashton, Lancaster's celebrated linoleum mogul who made his fortune covering the floors of working people in oilcloth before they could afford carpets. Williamson was Mr Lancaster and he took his philanthropy very seriously indeed, gifting a great deal to the city: schools, hospitals and parks. But he was a Trumpian

man, an egoist taken to self-aggrandisement, and the Ashton
Memorial – which he is said to have built as a memorial to his
second wife Jesse but which in truth is more a monument to
him – was his most controversial gift to Lancaster. This 150ft
(45.7m)-high cenotaph is like the amputated crown of St Paul's
cathedral in London, with balustraded balconies, a copper dome
and a weathervane instead of a cross at its apex. It stands high
on a hill in 54 acres (22 hectares) of parkland, a landmark that so
dominates the town I doubt there's anywhere within a 10 mile
(16km) radius you can't see it.

But it's a folly, with no function at all except that it's yet another
place in these parts where you can get married. Williamson did
a lot for Lancaster until his brand of self-regarding paternalism
dropped out of fashion towards the end of the 19th century.
After that, he fell out with Lancaster and it fell out with him.
He went on to become a penny-pinching recluse, a bitter anti-
trade-unionist who lived in his increasingly dilapidated mansion
in nearby Skerton, reluctant to spend money even to decorate it.

Having bought a pig in a poke ourselves in terms of our junkyard
of a boat, Em and I were saved from despair by the fact that she
took a new job in the north-east, which meant that the newly
bought wreck moored in an old gravel pit off the River Trent
in Shardlow found itself with a new role. Since it lay roughly
at a midway point between London and Newcastle, it became a
place where we could meet up most weekends. We'd christened
the boat *Pelekas*, after a memorable holiday we'd spent together
some years before in the village of the same name in Corfu in
Greece. Except that we misspelled it *Pelikas*, which we never
bothered to change. So much else about the boat was wrong, it
seemed appropriate. Instead, we changed the curtains and the
internal woodwork, and began to tidy up what laughably passed
as the galley. We only knew it was the galley because there was

a small two-ring Calor gas cooker-cum-oven built into what looked remarkably like a worktop – though both were so covered in grease we couldn't be entirely sure until we'd cleaned them down. Miraculously, under the grime we discovered the oven was still serviceable and that the worktop only needed covering with a sheet of Formica for us to be able to use it without risk of disease. The only other thing that functioned on the boat was a light, which worked from a gas bottle by heating a mantle, a sort of fragile ceramic mesh. Even in those days, it was a relic of another age – something that ought to have been preserved in a museum, not still in use. Even so, with a few candles burning in the background, it gave out a comforting light so that once we'd got the place shipshape it actually began to feel quite cosy in the evenings.

As we'd been working on the boat, our progress had been closely monitored by the owners of the handful of other craft scattered around the gravel pit. Today, the place has been developed as a high-end marina, with boats crammed together in rows along jetties like a municipal car park, so there's hardly any privacy. In those days, the problem was the opposite: there were so few boats around that it felt uncomfortably remote, not helped by the fact that the owners of the other boats at first appeared stand-offish. We put this down to the fact they pitied us. They, after all, knew the state of the boat we'd bought; they probably had some idea of what we'd paid for it, too. After two or three months, though, as they began to warm to us, we realised that we'd completely misinterpreted their first reaction, which wasn't personal at all, let alone anything specifically to do with our boat. It was just the way folk reacted to newcomers on the waterways in those days. The canals then weren't by any means an exclusive community, but people liked to know who they were dealing with before they engaged with you. In the words of that 17th-century naval idiom, they wanted to know the cut of your jib before they took the trouble to get to know you. This was because they were a self-reliant crowd and they needed to be persuaded that you could help yourself before they started offering to help you. They liked to see you rolling up your sleeves and getting your hands dirty. That was the membership fee they demanded to join their club.

Moored close to us was a couple about our age, perhaps a little older, who owned a disused wooden working boat of the sort that would probably have been hauling coal a couple of decades before. It had been cut down at the stern, probably because it had worn out or rotted away, but they'd repaired it and converted it into an attractive and homely leisure boat. We soon became friends, and one chilly evening I remember sitting in armchairs in their saloon in front of their blazing fire, drinking beer together, and suddenly realising just how comfortable boats could be with a little TLC. We went on a short trip with them one day, down the Trent to where it joins the Trent and Mersey Canal. From there, we cruised into Shardlow itself, to the Malt Shovel pub where they served Marston's Pedigree and Pimm's fruit cups in the summer. That's when I grasped the other main attraction of the waterways, which I sort of knew from our holidays but still hadn't entirely appreciated. Not only could boats be snug and cosy, but they could also take you to remote places too, places you'd never even have heard about other than through the canal. Poring over maps of the system, as we did constantly in those days, the extent of the waterways seemed limitless. They stretch from the Lake District in the north to Bristol in the south, from the hills of Llangollen in the west to the flatlands of Ely in the east – a whole world of new places waiting to be explored, yet astonishingly a world contained within the boundaries of the small island on which we live. Just thinking about the possibilities left us with an irrepressible desire to discover our own country. We had developed what you might call itchy feet, except we wanted to travel on water and didn't want to use our feet at all.

I have to concede that my grandfather was very helpful to us in these early days – but he ought to have been helpful, given that it was him who'd got us into this mess in the first place. In time, he found us an engine for the boat, although it wasn't from a boatyard or other authorised sales outlet: it was from the classified columns of the *Derby Evening Telegraph*. Again, I should have been cautious about him interfering since my grandfather's knowledge of marine propulsion was on a par with my grasp of thermonuclear physics. As might have been predicted, it turned out to be entirely unsuited to the demands of inland waterways. In fact, it would have been difficult to imagine an engine that could be less suited. It was an upright single-cylinder engine made by Hatz, a German company; and while the robustness of its manufacture might have equipped it for a lifetime reliably powering a cement mixer, I could see from the outset that it was going to be trouble in a canal boat.

We were on one bank of the gravel pit, on a sort of landing platform made out of old pallets, when we unloaded the engine from a trailer and fired it up for the first time. It exploded into life, leapt sideways like a startled hare and bolted towards the water where only some nifty footwork on my part prevented it from drowning itself. This preference of the engine for moving laterally, rather than in a straight line, was one of its drawbacks. Sadly, it wasn't the only one. When we'd installed it in the boat, it was unspeakably noisy, like a series of synchronised grenades detonating under your feet. But I'll say this in its favour: you never had to put up with the noise for long. That was because it never ran for long. The fact was it had a proclivity to cut out for no reason, generally in the most inconvenient of places and at the worst possible time, such as coming into a lock or going through a tunnel. It was years before we could bring ourselves to accept the painful reality of our relationship with the thing, and that was only after it had nearly sunk the boat in Shropshire when its relentless pounding fractured a weld below the waterline. We finally had to accept that this wasn't an engine we could rely on. We both felt a great sense of relief when we got to that stage. It was as if after a long period of therapy we'd finally come to terms with an essential truth of boat mechanics. Before then, you see, we used to depend on it to get us to places and it always let us down. Afterwards it still let us down, but we had no expectations that it would do otherwise. And for some reason that didn't feel quite as bad...

The Lancaster Canal is unusual in being a coastal canal, and at Hest Bank as you cruise north you can tie up and watch the sun set over the 120 square miles (310 square km) of Morecambe Bay, the largest area of sand and mudflat in the UK. Populated by vast flocks of waders and other wildfowl, the bay is a beautiful and spectacular part of the country. However, it's much underrated, mainly because it's in the shadow of the Lake District National Park, its more renowned northern neighbour, but partly because it's very dangerous, too. OK, the Lake District can be dangerous as well, and you'd be foolish to go wandering unprepared across Helvellyn in the middle of winter. But you wouldn't wander across Morecambe Bay at any time of the year, whatever your state of preparedness. Morecambe Bay is habitually treacherous. There are hazardous quicksands and unpredictable tides that race in at terrifying speeds; there are swirling currents and deep, fast-moving rivers that drain into it and that can sweep you away in the twinkling of an eye. You don't mess with Morecambe Bay, and if you're tempted, just remind yourself that in 2004, 23 Chinese cockle pickers, immigrants working under a Triad gang master, died when they were cut off by the tide at

Wharton Sands not more than a stone's throw from Hest Bank where we'd moored *Justice*.

However, there is a safe way of walking Morecambe Bay – although this being England, with all its quaint ways, it requires you to enlist the help of the Queen's Guide to the Sands. This royal sinecure, which has existed since the 16th century, pays the princely sum of £15 a year with the use of a ramshackle 700-year-old cottage thrown in for good measure. It probably includes invitations to royal weddings, too, for all I know. At the time, the post was held by Cedric Robinson, an ex-fisherman who was appointed in 1963 and who is a celebrity in these parts, despite the fact he's now retired. He knows these shifting sands like the back of his hand, and has written books about them – although the main part of his work was leading walks across the bay, which he did a couple of times a week for more than 50 years. This involved a lot of walking for him, since any trip he led involved him surveying the safest route by walking it himself in advance the night before and sticking laurel branches in the sand to mark his course.

Many of the walks he led were well-publicised charity hikes that attracted upwards of 500 participants, but even less well-advertised crossings were popular and places on them were limited. We were advised to book a walk with Cedric as soon as possible since it might be our last opportunity to do it. Cedric, you see, was in his 80s and had been on the verge of retirement for some time. Not that anyone took this too seriously. Cedric, we knew, had retired many times over the previous decade and probably a few times before that, too. Indeed, he'd retired more times than Frank Sinatra, which added to his celebrity and, presumably, kept the books selling and the crowds rolling in. And who can blame him, because the bay is an incredibly beautiful location by anyone's standards. Cedric's walks began at Arnside where the Barrow-to-Lancaster railway – the 'Furness

Line', as it's known – crosses the estuary of the River Kent on an elegant 500 yard (457m)-long viaduct set on 50 piers, so low to the water that passing trains appear to be floating over it. On a decent day, the snow-covered peaks of the Lake District seem to rise out of the sea, which can sometimes be a sapphire blue.

Unfortunately, the day on which we did the walk wasn't a decent day. Indeed, it wasn't even a half-decent day. In fact, the only reason I know what the bay looks like in reasonable weather is that I've seen pictures of it on Google. On our walk, the rain was lagging down so hard that you couldn't see your hand in front of your face: no elegant viaduct, no snow-covered peaks, no sapphire-coloured water. Nothing. Nothing but driving rain stabbing from above and ice-cold seawater sloshing about underfoot. And it got worse. I was aware that in doing the walk we'd be paddling ankle deep most of the time. I was aware, too, that we'd have to ford the River Kent, but I'd imagined this as a sort of extension of the paddling – a frivolous, knee-high gambol through something not much deeper than a village brook. What I hadn't imagined was that the water would be so deep it would reach that critical boundary at the top of my leg where my thigh ends and my intimate parts begin. It was excruciating – at one and the same time glacially cold and impertinently invasive. And it got worse yet. We had to ford not one river but three, the final one almost chest high, the deepest of the lot, a sort of muddy drainage ditch that separates the beach from the railway station at Kents Bank where, mercifully, the walk ended.

We were with a group of about 50, at least a third of them kids – all dressed for the occasion. We all had suitable footwear, sturdy but light fleeces and anoraks. Even so, in those conditions you'd have needed to be dressed like a trawlerman to have any chance against the weather. It wasn't surprising that no one was really up for the walk or pleased to be on it. Everyone was sporting that 'how-on-earth-have-I-found-myself-in-this-position?' hangdog expression and looked as if they hadn't been able to find the right excuse to get out of it. Everyone, that is, except the kids. Once released on to the beach, the kids were like a clowder of cats that had been penned up for weeks. They couldn't wait to get free and went scampering across the sands in so many directions that poor Cedric, who controls these walks with the assistance of a whistle, was left sounding like an overenthusiastic referee at a park football match, desperately doing what he could to stop them drowning themselves.

Some 4 miles (6.4km) on, and halfway through the walk, the adults were getting tetchy and bad-tempered from the cold and tiredness. The kids, however, were as irrepressible as ever. Now they were less like cats than those irritating pink bunnies in the battery ads that go on and on and on forever. Despite the rain, most of them were so overheated by their exertions they'd stripped back to shorts and T-shirts so that when they came to the rivers they were in and out of the water like a shot before Cedric could even get his whistle to his lips. They were still partying on the platform hours later, bouncing around like supercharged balls, when the train pulled up to take us home. Em and I, like all the adults, barely had the strength to stand. We felt chilled to the bone and ashen-white with exhaustion. We felt very old. Most of all, we all felt like a cup of tea.

4

Back to the main system, with a detour to the past

Meanwhile, back cruising the Lancaster canal, our problems mooring in the shallow waters got worse the further north we went. We were getting close to the terminus at Tewitfield where the canal stops dead in its tracks, brought to a halt by the M6, which severs it abruptly and prevents it reaching Kendal just 15 miles (24km) away. Even so, this far up it's splendid countryside, so archetypically English it makes you want to break into a chorus of 'Jerusalem' and start waving the St George flag around. Isolated fields lie patchworked among lush undulating hills, beyond which the looming outline of the mountains stand grey on the horizon. That afternoon blackbirds and chaffinches flickered among the hedgerows, every now and again bursting noisily into random song. The occasional breeze brought with it essences of the nearby sea, which you could literally taste on your tongue.

Even though we knew there were moorings at the terminus we didn't want to spend the night too close to the motorway, so mid-afternoon we began to look for alternative places to stop. That was easier said than done. A couple of hours later we still hadn't found anywhere deep enough for us to get into. Our old trick of ramming *Justice*'s bow into the bank didn't work either. We tried this a dozen times, maybe more, but we never got anywhere close. It was almost as if there was a shelf in the canal stopping us from getting near the towpath. By now we were becoming anxious. It seemed we were pursuing a lost cause and that we'd be better accepting the inevitable and just going straight to the M6 moorings without any more messing about. But at the point at which we were feeling at our least optimistic, we rounded a bend and ahead of us – like an oasis suddenly appearing out of the dunes of the desert – were a couple of boats tied up in deep water on the towpath overlooking a pleasing vista of fields. Next to them was an empty space that had our name written all over it.

At that moment, it felt like God was in His heaven and all was well with the world – though the sentiment didn't last long. As we got closer, it became apparent that things weren't as they seemed. This time the problem wasn't depth, but length. The space was a tad too short for us to fit. It was exasperating. I could have screamed. There was *nearly* enough room, there was *almost* enough. But we were a tantalising few inches too long to squeeze in. What made it more frustrating was that the two boats already tied there had left a wasteful gap between them of a yard or so. I was all for doing the obvious and moving them closer to create the space we needed, except that on the cut there's a taboo about touching other people's boats and Em was wary of breaking it. We were still arguing the whys and wherefores of canal etiquette when a guy on the furthest of the boats suddenly appeared. He looked as if we'd woken him from sleep. Or maybe he always looked as unshaven and his eyes as bloated and bloodshot.

'You're not thinking of moving that boat, are you?' he shouted across at us. And without further ado he marched over and delivered a lecture, the guts of which seemed to be that it wasn't right to move a boat under any circumstance, that it was bad manners and that there were insurance implications if we were to reposition it and leave it badly tied. What if it were to work itself loose and it got damaged? What if it were to sink?

I listened to all this with growing irritation. I mean, what had manners got to do with it? If manners were the issue, then wasn't it bad manners on any canal to do what he'd done and tie up without regard for other boats? And if we were talking bad manners — real bad manners — forget the protocols of mooring a boat; wasn't it a hundred times worse to interrupt other people's conversations when they were talking between themselves and what they were saying had absolutely nothing to do with you? But of course I didn't respond. I didn't respond because I'm English and because I'd just been surveying a bucolic landscape, with 'Jerusalem' ringing around in my ears and the flag waving in the background of my mind; and because, being English, I wouldn't even consider betraying what I really felt unless I was under thumbscrews — and even then I'd only confess my innermost sentiments out of concern that by not doing so, I might somehow offend the guy tightening them.

So I shrugged, smiled, wished the bloke a polite good day and meekly cruised off into the sunset to Tewitfield where Em and I spent the night adjacent to the southbound carriageway of the busy motorway, HGV lorries, not songbirds, our goodnight lullaby, and the smell of traffic fumes filling the boat, not the scent of the boundless ocean.

I was exasperated by this incident, but on the cut you move on, as much literally as metaphorically. When a new day dawns, you start your engine and take off; what happens one day is history the next. The difficulty in this situation was that moving on wasn't quite the option it might have been under other circumstances. Tewitfield was at the northernmost limit of the canal, remember. We would have to turn round and go back down it — which meant that it was inevitable we'd pass the difficult boat and its zombie owner once more. This much we could predict. What we couldn't predict, and what wasn't inevitable – what was complete coincidence, in fact – was that he should be on the towpath as we went by. And, not just on the towpath, but on the towpath in the process of moving the boat he'd berated us for even thinking about touching the previous day.

I didn't have to puzzle long to realise why. It was because he was helping another boat get into the mooring next to him – the spot we'd been trying to get into the previous evening. This other boat was steered by a woman on her own – a remarkably attractive woman, I couldn't help but notice. There was no doubt the unshaven boater with the bloodshot eyes had been saving the space for her, and it was obvious he'd been anticipating her arrival, too, since I couldn't help noticing that this morning he was as clean-shaven as an egg. And – was it my imagination – or was that a smell of aftershave in the air?

I wasn't happy seeing this, but I wasn't going to let him know. I put on my best Sunday smile and wished him a cheery good morning as we passed. But he didn't say a word. He didn't even look in my direction. For some reason, even though we were only feet away, he didn't seem to have heard me...

We'd had enough of the Lancaster Canal, that's what it came down to. We yearned for deeper waters and emptier towpaths where boats weren't taking up space while waiting to be sold. Our hearts craved canals you could reach without hazardous coastal crossings, canals that led to other canals which promised unknown territories to be explored and journeys yet to be had. We thought we might cruise to the centre of Liverpool, where we'd never been before in all our years of boating, because during that time it had never been possible by canal. Or perhaps we might go to York. Or Leeds. Or maybe even Manchester.

All these are canal cities with histories woven around the water. They're all worth exploring.

Leaving the Lancaster wasn't that easy, however. We booked our passage back over the Ribble Link, as you're required to do, and cruised back to Garstang where we'd been instructed to await further instructions. This should have been a formality but we didn't hear anything for days, and meanwhile a queue of boats like ours awaiting a return passage began to build up along the towpath. Soon, it became clear to us all that there was some sort of hold-up. Officially, no one told us anything, but through the 'towpath telegraph' – that irrepressible conduit of gossip by which news passes from one boater to another with the speed of a forest fire – we soon discovered that the cause of the obstruction was … well, a lack of water. What a surprise that was to those of us who'd been cruising the canal in recent weeks.

The water that supplies the Lancaster Canal comes from the Lake District by way of the unnavigable northern sections of the cut towards Kendal, but it had seemingly become blocked by a build-up of excessive weed in a culvert. To conserve water already in the canal, the Canal and River Trust had first closed the locks down to Glasson Basin, and then, when the situation became worse, it had closed the Ribble Link entirely. It wouldn't have been so bad if someone had at least kept those of us on boats informed of what was happening, but the Trust is commonly referred to by its acronym CART, and this is as much for its tendency to do things in the wrong order as having to get your tongue round its full name. It had acted without telling any of us what it had done, cutting off the Lancaster from the rest of the system and effectively leaving us all stranded.

What made it worse is that not only had the Trust put the cart before the horse, but its left hand didn't seem to know what its right was doing either. A small group of us from waiting boats stood around the towpath one morning, our eyes fixed on a laptop, while chief executive Richard Parry did an internet Q&A session with boaters about any problems they might be having. When the question of the stoppage on the Ribble Link came up he seemed, embarrassingly, not even to be aware that there *was* a stoppage. However, the public mortification he must have felt at the poor quality of his briefing did lead to positive action, for it was announced almost immediately that the Link would open in a couple of days.

Even then, finally getting away from the canal was a gruelling process, like trying to tunnel under a prison wall. The water was so low and the mud so thick that making any progress at all was like mining. Boaters on the Midlands' canals always complain about water depth. Honestly, they don't know they're born. So many of the canals away from the main routes are like this; it's what all canals used to be like in the past when they were rarely, if ever, dredged. Eventually, we managed to struggle back to Savick Brook and on to the River Ribble where, relieved at last to finally be on deep water, *Justice* coughed, spluttered and belched a great cloud of exhaust smoke before setting off like Usain Bolt out of the starting blocks.

Sadly, this wasn't an omen of a smooth crossing. Six of us came out together on the ebbing tide towards Tarleton Lock, with *Justice* bringing up the rear; but we hadn't even passed the Astland Lamp or turned into the River Douglas when one of the boats in front dropped anchor with engine trouble, clearly in some distress. We couldn't have gone on as if nothing had happened. If we'd left them, the crew would have had to call out the lifeboat to rescue them. Worse – depending on whether their anchor held – they could have been flushed on to a mudbank, or back into the main flow of the river where, without power, God-knows-what might have happened to them. Without even discussing it, we did a wide sweep across the river and turned back to see what we could do to help. The stranded boat was one we'd encountered a few times as we'd been cruising the Lancaster. It was home to an affable couple, both experienced boaters, but who at that moment were visibly shaken by the fact their engine had failed. We quickly breasted up – that is, tied up together, side by side – and headed off, following the rest of the flotilla, which we could just about see disappearing into the distance.

With us powering both boats we were in a potentially perilous position ourselves now. Admittedly, *Justice*'s engine is a large one with plenty of torque, and in still water the task of pulling another boat wouldn't be a problem for her. But this wasn't still water. Going down the River Ribble we'd been running with the tide and the flow. Now, having turned into the Douglas, we were against both. This posed a critical problem of timing, for we'd been let out of Savick Brook at a point precisely judged so that when we arrived at Tarleton there'd be enough water on the receding tide to allow us to get over the sill of the lock. If we missed that chance, I was at a loss to know what we'd do. We'd have to find somewhere nearby to moor and wait for the next tide – although I had no idea where that would be on this muddy and featureless river.

Even with everything going to plan, our schedule had been tight – but now, with the rescue, the plan had been shot to pieces. We were cruising against the clock in a couple of boats that had become one, twice the normal width and weight. Making any sort of headway was a slow and arduous process. As the implications of our situation began to gradually dawn, a walkie-talkie bleeped on *Justice*'s roof, startling us all. I'd forgotten it was there. It had been tossed across to us almost apologetically by Pete on one of the other boats crossing the Link. 'Well, you never know, it might come in useful,' he'd said as we left.

The caller was Harry, the lock keeper at Tarleton. 'Where are you?' he asked, his lack of introductory civilities betraying his anxiety. We gave him our bearings as best we could. 'Over and out,' he said. Twenty minutes later the intercom rang again. 'Have you passed under the power lines yet?' Harry asked. We looked around puzzled. The only power lines we could see crossing the river were at least a mile ahead of us. This didn't seem good news; whatever schedule we were on, we were obviously behind it.

After another 20 minutes or so, I decided I couldn't stand the worry of not knowing the worst, and so I rang Harry myself. The radio was answered by Pete. 'Harry's at the lock, standing by. He's expecting you any time soon. Where are you anyway…?'

But I never needed to answer the question. Suddenly, everyone on our two boats started shouting excitedly, Em the loudest of them all. They'd all seen the lock in the distance. At the same time, from the lock, Pete saw us. He started shouting down the walkie-talkie. 'I'm clocking you now,' he said, 'I've got you eyeballed. Aim for the far wall to the left…'

The entry to Tarleton from this direction is tricky to say the least. Thus far, you've been punching the combined might of the river flow and the ebbing tide, confronting it head-on. But at the very point you have to leave the river to enter the lock, the river swings sharply to the left and as a result the force of water coming round the bend hits your hull like someone angrily slapping your face, sending you wildly off course. The only way to navigate into the lock at this point is to do what Pete was urging us to do and aim at the brick wall to the far side of it and hope you've judged it sufficiently well for the current to flush you in the direction you want to go. As we edged closer to the lock I wasn't certain we could do this. I felt as I had when we'd left Tarleton weeks before – that the throttle on *Justice* wasn't adjusted enough for us to get to the power needed to complete the manoeuvre. I felt, as I'd done then, that I needed to regulate the revs manually. Em had been doing the steering since we'd lashed the two boats together. Now I left her to it while I went down to the engine room.

Inside, it was deafening and oppressively hot, a wall of noise and heat. The side-hatch doors were open, but it was gloomy after the bright day outside. I tinkered with the engine to tease more power from it, and as I felt the boat surge forwards I braced myself for the impact of what I thought would be an inevitable collision with the lock wall. The thunderous din of the engine became almost unbearable. But then a shadow passed across the engine room and, oddly, the collision didn't happen. I couldn't understand it. I put my head out of the hatch to see what was happening.

Em screamed at me. 'Get back in. Do you want to kill yourself?'

I was baffled. What did she mean kill myself? Then a wall loomed against the side doors. It was the wall of the lock. That could only mean we were already in the lock. It explained why Em had screamed. She'd been alarmed I might brain myself.

It took me a moment or two to fully grasp what had happened. What was clear was that she'd brought us into the lock safely even though we were breasted to another boat and fighting the tide and the flow; she'd brought us into a lock with barely a foot to spare on either side, and – astonishingly – she'd brought us in without even a scrape. It was an amazing feat of steering. I went up on deck where the crews of other boats who'd been part of our flotilla and who'd already moored were gathered around the lock sides to see us safely home. They were applauding. Even Harry was nodding his head in appreciation at what Em had done.

Unbelievably, this wasn't the last problem we had that day at Tarleton. The four of us on the boats in the lock were all so relieved to be safe that when Harry closed the gates to the river and opened the top paddles, we didn't register that the lock wasn't working in the way it should. Water flooded into the chamber from the canal above, cascading around us in its familiar tumult of seething spume. But it took some time before it struck us that the level wasn't rising – and neither were we.

Eventually, Harry noticed that something was jammed in the gates, preventing them from closing properly. He shouted down to us that he was going to have to wait for the tide to recede so that he could drain the lock completely and get a better idea of what the obstruction was. This would be a long delay. We were going to have to be patient. Someone suggested tea and went off to the galley to make a pot for us all, and we settled down for the wait. It turned out to be more than two hours – an uncomfortable interlude during which the two boats scraped and creaked their way down the lock wall until eventually the lock had drained and we finished up on the concrete bottom, leaning against each other at a precarious angle. Now we could all see what the problem was. A huge piece of sodden timber, part of the hull of some long-since sunken barge, had been flushed into the lock with us.

Harry tried to move it by batting it out of the way with the lock gates; I tried to dislodge it with our bargepole; someone else tried throwing a rope around it. But there was no shifting the thing. I could see us being trapped in the lock while CART consulted statutory health and safety regulations and completed several risk assessment analyses. Maybe – possibly – if we were lucky – in a week or so they might finally give the go-ahead for a member of staff kitted in lifejacket, harness and helmet to descend the lock ladder to move the obstruction...

However, common sense prevailed. Harry chose that moment to take his lunch break and while he wandered off for a sandwich, someone from a local boat who'd been watching proceedings – a boat aptly, if unusually, called *May Contain Nuts* – hopped down the ladder and, fully dressed in boots, jeans and T-shirt, dragged the wood out the way. 'It got shifted,' I explained judiciously to Harry when he got back. Harry nodded knowingly. 'Save a lot of paperwork,' he said.

While the lock had been draining, Pete set his mind to repairing the broken-down boat, which turned out to be a blocked fuel filter and not too difficult a task. The owners were beside themselves with gratitude, and by way of thanks for the help they'd had that day they offered to stand drinks for us all that night at the Hesketh Arms, further up the canal, near an entirely unremarkable manor house called Rufford Old Hall, its only redeeming feature being the Tudor great hall it's named after. This ramshackle pile was once the ancestral home of the Hesketh family, the local lords, who lived in the place until it was falling around about their ears, after which they offloaded it to the National Trust as a way of getting it off their hands. The hall is said to be haunted by a ghost that's been reported hovering above the canal which borders the grounds.

We certainly weren't troubled by ghosts as we sat outside in the sunshine drinking on the pub patio – although there were a few spirits floating around in glasses later that night when it got so chilly we all had to repair indoors. If truth be told, we were pickled by that stage, and in that condition, when reality was fast becoming a tentative concept, what we found inside was surreal, like something out of a dream so you had to blink twice to believe it. The whole bar was filled with people playing ukuleles. Every last one of them. It was bizarre. Weird. Like the type of dream you get after eating bad fish. It turned out to be the fortnightly Monday meeting of the Wigan Ukulele Orchestra. Like us, they were all a bit tipsy, so much so that they handed us ukuleles and invited us to play with them. I was so out of my head I almost agreed. In fact, looking back, I'm sorry I didn't. Though I'd never played a ukulele in my life before, I think that after the day I'd had I could have given George Formby a run for his money.

(And if you're not old enough to know who he is, you'll be young enough to use Google to find out.)

The maiden trip in our first boat *Pelikas* may not have been as demanding as crossing the Ribble Link, but to a couple of canal novices not long out of nappies, going out of the gravel pit on to the River Trent with an underpowered and badly installed engine certainly felt dicey. Fortunately, a number of more experienced friends and acquaintances we'd made could see the potential risks too, and they were troubled enough about our welfare to make themselves available for possible rescue duties as we left. One friend who worked as an engineer at a local boatyard insisted on accompanying us down the river to where we turned on to the Trent and Mersey Canal. Our friends in the cut-down wooden boat helped by stationing themselves at the junction in case our engine proved too frail to deal with the current and we were swept away.

As it transpired, we didn't need assistance; and as we passed Shardlow's famous Mill Number 2 – better known nowadays as the Clock Warehouse – I remember the sense of breathless elation I felt at finally breaking free of the place after so many months being psychologically anchored by the demands of the boat.

Shardlow today is a conservation area, widely recognised as one of the most complete examples of a canal settlement in the UK. It encompasses more than 50 listed buildings: former wharves and warehouses, stylish town houses of the well-to-do, artisans' cottages and all the rest of the surviving trappings of what had once been a busy transport interchange where heavy river barges transferred their cargoes to smaller canal craft. Unsurprisingly, today it has its own heritage centre – although given how heritage has become so much a part of how we English define ourselves in the 21st century you wonder if the place needs it, particularly since the whole of present-day Shardlow is itself a shrine to past industrial glory.

At the time I'm talking about in the 1970s, the village was dilapidated, parts of it not far off being in ruins. Everything about the place seemed neglected. The state of the brickwork on the warehouses was atrocious, stained with damp and badly in need of repointing. Some barely had roofs and those that did were scarred with gaping holes, tiles broken and displaced. One or two of the warehouses had been cheaply renovated, but some had already been demolished along with a stable block capable of accommodating a hundred or so of the horses once used to tow narrowboats. Judging by other smaller examples of canal stables that survive, this must have been an extraordinary structure, and it's a great shame it's been lost. But I guess we should be grateful that for the most part Shardlow has survived.

The exception to all this dereliction was the Clock Warehouse, a former grain store built in 1780, which was an icon of the waterways even then. It's an elegant four-storey redbrick building divided into three bays, the central one projecting outwards over an arch spanning a short loading arm, which at the time was home to a constantly squabbling flock of doves. It was built so unloading work could be done undercover and goods hauled directly into the warehouse; although at the time the arm had long since silted up and a couple of boats were rotting away in the mud, one of them an old wooden day boat called *Sally* that has stuck in my mind because it was the name of a friend.

What characterised the building most though – then as now – was its prominent sign, one that featured in numerous travel books even before canals were as popular as they are today. At the very top of the central bay, beneath the clock that gave the warehouse its name, was the legend 'NAVIGATION' in letters a foot high. Underneath that, below a window, is the proud announcement, capital letters and all, 'FROM the TRENT to the MERSEY' – this latter information a statement of pride presumably, a sort of advertisement for the canal since I can't for one moment imagine boatmen at the time it was built not knowing precisely which navigation they were on.

For a while, it housed a small museum and then a tea room. Later, it became a canal shop and chandlery. Finally, the place was revamped as a pub/restaurant, though who knows what will happen to it now after all the problems with Covid. I can only wish it well. We fell in love with the Clock Warehouse during our time in Shardlow and I still have a soft spot for it now, although the day we were leaving on our maiden trip, I was pleased to see the back of it. My concern then wasn't with the past but the future. There were adventures ahead for both of us and we plotted a course north with the sort of confidence that only the young possess.

An hour later, we broke down.

It was the first of a series of similar incidents on that trip, one merging into the other with such frequency that I can't recall with any accuracy what caused most of them – except it was always something to do with the engine, either its complete unsuitability for the job, or the cack-handed way my grandfather and I had installed it. The engine regularly parted company with its mountings, and once – probably tiring of the predictability of its own behaviour – it parted company from the gearbox too. On one particularly memorable occasion in Knowle Locks near Solihull the propeller came off and I had to get into the freezing water to retrieve it. Em thought this was hilarious. As I emerged from the water dripping with weed and oily slime, her contribution to helping me in my hour of need was to take a photo.

Eventually, a couple of weeks later into our maiden trip, we limped by some means or another to the top of the 21 double locks at Hatton, which drop down from above Warwick to the valley of the River Avon, like a giant staircase hewn from the hill. There, we shared the descent with another boat until the crew tired of our incompetence and roped us to them so that they could tow us down without us slowing them down.

At the bottom, they untied us and motored off while we staggered on, making what headway we could with an engine that once again had started to play up. It was dark by the time we tied up for the night in Leamington Spa, tucking ourselves in behind a small cluster of boats in a scuzzy mooring between a scrap yard and a gasometer. The following morning, once they discovered they had new neighbours, the people on the other boats were all over us as if we'd been celebrities, sociable and welcoming. They gave us coffee and biscuits and we sat around chatting and gossiping about boating and canals in a way that over the years we'd learn was what people did on the cut, wherever you stopped. However, when the time came to leave and I attempted to prepare *Pelikas* for departure, it was only to discover that I couldn't get the engine started. It had given up the ghost yet again. Dispirited and dejected from so many mishaps, we decided to rest up for a few days and stay where we were.

In fact, we made Leamington Spa our base and stayed there for the rest of the decade, establishing a troubling pattern by which our mooring was decided more by the state of our engine than any opinion we had on the matter.

5

To Yorkshire

In the 1970s, when I first visited Leeds by boat, it generated in me an awful sense of foreboding. But I can be forgiven for it. Anyone cruising up the River Aire in those days would have felt the same way. The place was a manifestation of industrial decline, littered with the ruins of factories, mills and the remnants of crumbling warehouses, some of them used as car repair garages or paint shops, judging from the acrid smell of solvents emanating from them. Along the bank were dilapidated wharves half submerged in the murky river water, which shimmered with an oily residue, like a dirtier version of those psychedelic paraffin slides Pink Floyd used in their early light shows.

It reminded me of nothing more than that famous picture painted in 1801 of the Bedlam Furnaces, just downstream from Ironbridge in Shropshire on the River Severn. The canvas is dominated by a massive inferno belching flames across a landscape that must have once been a rural idyll, but which by then was besmirched by industrial debris: huge cylinders the size of gigantic oil drums, fragments of unidentifiable machinery and massive pipes. Without any irony whatsoever, this painting is viewed nowadays with some pride: it is seen as a symbol of the birth of the Industrial Revolution and the way it heralded the commercial dominance of England and English culture. Cruising up the River Aire towards Leeds at the time I'm talking about, the Industrial Revolution was well and truly over, its fires long since burned out, and what we were left with was the filth afterwards, like the detritus from a riotous party. A quest for wealth born out of environmental devastation had, by its conclusion, wreaked ecological ruin. It's a sad comment on the Industrial Revolution, but sadder by far is the way we still triumph in its excesses, proud that we were the first country in the world to do it.

But it's not all bad news. Recently, when I cruised the river, it had transformed so unrecognisably that I was caught off guard by Leeds, which suddenly appeared out of nowhere from a sea of greenery. I was cruising alone, sitting on the top of the steering hatch, one leg dangling over the side and the other crooked on top of the boat. It was a close and muggy day and I was almost dropping off to sleep, lulled by the gentle beat of the engine. There was nothing else on the river and I'd thought I was about half an hour from the city. But suddenly, without warning, I rounded a bend and found myself at River Lock Number 1, where the Aire connects to the Leeds and Liverpool Canal. I was so taken aback I jumped from the hatch and almost fell in – although that wouldn't have been as miserable an experience as it might have been in the past, because in the intervening years the river has been cleaned up. Today, there are reports of salmon in the lower reaches, only prevented by weirs and other obstructions from reaching their traditional spawning grounds in the Dales towards Malham Cove where the river rises.

At least in Leeds itself I have something tangible to corroborate my impressions of that first visit, for Em took a picture of the canal basin, and I have it before me as I write. It shows a bleak urban landscape, a row of ruined Victorian warehouses lining the edge of a lock: an industrial terrace without function, but still strangely graceful in its own timeless way. The towpath is dusty and brown after a hot summer, and the only colour evident in the scene is a single brightly coloured narrowboat in the foreground. That boat is the repainted *Pelikas* in which we'd finally installed a different engine and cruised to the city via the Aire and Calder, mixing it with snaking trains of coal barges nicknamed Tom Puddings that plied the rivers then, feeding coal to the three massive power stations at Ferrybridge, all now long since decommissioned.

The derelict waterfront at Leeds that Em captured on camera all those years ago is unrecognisable from the city of today. There is no Royal Armouries Museum, no gilt and glass facade at the rear of the station, no blocks of upmarket waterside apartments, no smart hotels. Most of all, there's no one around except us. But this was before planners began to realise the role the waterways could play in urban renaissance, before waterside loft-living became the ambition of the iPhone generation. It was in the days when a bar wasn't a riot of glass and chrome serving exotic cocktails, but a gloomy backstreet dive doling out pints of keg bitter in sticky glasses.

And the pattern for Leeds has been the pattern for the rest of Britain, too. Wherever you go today, these leftover remnants of Britain's manufacturing past have become corridors of regeneration, the basis of a new Canal Age centred on leisure rather than industry. Sometimes I find the scale and speed of the transformation disturbing, as if a world that was exclusively mine has been stolen from me while I was dozing in front of the telly one night. Yet at the same time I feel proud to have been a part of the process and vindicated by what has happened. In the 1970s, people thought I was crazy to spend time messing around on these filthy ditches. Crazier still was when I started evangelising about how waterways could be used in the future, how they could be the focus for urban renewal. It wasn't a popular subject, and I wasn't popular advocating it. Whenever the topic came up at work, I could sense colleagues shuffling away from me, their eyes glazing over as if I were some nerd about to talk about trainspotting or stamp collecting or some other geeky pastime.

Which, looking back on it, I suppose I was.

Not that the attitudes of other people has ever worried me much. At a time when I doubt any more than a few thousand of us would have cared if the whole canal system had been left to rot, I was zealous in my belief that there was a bright future for it. And like most zealots, I was convinced, not just of my vision but its moral righteousness. I *knew* not only that my world view would eventually prevail, but that it was right that it should. I had lived in Bangkok before they destroyed the city by filling in the *klongs*; I had been to Venice many times. I could imagine British towns as they could be, making a feature of these industrial arteries they had inherited.

In 1980, working for London's *Time Out* magazine, I managed to persuade the editor to commission a cover feature from me on waterways in the city. The magazine prided itself on having its journalistic finger on the pulse of life in the capital, yet it had been five years since it had even mentioned the city's canals, apart from listing gigs at Dingwalls at Camden Lock, which had opened a few years before on the derelict site of some former gin distilleries, round the corner from old canal stables where one or two ex-hippies had taken to selling home-made jewellery at a Saturday market. Yet the waterways were a massive feature of the London landscape. They stretched from Brentford in the west to Limehouse in the east, where they headed north through Hackney, Walthamstow and Enfield to join with the rivers Lea and Stort. This is a distance of almost 30 miles (48km). It traversed the city. It split it in two.

What I found researching my 1980 feature was an almost completely forsaken network of waterways. Just a step out from Bromley-by-Bow tube station were the Bow Back Rivers, a scene of desolate beauty, so cut off from the city that I had to hack my way along the overgrown towpath to get to them. I remember particularly how quiet the area was apart from birdsong, which, I wrote, was 'almost deafening'. Tucked away there I discovered Three Mills, which had once been another gin distillery, but which at the time was being used by the wine importers Hedges & Butler. Not far away was the ornate and turreted Abbey Mills Pumping Station, which I described, with only a touch of exaggeration, as the East End's answer to Brighton's Royal Pavilion. Yet except for a few intrepid kids fishing, the whole area was forlorn. I walked to Limehouse Basin, where the Regents Canal converges on the Thames. It's a huge stretch of water, and as recently as the 1940s you could have walked across it entirely on narrowboats waiting to offload cargoes brought in by seagoing ships. Yet at the time I was researching the article there were just a couple of beat-up barges servicing Cohen's Scrap Yard on one bank. Beyond Commercial Locks towards Hackney it was the same story. For mile after depressing mile the canal cut through a neglected landscape of abandoned factories and council estates, most of which had turned their back on the cut except as a sort of linear rubbish tip for old prams, mattresses and TV sets. Of boats, however, there was no sign – although as a boatowner myself at that time, this was no surprise to me. No one would have moored around here. Not if they had a brain as well as a boat. If they had moored, they wouldn't have had a boat the next morning. It would have been ripped apart by vandals.

Today, if you walked that same stretch you'd be lucky to see the canal at all because so many craft of various sorts are jammed into every half-metre of space, double and sometimes triple moored. People live on boats in the capital in ever-increasing numbers, mainly because with property being so prohibitively expensive it's the cheapest way of owning a home in London.

The result has been the creation of a huge canal community with its own customs, its own culture and its own unique energy. Walking the London towpath these days in summer, especially around London Fields, is like looking at a gallery of contemporary youth: Goths and Stylers, Ravers and Sick Boys are splayed across the top of their boats for mile after mile, drinking, smoking and socialising in what seems to be an endless towpath party. These days on the London cut you're as likely to come across a Book Barge or a boat used as a performance space, with acrobats on the roof, as one used to carry anything remotely industrial. There are waterside cafes, permanent and pop-up, and old East End pubs that have been ponced up beyond recognition. Camden Market has grown to become one of London's must-see tourist sites; and the 2012 Olympics were, of course, held on an island formed by the Bow Back Rivers. Three Mills, which I stumbled across all those years ago, is now a TV and film studio.

If you were young, why wouldn't you want to live on a boat in London when the alternative was some pokey, overpriced bedsit in a crime-ridden corner of the city so far off the beaten track you'd need a compass to find it?

The ultimate acknowledgement of London's waterways, the definitive endorsement of their contemporary status, is that on the canal behind King's Cross station, near the restored and reconstructed gas holder (which of all things has become a new park) is Kings Place, an arts complex that houses the corporate HQ of the *Guardian* newspaper, that iconic weathervane of liberal fashionistas.

It was bound to happen – it had to. With 3,000 miles (4,828km) of canals and rivers permeating the country like the roots of an oak tree, the British waterways system offered too much to be ignored. Waterways went everywhere, and everywhere was close to one. Forget cities – out in the countryside there were mile upon mile of them, corridors through a covert, rural England that was remarkably unspoiled: they were conduits to a forgotten Albion, pathways to a past that had lain virtually untouched for generations.

Yorkshire, as with so many other things, is better endowed with waterways than other places, but even an area renowned for its hard-headed approach to commerce took a while to wake up to the potential benefits, economic and social, of the 128 miles (206km) of canal that linked Leeds to Liverpool, and that for years was the jewel in the crown of the system. When we first visited, it was the only surviving canal of the three that had once crossed the Pennines, threading its way out of Leeds, past the majestic five-lock staircase at Bingley to reach Skipton, the gateway to the Dales.

It's a startling waterway, part of it so rural that the celebrated Pennine Way footpath runs along the towpath. But it has got a compelling industrial face, too; and after it's crossed from Yorkshire into Lancashire it passes through towns like Blackburn, Burnley and Wigan. You couldn't call the canal in these places beautiful, although it does have a certain grandeur to it, sweeping ostentatiously through these municipalities as if it were built not for industrial traffic but to host mayoral flotillas for some festival or another. It is wide and deep and trees line its course, and where there aren't trees there are always fishermen in their droves arching their fishing poles over boats as they pass in a constant guard of honour. Blackburn was the last conurbation to be connected to the canal system and 39 mills grew up in its wake; some of them, like the vast and magnificent Imperial Mill, still stand as an imposing monument to the past. In Burnley, in a more modest accolade to bygone years, a cluster of mainly 19th-century industrial buildings adjoining the canal have been meticulously restored and designated as The Weavers' Triangle.

The canal towpath here is constructed of traditional stone slabs, and the roofs of loading sheds still hang over the water.

Today, however, the Leeds and Liverpool has competitors. After long and costly restoration work you can now cruise the two other trans-Pennine canals that have been reopened. The first of these – the Huddersfield Narrow Canal or the 'HNC', as it's known among boaters – starts close to the centre of the town, behind the university, and it storms the Pennines like a squaddie in training with his sergeant major barking instructions behind him. At Standedge, it burrows under the mountains towards Manchester through Britain's highest, deepest and longest tunnel, which at 6,484 yards (5,929m) – nearly 4 miles (6.4km) in old money – is a daunting length in a boat however you measure it.

What's more, this isn't the most extraordinary aspect of the canal. This is the fact that it goes right through the middle of Stalybridge. Now, I recognise that to those untutored in the ways of the cut, this may not exactly sound like a spectacular achievement. But believe me, if you looked at pictures of the town just before the canal was restored, you'd be hard-pressed to know that there'd ever been a canal running through it. Most of its original course had been filled in to become a car park, and a couple of factories had been built over what was left. Yet today you can cruise right into the centre through a specially dug channel and a rebuilt lock to a brand-new plaza called Armentieres Square. Considering that a couple of years after it was formed, the Huddersfield Canal Society, which pioneered the restoration, had just 40 quid in its bank account, and that this section of the restoration alone cost millions, you can understand that getting boats moving along the HNC again wasn't a run-of-the-mill achievement so much as a miracle.

The second of the restored Pennine waterways, the Rochdale Canal, by comparison rises more gradually, ambling out of

Manchester through some its most unprepossessing suburbs until just beyond Littleborough it abruptly reaches its summit in West Yorkshire, where the landscape changes dramatically. Suddenly, the purple heather-clad hills drop into the canal, which in turn drops down to the lovely town of Hebden Bridge and on to Mytholmroyd, the childhood home of the poet Ted Hughes.

I cruised these waterways soon after their restoration and I wouldn't have missed the opportunity to do it – but it was far from easy. After the undulating shires of the South and Midlands where I'd done most of my boating, all this locking wasn't what I was used to. On the HNC, I don't think there's a single point at any lock where you can't see the next one in front of you, inviting you to come and have a go at it like some provocative drunk looking for trouble on a Saturday night. At that time, not long after it had reopened, the paddle gear was more often than not rusted solid. Things have improved a lot since, but in those early years getting the locks to work was like trying to jemmy open an old safe. It took you into hernia territory. Far worse was the lack of water. When these canals were first planned in the late 18th century, they were designed with a comprehensive system of reservoirs to feed the locks; but over the years, the reservoirs fell into disrepair, or worse, they were sold off to Yorkshire Water. I would often find myself suffering the worst effects of a Pennine summer – which is to say, suffering a characteristically long period of persistent, driving rain – only to be sitting on the bottom of the canal with insufficient water on which to float. On more than one occasion I got stuck in a lock chamber for lack of water, once having to be rescued by a snotty-nosed 12-year-old. Seeing what a pickle I was in, and being a true son of Yorkshire, he screwed a tenner out of me for the privilege.

You couldn't help but smile. And it was a good job I did, because smiling was often the only thing that kept me going through all the travails I faced. There's something about a canal

– any canal – that attracts oddballs, whether they're boaters, dog-walkers or ubiquitous fishermen. It is part of the charm of the waterways, but it seems to be magnified in the north. One sunny afternoon in Marsden on the HNC, I watched as a young bloke in designer jeans and a white T-shirt, with a mobile phone glued to his ear, walked straight into the canal. And when I say that, I don't mean he strayed over the edge and gave himself a wet foot, or that he slipped and went tumbling. I mean that he walked straight into the water up to his waist as if it was on his route, striding into it with such purpose you'd think he'd got an appointment with the bottom.

One lunchtime, on the HNC again, I stopped briefly for a pie and a pint at a pub and came back to the boat to find an angler had set up camp on my deck, his paraphernalia laid out all around him as if he were there for the week. I'd had it bad the previous night, unable to get into the side because the canal was so shallow. Finally, I'd just thrown in the towel and moored in the centre of the channel, being pretty sure that there wasn't another boat on the whole canal, and that I was thus unlikely to pose much of an obstruction to anyone or anything, except perhaps bewildered fish unfamiliar with the submerged hulls of boats. Even so, I slept fitfully and so was in no mood for confrontational fishermen out to make my life difficult. 'What on earth are you doing, for God's sake?' I said when I saw him. 'You're on my boat.'

'And your boat's on my fishing spot,' he replied with a logic that was impeccable and not unfriendly. I could see his point. He was an old bloke and he'd probably been fishing in that spot since the Boer War. Suddenly, what had been his own personal fiefdom had been invaded by an alien in a 60-foot-long cigar tube made of steel. In his position, I'd have felt hacked-off too.

All the way down the HNC that year there was evidence of this sort of passive resistance to boats navigating the canal.

And as with the fisherman, I couldn't really blame people for feeling the way they did. Many of them in properties bordering the canal bought their homes believing that the ribbon of water at the bottom of their garden was somehow included in the deeds. Anyway, they treated it like it was. They colonised it. They planted it with flower beds and behaved as if the bank was an extension of their lawn, the canal a private pond.

Attempting to navigate the HNC, the water was so shallow at times that, even when the boat was afloat, there was barely enough depth for the tiller to function as a feasible mode of steering. I found the only way of making any progress was to engage the engine in forward gear on a gentle tickover, and then steer from the front deck with my bargepole, fending off from the banks when it looked like the boat was going off course. I was doing this one afternoon when I was set upon by a woman in one of the adjoining houses who'd seen me from her kitchen window as she'd been washing up and rushed out to confront me. 'You're putting holes in my lawn,' she said angrily, writing down the name and number of the boat on the back of an envelope she'd brought with her for the purpose. 'I'm going to report you to the authorities and make a formal complaint.'

I didn't know what to say. A row of geometrically precise puncture marks blighting the otherwise unblemished surface of her grass was incontrovertible evidence of the truth of what she was alleging. But there was another truth, as there so often is in such circumstances; although I judged that with her in such high dudgeon and me somewhat preoccupied with navigating a 20-ton lump of steel across a puddle, it perhaps wasn't the best time to open a discussion about the finer points of land tenure. I didn't want a row with her is what I'm saying. Not when I could see so plainly where she was coming from. Not when there was a part of me that sympathised with her. Besides, I'd come to rather like the people of this part of

West Yorkshire, as I'd come to like the wonderful countryside of West Yorkshire itself. And it *is* wonderful. Not twee and pretty like Oxfordshire or Kent, nor a wilderness either, like Dartmoor or the Scottish Highlands; but hard, functional and utilitarian, a landscape of swelling hills topped by dark moorland and threaded with rows of stout grey houses built of stone to withstand proper weather, not that mollycoddling stuff we call weather south of the Trent.

I suppose I should have been happy that at least the lady complaining about her lawn didn't take direct action to signal her disapproval of the canal like some did on the Rochdale Canal, the other newly restored Pennine crossing. There, a farmer who'd come to believe that the disused canal bed was part of his land, took to sawing the balance beams off restored locks so they couldn't be used. Balance beams, for those unfamiliar with them, are the long timbers that protrude from locks like arms, their function being to balance the weight of the gates, allowing them to pivot on their hinges and open easily. The gates are massive things, so the balance beams have to be equally heavy. They're enormous pieces of wood, at least a foot thick, sometimes twice that. Even using power tools, sawing through a balance beam would be a demanding job. It's certainly not the sort of task you could knock off in the odd ten minutes before lunch. To cut through a balance beam requires commitment and dedication. It requires serious effort. Yet this farmer did it repeatedly until eventually, having lived with his eccentricity long enough, the police took him to court, where the magistrate started fining him on an escalating scale that rose with every eviscerated lock beam they found lying mutilated on the towpath. When that still didn't cure him of this incorrigible habit of attacking blameless blocks of wood, they finally had to put him in prison where, for all I know, he may still be languishing to this day.

The kids in north Manchester weren't that keen on the Rochdale Canal, either. Or maybe they didn't have strong feelings one way or another, but just saw the newly restored canal as a fresh challenge to their destructive ingenuity. At first, they took to opening all the paddles on the locks, causing waterfalls down the canal that flooded Failsworth a few times. Eventually, all this grunt work must have become too strenuous for them, so after a rest period during which they took to indulging their artistic side in graffiti, they finally came up with the idea of removing the paddle gear from the locks completely. This at any rate had its positive side, in that the antique iron must have had value at some dodgy scrap yard somewhere, so that they could make themselves a bob or two from their endeavours.

But even when they weren't attacking the locks, the kids were hardly welcoming ambassadors to visiting boats. During my trip, I got spat at, attacked with bricks and regularly sworn at – the latter for no better reason, it seemed to me, than because I was a sentient being in a deserted place and the kids cursing me were pissed off at something and felt the need to express it to someone. Anyone.

On one bridge near Rochdale, a bloke too old to be called a kid balanced precariously on the parapet, out of his mind on something or another. Once I was under him, he tried to pee on me – although not very successfully, I recall, most of it dribbling down his trousers. There were reports of 'steaming' as well – gangs of kids boarding a boat at the bow and running out at the stern, grabbing anything valuable on the way through. Urban myth or not, the situation became so bad that boaters wouldn't navigate this part of the canal, so that to justify the time and money they'd spent restoring it, the waterways' authority had to arrange for those navigating into Manchester to be accompanied by minders riding shotgun until they got past the worst areas. Ah, the joys of canals. You don't see this sort of thing when the celebrities are travelling about on their telly programmes, do you? And they don't tell the newbies about it either when they shell out a hundred grand and more at the boat shows.

But what did I expect of the north, what does anyone expect who doesn't live there or know it or feel for it? The south with funny accents? The Home Counties with better beer? Weren't there bound to be casualties from an industrial system that had exploited the region when there was money to be made out of it, and discarded it so unthinkingly when there wasn't? For God's sake, had I expected Jerusalem in this green and pleasant land of ours?

It was sad, really, because when I got the chance of speaking to local people I discovered that the reappearance of moving boats on the canal after so many years of it being derelict touched some of them more deeply than I'd have thought possible. Coming through a lock at one dreary suburb with nothing much to commend it except a discount furniture shop on one corner and a shuttered Tandoori curry house on the other, boats were such an unusual and colourful sight that a couple of dozen people interrupted their day to watch me. It was so odd for me to excite such attention that I took a picture of the scene. There are old people in the photograph, toddlers, teenagers, and young mums holding up their babies to show them what in so many places would be an unremarkable commonplace, but which in that drab neighbourhood – a place where you just knew there'd be no libraries, no jobs and no decent schools – it was a sight of unexpected vibrancy. And, of course, a sight of unaccustomed affluence, too. I couldn't help but wonder how much a local house would fetch and how that would compare to the cost of my boat.

With the security men operating the locks for me, I had time to chat before the last part of the trip into the city centre. One bloke saw from the boat's livery that it came from Banbury and he wanted to know if I'd travelled all the way by canal. My insistence that I had did little to reassure him: he was convinced I'd had it craned out of the water at some stage. Other people were more curious about my domestic arrangements. Had I got a cooker in the boat? A lavatory? Was there a sink where I could wash? One woman sticks in my mind in particular. She was in her 80s, a small, chirpy lady with a perm like a plaster cast. She told me how she remembered commercial barges coming down the canal to Manchester, and how as a girl she and her friends had taken bottles of cold tea and sandwiches to have picnics on the towpath, where they'd get chased away if anyone from the canal company caught them. As she talked, tears welled in her eyes as memories kept flooding back to her across forgotten years. For me, this was just a restored canal, but for her, being part of her youth, it was thronged with ghosts from long ago, an important feature on the landscape of her past. I found it very moving.

6

Manchester and Liverpool

We spent the dog days of summer after our trip up the Lancaster ostensibly crossing the Pennines to Manchester. What that meant in reality was that we spent most of it in the Yorkshire Dales, bouncing between the wonderful old market town of Skipton and the village of Gargrave 4 miles (6.4km) away. This became a convenient base for us to explore the National Park, cycling or walking the miles of public footpaths that criss-cross the countryside in these parts.

When we finally did arrive in Manchester it was an eye-opener in more ways than one. I lived for a while in the city during the early 80s just after the famous Haçienda nightclub had opened. This wasn't long after Ian Curtis of Joy Division had hanged himself, marking the end of the road not just for him but for the band, too. Afterwards, the remaining members regrouped as New Order before they went on to invent the 1980s. Sadly, though, by the time I arrived in the city they hadn't quite got to grips with the task in hand and their music still felt like, well, like Joy Division, actually. But then the whole of Manchester felt like Joy Division at that time – which is to say it felt far from joyful. One journalist described the band's music as 'brooding, droning, dire' – which is as good a description I can think of for Manchester in that era, too, except that as a Midlander I'd want to add that it was also very wet as well, and very cold, particularly in the Haçienda on weekday nights when they couldn't afford to heat the place.

But what a different city it is now, a complete revelation. Most of the filthy canals I remembered from the past had been cleaned up and were unrecognisable from those I used to wistfully wander around when I lived there, constantly bemoaning the waste of such a unique resource. Like every major city in the country with a canal, Manchester's had a spate of recently built high-rise apartments and offices springing up along the towpath like uncontrollable weeds. But I'm not complaining. In this city more than all others, it makes for a dramatic mix of old and new, with a tangle of waterways, roads and railways layered on top of each other like rock strata. An elegant steel bridge, the height of contemporary design, is dwarfed by a nearby Victorian viaduct, a highly decorated confection with abutments like castle turrets, and cast-iron railings shaped like Gothic arches. Above that, viaducts stretch over other viaducts, each of them the relic of a separate period of rail history. Above them all – the icing on the cake, as it were – is the Great Northern viaduct erected in 1894, the cavernous arches of which are supported by enormous tubular steel columns, built to withstand earthquakes.

We moored in Castlefield for a couple of weeks, and you couldn't get a more central location, just a step away from Chinatown and Piccadilly and literally round the corner from the Science and Industry Museum; the moorings there are on an arm of the Bridgewater Canal, which is an unusual canal in being privately owned, one of the few in the country that are. It's the property of Peel Holdings, one of those secretive companies that few have ever heard of, and yet that control vast swathes of our country. Some 37,000 acres (15,000 hectares) of it, in fact, administered through a complex network of more than 300 separately registered companies, a structure designed according to the *Guardian* 'like a series of Russian dolls, one nested inside another', their purpose being 'to keep its corporate structures obscure and its landholdings hidden.'

Not entirely hidden though and we know its £2.3bn property portfolio includes farmland in the Medway, an industrial estate in the Cotswolds, shopping centres, ports and even Liverpool John Lennon Airport. Around the corner from the moorings at Castlefield is the Rochdale Canal, which rises to the Pennines out of the city through a flight of locks and a dark passageway under Piccadilly station. It's a fearsome stretch of canal. You navigate through a network of damp subterranean culverts that could be a leftover set from *Blade Runner*. There are dark, low archways of Victorian bridges supporting roads above; there are foundations of more contemporary structures built on pillars and emerging from the water like the columns of a submerged cloister. Piccadilly Lock is completely underground, its roof a series of wide steel girders bearing the weight of the city on top of it. At one point, the canal opens to daylight, which pierces the gloom with a jolt, like a blast of freezing cold air in a warm room. Maybe there was once a loading bay here. Maybe it was the wharf for a long-forgotten mill.

It's a grim stretch of canal even now, but it's nothing compared to what it used to be in the 1980s. Back then, the towpath would crunch with hypodermic needles discarded by addicts who used to gather under a series of yawning arches bordering the water, shooting up in front of your eyes. It was a sort of social club-cum-doss house for them and meths drinkers who were forever screaming at you as you went by. Menacing? Mmmm, a bit. I think it was supposed to be menacing. They were an urban tribe, refugees from the contemporary world until the contemporary world couldn't accommodate them, even underground and out of sight, and they were cleared out. The authorities blocked off the arches they'd once occupied. They installed new lighting and covered the openings to their squalid haunts with a cheerful mural of barges and flowers, which, apparently, was supposed to be something to do with celebrating Manchester's cultural heritage since the Industrial Revolution. But it's always easier to celebrate a success than remedy a failure, isn't it? I wonder where those addicts have gone, because it seems to me they also represent at least a part of the city's industrial heritage. And one thing's for sure, and that's that they won't have disappeared.

Navigating out of the city in this direction is particularly unnerving for other reasons, too. At certain times of the year when there's been heavy rain, the overflow buckets off the Pennines and down this flight of nine locks, which cascade with water. This is because there are no by-weirs to drain the overflow. The land on which they were built was sold off by the Rochdale Canal Company years ago when this short flight of only 1.5 miles (2.4km) was the only section of the whole canal that remained in use after most of it had been closed in 1952. I made the mistake of going up the flight on my own once after heavy rain and I was lucky not to sink the boat. It seems counterintuitive, but water flooding over lock gates into pounds below doesn't push boats backwards as you'd expect; on the contrary, it creates a vortex that draws craft towards it. Navigating a flight like this is nerve-racking because there's always the risk of getting pulled under what are essentially a series of tumultuous waterfalls. Approaching a lock on your own, you have to jump off the boat with a rope and tie it to a bollard as quickly as you can to prevent being sucked forwards. Only then can you open the paddles to empty the lock. On one occasion, my knot slipped and the boat went careering towards the torrent, where it would have sunk in seconds if I hadn't managed to haul it back from the brink.

Things get even worse once the lock's emptied and you're preparing to steer in. Now the waterfall that had been pouring over the bottom gates is surging over the top ones. Single-handing in these conditions is a nightmare. You have to edge the boat into the lock without getting too close to the wall of water ahead of you. It's a nail-biting process that requires split-second decision making, for when you think the time's right you have to scramble on to the boat roof carrying a rope, leap on to the lock side and tie up as fast as you can. A couple of times I got it wrong and could only watch in horror as the boat edged towards catastrophe. Once I made such a hash of it I misjudged my course completely and the boat grazed the edge of the waterfall. It immediately lurched with the power of the flow and my front deck flooded faster than the scuppers could take it out. Luckily, despite being in a blind panic, I managed to reverse to safety before I sank. Much good it did me. All I had achieved was a second chance – the opportunity to do the whole harrowing manoeuvre again.

By the time I got to the top I wasn't just physically exhausted by all this, I was mentally exhausted too. Believe me, this sort of boating takes a lot of concentration. I could have done with an hour with my feet up. Or failing that, maybe a pint or two. What I didn't want was some wisecracking smartass sitting on a bench at the lockside wanting to engage me in conversation. But that, of course, was exactly what I did get. 'That looks like fun and games,' he said. 'Still, a bloke of your age, I suppose it keeps you active?'

I gave him a forced smile. He couldn't have been more than 18 or 19 and there's nothing those of us in our later years enjoy more than being patronised by the young.

'Mind you, it's got to be better than the gym,' he went on, 'I guess it's a good workout doing all that exercise. And not so many sweaty bodies around either, eh? Not so many babes to distract you.'

He sat on the bench kicking his heels, a smutty smile on his face. Maybe this exchange was just his way of being friendly, but I wasn't in the mood for it. Inside, I felt irascible and unsociable.

I'd have liked him to ignore me completely. Failing that, I wondered if he'd mind awfully if I wrung his neck and threw him in the lock.

'Yes, it has been tough going, this flight,' I said, attempting to veneer my response with politeness, but not really wanting to encourage conversation.

He wasn't to be so easily deterred. 'So what now?' he said, genially. 'Are you going back into town again? At least it'll be easier downhill.'

I gave him another wan smile. This gag about locks being easier downhill than uphill has to be the oldest one-liner in the Inland Waterways Joke Book. I'm sure the old 18th-century boatmen must have heard it as often as I had, and I've heard it every year I've been cruising at every lock flight from Bath to Bingley.

Suddenly, a way of ridding myself of his irritating presence occurred to me: a way of getting rid of him without being provocatively rude. I said, 'I've got to press on. I've got a good few more locks to do today. In fact, if you're not busy, you could always give me a hand...?'

I expected he'd be off like a shot, and I was surprised he wasn't. Instead he stood up shaking his head with what seemed like genuine regret. 'Sadly, can't do, my friend,' he said, 'though there's nothing I'd like more. Disappointed though I am, my attendance is required at an important engagement...'

It turned out the engagement was at the police station where he had to report twice a day after some dispute over the ownership of a television set he was caught carrying close to a house that had just been burgled and had one stolen. It seemed he was wearing a security tag, what he called his 'Rolex.' He lifted up his leg to show me.

'Thanks, anyhow,' he said as he left.

'Thanks?'

'Well, you know, for talking to me, for being civil. I often chat to people in boats when they're coming this way but most of them don't exactly warm to me. You're different,' he said. 'You're friendly.'

The most famous section of Manchester's canal system runs parallel to the Rochdale along Canal Street. This area is marketed now as the heart of Manchester's gay village, and the towpath's used as a short cut between bars and clubs. Sadly, for a place where so many come for a good night out, an unprecedented number of people have lost their lives around here as they've slipped on the towpath or lost their footing crossing the canal by the lock gates. At one time, it was estimated an astonishing 61 people had drowned on Manchester's canals over six years – so many that the idea of a serial killer at large, knocking people into the water, took hold. The police investigated this theory of the 'Manchester Pusher' more seriously than you'd have thought it warranted, given that as a Manchester friend of mine observed, if a killer had been at large for that length of time, surely at least one person would've survived a ducking to be witness to what had happened to him. If we're looking for a more likely culprit for the tragedies, most of which involved young people, alcohol would be top of the list, and indeed a recent research project by the Royal Society for the Prevention of Accidents identified this as a factor in two-thirds of the deaths.

One way or another, what's happened hasn't materially affected the attractions for visitors to an area that, despite its label, is a magnet for young people of all persuasions – gay, straight or transgender – who flock here in their droves. The place crackles with an earthy energy. You can sense it around you. You can feel it in the air. But then it's the same across the whole of the centre of Manchester, which attracts the young in a way London hasn't for years. This is because London's shot itself in the foot with its high property prices. It's so expensive that barely anyone young can afford to live in the place any more, let alone go out at night drinking and clubbing.

It was the same in Liverpool, where we stopped for another couple of weeks. The place fizzed. You felt it was only ever a random spark away from spontaneously combusting. If possible, there were even more young people on the streets than in Manchester – so many in fact that you'd think the manufacture of them was a local industry rather than simply the by-product of an engaging pastime. Again, it didn't seem that going out on the town was prohibitively expensive. Most nights of the week there'd be swarms of pimply faced lads in trousers too tight for them, pursuing bevies of shrieking women tottering along the pavements in vertiginous heels. And hen nights, so many hen nights! Wherever you looked. Hen nights where everyone dressed as schoolgirls. Or as nuns. Or fairies. My God, I have never seen so many hen nights in my whole life as I did that fortnight in Liverpool – although I suppose if the city's going to meet its production targets for kids, this is a key part of the entire process and should probably warrant a development grant.

This constantly festive culture in Liverpool wasn't as much of a surprise to me as the changes in Manchester. Maybe this was because, although Liverpool has changed physically, the mentality of the place hasn't altered much in 40 years. Even when I knew the city in the worst days of the 1980s, when the economy was in recession, with national unemployment at a 50-year high and the north-west suffering more than most, there was an irrepressible spirit about the place, positive and life-affirming. Liverpool has such a history of accomplishment that if it can't articulate its aspirations through commerce, trade or artistic creativity, its inherent energy is just as likely to burst out in political protest, as it did in the summer of 1981 when there was widespread rioting.

I was working for the BBC at the time, based in Manchester for a programme called *Nationwide,* which no one under the age of 40 will ever have heard of even though they've been watching a paler, less contentious version of it for years called *The One Show.* I was based at the Oxford Road studios – now demolished as part of the Corporation's move to production line television at Media City in Salford. Before the days of hot desking, I had one all to myself next to an old stager of a journo, 20 years or so my senior, who was responsible for funnelling news from the area to the national newsdesk at TV Centre. I liked him a lot. He was a sort of father figure to me, and I had a great deal of respect for him. Or at least I did until the time of the Liverpool riots when I overheard him briefing London about events. 'Oh, it's not worth bothering with,' he said. 'Just a load of blacks kicking up.' I don't need to tell you that the word 'blacks' wasn't the one he used.

Curiosity excited, I went over to Liverpool that night to see for myself what all the fuss was about. I'd already been on the front line, reporting on London riots in Lewisham, Brixton and Notting Hill, so I wasn't unfamiliar with violent disturbances on the streets. Even so, the damage I witnessed that day was on a scale totally in excess of anything I'd seen before. The media christened what happened the 'Toxteth' Riots, although in reality the riots happened right across the district of Liverpool 8, which stretches from Toxteth down Upper Parliament Street towards the old Cathedral and the area now christened the Georgian Quarter for the simple reason it's said to contain more Georgian buildings than Bath. It was summer, and I arrived after the worst of the action had finished. It was getting dark and vans of police were parked randomly along the street, suspiciously eyeing restive groups of young black guys who, in turn, were suspiciously eyeing them. There was a palpable tension in the air, yet everything was eerily quiet, except for odd sirens in the distance splintering the silence. Around me, buildings were blazing, and not just buildings either, for the very streets themselves were on fire – something I'd never seen before or since. Whether this was because of a recently thrown petrol bomb, or because the asphalt covering the 18th-century cobblestones was actually burning itself, I couldn't say.

The city today is a completely different experience, but that's because it's a completely different city. In the past, it was focused around Lime Street station, just down from the famous Liverpool Empire and around the corner from the equally famous Adelphi Hotel, which is where, in the Golden Age of transatlantic liners, the well-heeled elite would stay before setting sail for New York. I stayed there once or twice when I'd been out on the tiles and was too drunk to make it back to Manchester but by then it had turned into a sort of upmarket doss house that, like the city's iconic sex worker Maggie May, had obviously been around a bit and seen better days. Great ceiling-to-floor mirrors, once the height of opulence, were flaking brown, like books singed in a fire. Plaster was falling off the walls of most rooms, and the once-splendid marbled washbasins in the bathrooms were invariably cracked and stained.

Today, the focus of the city has moved further west towards Albert Dock, where 42 acres (17 hectares) of land have been developed into a huge residential, shopping and leisure complex called Liverpool One, which advertises itself as the largest open-air shopping centre in the UK. It takes some getting used to. The scale of it is prodigious, even for someone like me, familiar with some of the grosser southern temples of consumerism like Bluewater or Westfield. It so dominates the city centre that in many ways it *is* the city centre, completely redefining the balance and layout of the old Liverpool I used to know.

The development had fortuitous benefits for the inland waterways, however, for in the past narrowboats weren't able to get much further into Liverpool than Stanley Dock, where a short flight of four locks takes the Leeds and Liverpool Canal down to the Mersey. This is about a half-hour walk from the city centre – far enough away not to feel in the city centre at all. But in 2009, an extraordinary link was opened, extending the canal through a series of culverts, locks and tunnels to the heart of tourist Liverpool at Albert Dock, where the Mersey Maritime Museum, Tate Liverpool and a Beatles museum are situated. Beyond that is Salthouse Dock, where we moored amid great blooms of jellyfish that had taken up residence around the boat as a result of the unusually hot summer. One evening, we stood on the deck with a torch and counted nearly 30 of them surrounding our hull, like translucent phantoms hovering in the dark water.

The most impressive part of the new link without doubt is the tunnel parallel to the city's famous Pier Head, which emerges under Liverpool's three most iconic structures – the 'Three Graces' as they're known – which tower above you. The Royal Liver Building, the Cunard Building, and the Port of Liverpool Building are extraordinarily beautiful vestiges of Liverpool's shipping past and they dominate the waterfront in a way that's unmatched by any cityscape anywhere else in the world. Emerging from a gloomy tunnel hanging with cobwebs, and seeing them glinting in the sunshine, my first view of them for many years, it felt like I was renewing my acquaintance with old girlfriends from the past whom I'd loved and left and whose allure I'd forgotten.

We made good use of our time in Liverpool. We took a ferry across the Mersey, and a train to Crosby to see Antony Gormley's life-sized cast-iron figures spread across the beach. And we went to the Africa Oyé festival in Sefton Park, which – can you believe it? – was and still is – free. Free! You remember free? When you didn't have to pay any money to hear music? When you weren't stopped by officious stewards at some hastily erected barrier wanting to relieve you of wads of currency in exchange for some wristband you wouldn't be able to take off until you were festering underneath with sweaty ulcers?

'Please,' the commentator begged us over a tannoy. 'We depend on your generosity for our funding. Please buy a beer to help us out.' I found this no great hardship. In fact, I recall being in a particularly generous mood that afternoon, and with the responsibility of the festival weighing heavily on my shoulders, I set about my task with serious commitment, drinking several bottles of the stuff as I lay on the grass soaking up the sun and enjoying the vibes.

On another day we took the National Trust Transit bus to visit the childhood homes of John Lennon and Paul McCartney, where we sat crammed in with a bevy of young Japanese women, squealing along to a recording of 'Yellow Submarine' as we crawled through the traffic. John's house was much posher than I'd imagined; Paul's much poorer. Paul's brother Mike, a talented photographer, snapped his brother in the sitting room of the small council house where they lived just before the Beatles took off on their extraordinary rise to musical celebrity. A print of that picture hangs on the wall. Paul is splayed awkwardly across a shabby armchair, a caption underneath explaining that he was ashamed of the family's poverty and only agreed to pose if he could position himself to hide the holes and tears in the upholstery.

While in Liverpool, we were only a short distance from another place on the Mersey we'd visited earlier in our canal odyssey.

During our first year living on *Justice* we'd travelled up the Shropshire Union Canal to Llangollen, where we spent our first winter. 'The Shroppie', as it's generally known among canal folk, runs as straight as a railway from Wolverhampton to Ellesmere Port on the River Mersey, slicing through high cuttings or balancing precariously on steep embankments from which occasionally you can catch a glimpse of the surrounding countryside through the tree cover. This is prime farming land and remarkably flat. Fields lie around you in formation, like regiments lined up waiting for battle at Waterloo. Every now and then the vista is punctuated by a small wood or copse, their foliage like puffs of artillery smoke on the horizon.

We stopped at the old, mostly Georgian town of Market Drayton, which was rebuilt in 1651 after most of it had been destroyed by fire. It has some lovely narrow streets and one or two particularly fine buildings. The place gets its name from a charter for a market granted to it by Henry III in 1245, and there's still a market of sorts functioning today, though it's nothing like as flourishing as it was when Em and I first visited 40 years ago. Then, it was vibrant and thronged with people who seemed to be as much attracted to it as a social facility as a place to shop, judging by the groups of people gossiping in the street or chatting over tea and buns at the tables of adjoining cafes. Today, sadly, it's been reduced to a handful of stalls fighting a losing battle with two supermarkets down the road. Barely anyone seems to be using it. But that's the way it is in Britain today. We don't value what we have, and we complain when it's gone. Yet we seem incapable of grasping the connection between the two.

Along with too many other similar small towns, modern life has not treated poor old Market Drayton well; and despite constant efforts to revitalise it, it feels tired and run-down and somewhat confused to have found itself in a backwater of the 21st century without any escape route to the future.

After we left, we moored for a week or so in the pretty village of Audlem in Cheshire, 6 or 7 miles (10–11km) away, which is having to face its own problems with the present. On the surface, Audlem encapsulates so many elements of Old Albion it's an archetype. It straggles a long flight of pretty locks, and has a prosperous centre, with charming cottages clustered around a war memorial and the village church, which stands on a dominating hillock. To read the village website you'd think the biggest problem Audlem faced was dogs fouling the rec where the kids play. But Audlem, like Market Drayton, is not what it first seems. On the outside, it may appear the epitome of Middle England, but the truth is you don't have to scratch far below the surface to realise it's got the same sort of problems as anywhere else in the country, what with poverty, lack of opportunity and, at one time, a serious drug problem that plagued one of its apparently idyllic canalside pubs.

The drug problem hasn't entirely gone away. Searching for a mooring spot, we considered tying up next to a boat that for all intents and purposes looked unoccupied, its rear deck draped with a fine gossamer of cobwebs and its curtains tightly drawn, suggesting no one had been on it for weeks. However, as we dropped speed, they started twitching and before we could even start our approach a hollow-eyed couple appeared at the windows accusing us of colliding with them. Their voices were slurred, their pupils the size of pinheads. Blimey. I don't know about colliding with them, but the smell of dope coming from their boat hit me like a cosh. But an advantage of boats is that you choose your neighbours. We decided we didn't want to be near this querulous pair and we drove on. It was a wonder I could steer straight afterwards.

Over the next few weeks, we ambled up the canal to its terminus at Ellesmere Port, where it meets the Mersey, 20 miles (32km) or so upriver from Liverpool. On the way, it passes the walled city of Chester, where the canal winds around what once used to be the old castle moat. Chester has its Roman ruins and its medieval streets and its unique two-storied arcades called 'rows', which you enter by way of creaky old staircases that lead you either up to a continuous gallery where you can walk overlooking the street or down to shops buried in dark crypts where you might imagine having to go to buy the school uniform for Hogwarts. Chester even has its old port area, since in the past the River Dee used to be an important commercial waterway; until it got silted up, sizeable ships used to load and unload cargoes at wharves situated just outside the city walls where the racecourse is now.

With all this on offer, why would anyone want to push on further into the industrialised hinterland of Merseyside, risking themselves in the process to a fearful set of what are called 'staircase' locks, where the front gates of one lock become the back of another, dropping so steeply that the canal seems to fall precipitously off a cliff edge?

Well, that's a difficult one to answer. As far as we were concerned, it was because like so many boaters we'd been to Chester a number of times before but had never got around to visiting Ellesmere Port. One of the reasons for our odyssey trip was to go to these sorts of places that had slipped through the net despite our decades cruising the waterways. However, there was a secondary reason for going that particular year. We'd booked ourselves into a festival at the National Waterways Museum that is based there. It was an unusual sort of festival, in part a music festival – or to be more precise, a Festival of Sea Shanties – and partly a boat festival. There was also a rally of old Morris Minor cars taking place, which we didn't know about until we arrived and found all manner of these Moggies milling around the site in all their modest glory: soft tops, vans, and estate cars you never knew they'd made. Tacked on to all this was a beer festival, appended to add to the general gaiety of the event (which, with 40 or more types of real ale available at a couple of quid a pint, it succeeded in doing very successfully, thank you very much).

Our arrival wasn't distinguished. No sooner had we checked in and negotiated the couple of locks that drop to the Lower Basin where we were scheduled to moor than our engine stopped dead without warning. Our propeller had fouled. Fouled propellers are not unusual on inland waterways. In fact, they're the bane of the boaters' lives. If it isn't clumps of river weed then it's lengths of rope that other boaters have unhelpfully discarded, or old supermarket bags in towns, or worse still those leathery fertiliser bags that farmers abandon so casually across the countryside. This latest problem was a bag, too. Except it was no ordinary bag. It was one of those huge industrial carriers made out of God-knows-what that building suppliers use to deliver materials to construction sites. This one contained rock, which I guess had been deposited in the basin years back to provide a quick fix to a bank collapse. Unfortunately, the whole caboodle, rocks and bag, had been dropped in the water as it was, leaving the bag handles floating like reeds in a stream, a trap for unwary navigators like us who might cruise over them. It took a couple of hours to get them off the propeller – although thankfully it wasn't a job I had to do entirely alone. Presumably embarrassed by a mishap they thought partly their responsibility, the festival organisers put the job in the hands of one of the site crew, a lad of no more than about 15 who set about the task with an enthusiasm that was exhausting to witness.

Even without the festival, Ellesmere Port is an intriguing location for a day out for anyone, especially anyone interested in the waterways. Its collection of traditional boats is rightly famous, but the real star of the show is without doubt the 7 acre (2.8 hectare) dock itself, designed by the great civil engineer

Thomas Telford. As late as the 1950s, this was a functioning industrial complex, with its own workshops, forges and stables, all of which have survived intact. Recently, they've renovated a street of dock workers' cottages too, so that it's now even more like stepping out of the Tardis into a *Call the Midwife* past when the whole site was busy with barges and narrowboats unloading from seagoing ships for distribution across the country.

You can see how the whole thing links up sitting on the grass in the sunshine as we did, looking across the locks of the dock to the Manchester Ship Canal and the Mersey Estuary beyond. A fuel tanker was being teased along the Ship Canal by a couple of tugs as we watched. Compared to the immense oil tankers that ply their trade out of the Gulf, this was small stuff; but that's like saying that 770ft (235m) Canary Wharf is small stuff compared to the 2,722ft (830m) Burj Khalifa building in Dubai. The fact is, both are huge buildings – just as a Gulf oil tanker and a ship navigating the Manchester Ship Canal are both massive boats. Put it this way: compared to either, *Justice* is a tiny tin can.

A lot of beer was drunk that weekend, a lot of songs sung. I nearly fell in the water coming out of a concert late one night, and one of the 1960s folk group The Spinners actually did – which I can tell you is no joke in the dark when you're getting on a bit and the banks of the dock are as high as they are.

7

York, the River Ouse and the Ripon Canal

OK, so let's make this much clear from the outset before you ask since I'm certain you will ask. You're going to think to yourself, 'They went up to York! That time of the year? Didn't they know what risks they were running? They've no one to blame but themselves.' And yes, it's true, Em and I *were* aware that the River Ouse at York has a tendency to flood in the winter. We were also aware this was so persistent and regular it might have been better to call it a habit rather than a tendency. Yes, we knew all that. But everyone who knows anything about geography knows that, don't they? Everyone's vaguely aware that York floods regularly. If you want to know how regularly then when you're next in town, take a look at the plaque on Ouse Bridge in Tower Gardens. There, you'll see marks representing flood levels in York going back to 1636, although it's known to have flooded as long ago as 1263, and probably before that too except there aren't records. More recently, there have been bad floods in 1947, 1978, 1982 and several since 2000. So you're in the picture now, yes? We were in the picture too before we made the trip. Not that it helped – we decided to do it anyhow.

Our thinking was that yes, York floods in the winter. But this wasn't the winter: it was autumn, early autumn at that. Why should we worry about the prospect of floods – we weren't planning on staying longer than a couple of weeks; we'd be in and out before anyone noticed we were there? Besides, it wasn't as if the floods happened *every* year without fail; they weren't *inevitable*. We thought there couldn't be that much of a flood risk at this time of year since no one warned us about it, or tried to deter us.

So, we headed for Selby along the surprisingly beautiful and secluded Selby Canal, where a lock opens on to the tidal river. We'd booked to go out on a 1.30pm tide, and if I blame myself for any aspect of the debacle that was to envelop us over the ensuing months, it was that I didn't read the runes sufficiently well. We arrived at the lock an hour ahead of time in bright sunshine after one of those gorgeous mornings that trick you into thinking summer isn't over. However, when the time came for us to leave, it was lagging it down – 'stair rodding', as they say in these parts. We really should have taken more notice. The gods were telling us something that day. Unfortunately, we weren't listening.

Generally speaking, tidal rivers make dull cruising. On a canal, any canal, whatever the prevailing conditions, you're at least able to see over the banks and watch the countryside passing by, but on a tidal river, even on a high tide, all you can usually see are the banks, which are either bland or menacing, depending on whether they're a mud beach, dropping from fields to the water's edge, or they're lined with the rocks the size of dustbins that are used to stabilise the shoreline. The Ouse, like most tidal rivers, had stretches of both, which was unsurprising. However, what *did* surprise us about it was the pace and force of the tide. I was on the tiller and the moment we exited the lock, the water swept us upstream, sending us hurtling towards York at a startling rate. Swinging round the sometimes-severe bends that characterise that part of the river, it took time to adjust to the pace and movement of the water and get the measure of the conditions – conditions that seemed particularly challenging after coming off an undemanding canal.

But undemanding is what canals always are by comparison with rivers. It's because they're artificial, a human construct. They work by feeding water from the summit in response to boats drawing from it as they move through locks. What little current there is on a canal really doesn't deserve the name: it's more of a trickle – controlled, gentle and steady, hardly discernable in normal weather conditions. Canals were built as a conduit for trade, and they were designed as far as possible to be reliable and predictable, not subject to extremes of weather or landscape. As a result, they're lifeless compared with rivers, which are the creation of nature and have a will of their own, no matter how humankind tries to control them. Most of the time, rivers are quiet and tranquil, occasionally almost playful as they dart around bends and plunge over weirs. But other times – more often than you'd think, especially in recent years – they are volatile and erratic, and it's no exaggeration to say that when they're in this sort of mood they're highly dangerous and you risk your life venturing on to them.

It didn't take me long to suss out that all it needed was a spell of bad weather for the Yorkshire Ouse to turn into that sort of river. The bad-tempered sort. The sort you have to respect. The sort you can't relax on for one minute.

The journey time from Selby to York is about five hours in a narrowboat, but with the tide pushing us along we were in Naburn – where a lock marks the limit of the tidal reach – in about half that time. At this stage, we had no concept of how important a role the place would play in our lives over the coming months; and if I have any first impressions of it worth recording, it was just the sense of relief we both felt at getting on to quieter water. At first sight, the place seemed pleasant enough, tidy and nicely kept. As well as the lock itself – which is actually two adjacent locks – there are a couple of grand semis that look as they were built in the 1920s, and an attractive complex of Victorian workshops replete with a blacksmith's shop, erected on the site of an old mill that was once a base for river maintenance work. Dominating all this is a peculiar building that looks like a congregational chapel, except that it's the size of a football pitch, swollen out of all proportion. It has an enormous front door and portico, and rows of excessively high windows on all sides. The place was built in 1823 with no more serious function than as a banqueting hall for the trustees of the river who used to meet there for a formal dinner a couple of times a year. A banqueting hall? For use just a couple of times a year? Really, what could they have been thinking of? We've all had jollies on the company's tab – maybe even a meal out at a restaurant – but this is the only example I've ever encountered of a company building its own restaurant for the purpose.

By now, the rain had cleared and the sun was beginning to peek through the avenue of trees that connect the lock approach to the main river. We booked our passage back with the lock keeper as we were required to do, and cruised on to York, where we moored before evening. After a few days' sightseeing and resupplying, we pressed on further north on to the River Ure and the Ripon Canal. Our final destination was the city of Ripon itself, home to the magnificent cathedral church of St Peter and St Wilfrid, founded in the 660s when the England we know didn't exist, but was a series of separate kingdoms under regional rulers.

Neither of us had been to Ripon before and usually, washing into a strange city like this, its history – especially a history going back so far – wouldn't have been at the forefront of our minds. But the saga of the city of Ripon is the chronicle of the cathedral, and you really can't ignore the cathedral in Ripon. It's one big bruiser of a building, take it from me. It dominates the city, especially at its west end, where two huge towers buttress the gables of the main part of the building, like a couple of burly policemen propping up a stout elderly lady who's taken a bad turn shopping. Inside, it's so high it makes your head spin; I swear you could paraglide from the top. The doors alone are more than 16ft (5m) tall, so heavy that until 2010 they hadn't been opened for 150 years.

We were even more aware of Ripon's history than we otherwise would have been because this period of time living on the boat was taking place during the run-up to the 2016 referendum on the UK's membership of the European Union, a key part of our own contemporary history. As a result, questions were being asked about the nature of England, and this was being reflected as much in scrutinising the relationship between the north and south of the country as it was in examining our links to the Continent. Touring the north by these old industrial arteries – remnants of a lost industrial past, or Britain's 'golden age', as some call it – you couldn't help but be struck by the amount of proudly independent towns and cities that felt themselves far enough removed from Westminster to be confident confronting current political orthodoxies, however many experts warned them it was probably not in their best social or economic interests.

As far as I was able, I tried to stay above the debate. I avoided voicing any strong opinions of my own, and restricted what little I said to occasional throwaway lines aimed more at encouraging conversation than making a point. In some places, this was the only way of having any sort of safe conversation about politics. After all, I was from London. I lived in a bubble and as a result anything I thought or said stood the risk of being rubbished for that reason alone. During some exchanges – not all, but more than I'd have predicted – I sensed a reservoir of antagonism against London and everything it was perceived to stand for, from the government's recent policy of austerity to England's failure to progress beyond the group stages in the 2014 World Cup. It wouldn't have been hard to have inadvertently said something that riled people; and so when I was asked where I was from, as I almost invariably was because my accent wasn't local, I sometimes said I was from Leicestershire. If I was more honest about where I came from I'd respond with some self-deprecating comment along the lines of, 'I live in London – well, someone has to' – which at least made them smile before they started having a go at me.

Most places were friendly, however. I remember in particular one dirt-poor town where we stopped as we were crossing the Pennines, the name of which I wouldn't mention even if I could remember it. It was winter and it had been a miserable day, wet and so stormy that we'd left the uplands, where we were being battered with winds, to seek sanctuary on lower ground. It wasn't that late in the day when we cast off, but even so, darkness was already beginning to fall when we gave up the search for anything better and pulled up at an unprepossessing mooring opposite a scrap yard. Regardless of weather, we always attempted as a matter of course to get off the boat sometime during the day, if only for a short time. Part of the reason was to explore where we were, or we'd have never seen anything of the places we were passing through. Mainly, though, it was because you have to. Living on a boat, you need to take every opportunity you can to get out and about. It's too easy to become stir crazy, especially during the short days of winter when cabin fever's a risk to your mental health, not to mention any relationship you might be struggling to maintain in a space only a tad bigger than an average bathroom. Besides, that day we had an added incentive to go for a walk. Forget all the scholarly stuff – the fact was, we'd run out of milk.

In so many ways, the place we'd found ourselves in was a cliché of a hundred similar places we'd stopped over the years.

The kindest thing you could say about it was that it had seen better days. A single main street led from the canal up a slope with maybe half a dozen short, terraced streets leading off it. Dotted along this were the usual suspects: a nail salon, a 24/7 grocery store run by South Asians, a chippie and the ubiquitous Chinese takeaway. Unusually, the place had a pub, a busy one at that as we could tell by the sounds emanating from inside. As much to avoid going back to the boat as wanting a drink, we went inside and ordered pints. We must have stood out like sore thumbs with our odd accents, our expensive rainwear and our nesh complexions, which – after our recent assault by the climate – spoke of a southern softness and affluence. Even so, people were welcoming and curious about us, and it wasn't long before we fell into conversation with a boisterous party who for all the world looked as if they'd just walked out of central casting after an audition for some gritty north country crime drama. To call this group politically alienated would do them no justice. They weren't alienated from anything. However, they'd rejected a good deal of the political pap they'd been fed over the years. No, they weren't keen on the EU, but they weren't too keen on the local council either. Most of all they weren't keen on London, which they thought leeched off the rest of the country and had too many foreigners living in it for it to be called England at all.

They insisted on buying us a drink. We insisted on buying them a drink back. The problem was, one explained to us, that no one cared about people like them. They'd had a lot of trouble with kids getting up to mischief recently, but the police weren't interested and the council took no notice of the damage they caused. Weren't their local councillors on side? I asked. Weren't they doing anything to help? A woman interrupted. Well, actually, yes, she said, recently they had been. After being ignored for as long as she could remember, never seeing a councillor from one year's end to the next, they'd at last got someone who'd been coming round regularly talking to them, listening to their problems. As a result, there'd even been some movement from the police on the kids.

'What party are they?' I asked out of curiosity. 'Labour? Liberal?'

'British Nationals, I think,' someone interrupted. 'Is that what they call themselves?'

I can't say we ran across much support for extreme right-wing parties in Ripon, though we did find similar, more nuanced, nationalistic attitudes that betrayed themselves in talk of autonomy from London or Brussels, it didn't seem to matter which. I didn't take a lot notice of it. As far as I could see, this resistance to outsiders, from wherever they came, and whatever they wanted to achieve, has been par for the course in Ripon since 948 when it was part of Northumbria, and King Edred torched it during his campaign to wrest the city from the Vikings and bring it under English rule. The place was just as resistant to the Normans when it was caught up in the rebellion against William the Conqueror. Its reward was to get another kicking in what's known as the Harrying of the North. This campaign by William to consolidate his invasion might sound like a small-town neighbourhood dispute, but the deaths that resulted from it amount to genocide by any contemporary standard. It's estimated about a third of the entire population of the north of England was wiped out either by slaughter or famine.

Paradoxically, Ripon benefitted from this pogrom, since as part of William's strategy of colonising his conquests, he encouraged the foundation of a number of religious houses in the north, one of which was at Fountains, a few miles from Ripon. The monks here were Cistercians, an order founded near Dijon in France. By 1300, Fountains Abbey virtually controlled the entire wool industry in England, utilising its network of religious contacts, which spanned Europe. Think of the place less as a religious foundation and more as the HQ of a successful and prosperous multinational company.

Em and I cycled there one bitterly cold but bright day by a route that took us along lonely public footpaths until we suddenly emerged at the crest of the gentle valley overlooking the River Skell, where the abbey ruins nestle. As idyllic locations go, you'd be hard-pressed to find a better one, regardless of whether you were looking for a place to trade wool or one in which to talk to God. Sheltered by the swelling hills around it and supplied with plentiful fresh water from the surrounding springs that gave the place its name, Fountains prospered. Even now, derelict, it's an imposing sight. Accustomed as we are these days to ever-higher skyscrapers, the prodigious scale and splendour of the ruins is still awe-inspiring, lying along the river valley like the ruins of a bombed town. The old tower of the abbey church looms over the hollow shell of innumerable Gothic arches, some of them windows, some the supporting buttresses of walls, or fragments of walls. Beneath, is a maze of crypts and vaults and cloisters tangled into an elegant pattern enhanced by the river that entwines it.

We went back for a second time one fine evening to see the place lit up in a display promoted as 'Fountains in Floodlight'. It was an enchanting and mystical visit, the illumination through the derelict windows and against the columns emphasising not just the inherent beauty of the crumbling buildings but their confident solidity – a sense of the eternal they generate, as if the place shouldn't be measured against the span of human lives but against the passage of time itself. A choir was singing in the vaulted crypt, and their haunting voices echoing across the lawns drew us in as night fell. Neither of us would have missed this second visit for the world, even though it was a swine getting back to the boat afterwards because the lamp on Em's bike gave up the ghost and we had to struggle along the eerie

111

footpaths using just mine. This was difficult enough on its own, but it became more difficult yet when my batteries began to fade, too. Eventually, we had to find our way in almost total darkness and in rain that began falling again as it seemed to have been falling for days.

The Reformation finally did for Fountains Abbey. Once Henry VIII and his thieving henchman Thomas Cromwell had got it in their sights, it didn't stand a chance. The abbot, William Thirsk, was expelled over some dodgy allegations about prostitutes and missing money, smoothing the way for the abbey itself to be confiscated a few years later. Afterwards, Thirsk threw in his lot with an insurgency called the Pilgrimage of Grace – the biggest uprising there ever was against the Tudors – when the north rose against Henry's policy of breaking from the Catholic Church in Rome. On the basis that this was the first time England had separated from the prevailing European culture, the event has been called the first Brexit. Thirsk, though, didn't just lose a vote – he lost his life, hanged, drawn and quartered at Tyburn.

It was late when we got to bed, so the next morning we weren't overjoyed at being woken early by the cheery voice of a woman knocking on the roof of the boat. She was cradling a clipboard and sheltering from a heavy rainstorm under a huge umbrella. She announced herself as the moorings' warden. The news she had to impart, like the weather she'd brought with her, was far from welcome. Apparently, we'd been in Ripon too long: there were restrictions prohibiting us from staying more than 48 hours.

'But there's nobody else here,' I protested plaintively. 'It's deserted, abandoned, desolate. There hasn't been another boat around the whole time we've been moored. In fact, I suspect there's not been another boat here since the summer.' My protestations were all to no avail. She was polite enough explaining the rules to us, but what it came down to was that they *were* the rules, and rules is rules and if we didn't like them then we could push off and go boil our heads in a vat of oil – though, of course, she didn't say that last bit but instead gave us one of those perma-smirks so beloved of politicians that said 'You can argue this as much as you like but you're still going to have to bugger off.'

We were thinking about going soon anyhow, for it was getting close to the time we'd booked our passage back to Selby, so we cast off later in the day and after stopping for a couple of farewell days in York, we headed downstream to Naburn in yet another rainstorm. There, devastating news awaited us. News that completely threw us and changed our plans definitively. It seemed that we couldn't get back to Selby Lock after all. Or rather we could get *back* to it, but we couldn't get *through* it: it was silted up by all the heavy rain there'd been and they couldn't get the gates open. They'd need to send down divers when the weather was better. And how long was that likely to be, we wanted to know?

The lock keeper – his name was Ken – shrugged his shoulders. 'How long's a piece of string?'

The full implications of what this meant for us didn't dawn for a while. Our immediate response was to bemoan the plans we'd made, which would have to be put on hold indefinitely, but later it struck us that the delay might have more serious consequences since it would take us into the peak season for floods. But what could we do? We were trapped now, through no fault of our own, completely cut off from the rest of the system. Once more, we cruised back upriver to York, where we moored in our usual spot on the steps adjacent to Museum Gardens, beneath the path named after that daughter of York and national treasure, Dame Judi Dench. We were beginning to know York and its riverside

113

very well by now. We liked York a lot – but how could anyone not like this old walled medieval city that is so chock full of ancient buildings it's more like a film set than anywhere real? We couldn't get enough of it, and despite what had now become a climate of constant heavy rain, we delighted in simply walking around its narrow streets exploring its cafes and countless little independent shops. It was good to have time to look up friends we had in York, too, and lovely to have the opportunity to spend time with them.

One day, however, I had to make a day trip away from the place. Months before, I'd agreed to speak at a literary festival in Staffordshire, and although it was inconvenient, I couldn't get out of it. However, in terms of the weather, it was probably the best day there'd been for weeks to have to do it. The rain that had been hammering down relentlessly since we left Fountains Abbey had at last abated, and the river, which had been unpredictable, seemed to have finally stabilised. Em, who often comes along to these things to lend moral support, couldn't face listening to me rabbit on for the umpteenth time, and had volunteered to stay on the boat in case there were problems – an act of selfless sacrifice that I couldn't help noticing coincided with her arrival at the final pages of a book she'd been engrossed in for weeks. I can't say I was entirely happy leaving her alone, and when I stepped on to the train I couldn't rid myself of an unsettling anxiety, a niggling, uncomfortable feeling that this wasn't the right thing to do in these circumstances, and that something was bound to go wrong.

The Staffordshire gig didn't go well. Perhaps I was fretting too much. Perhaps the audience picked up on my mood. One way or another, no one laughed at my jokes and I didn't sell many books either, which, after all, is the purpose of these things. To cap it all, when I went back to the station to catch the train back to York, it didn't turn up and there was no one around to explain its disappearance or to tell me whether the next one was likely to magically evaporate in the same way, too. It was turning cold now. A bitter wind had whipped up. Adventurers talk about the rigours of the frozen Arctic wastes or the icy wilderness of the snow-covered Russian Steppes. But they know nothing. They've never stood at Lichfield Trent Valley station on a glacial Wednesday night in October, struggling to come to terms with the prospect of dying of old age and hypothermia while waiting for a train.

I rang Em to apprise her of the situation. It was in my mind that I might have to stay the night, and on my walk to the station I'd seen a chintzy B&B with an open fire in the lounge and a sign on the door advertising vacancies. But at the first suggestion that I might not be back that night, her voice turned more glacial than the weather. It made me realise that I'd *have* to get back, even if I had to walk.

'The river's turning ugly,' she said. 'I've dropped the anchor but you need to get here as soon as you can.'

Looking down on the boat from Lendal Bridge as I walked across the Ouse after finally getting back to York in the early hours, I could see exactly what she meant. While I'd been away, the river had risen higher than I'd seen it before. Already, it had crept up the steps bordering Museum Gardens so that *Justice* was now floating *over* the ropes that restrained her, ascending the steps herself as the water levels rose. She was like an island in the river, quivering in the current.

To get back on to her, I had to wade through water that was already knee-deep and flowing so powerfully I could feel its cold pull against my legs. I clambered on board in the nick of time. Had I been any later I wouldn't have been able to manage it and Em would have been stranded on her own, a terrifying prospect for both of us. As it was, even with the two of us aboard the situation we were in was frightening. The river was surging downstream too powerfully for us to contemplate moving. We wouldn't have done it in daytime, let alone the middle of the night. We'd have been swept against the bridge arches where the build-up of water would have sunk us in seconds. There was nothing for it but to batten down and stay put. But the river was rising faster than ever now – so fast that it's no exaggeration to say you could see it getting higher as you watched.

Our first priority was to loosen the lines on which our safety depended. They were already starting to strain. On *Justice*, this presents more problems than it might on other boats. You can get to the bow and the anchor ropes easily enough, but getting to the one on the stern is more difficult because, unusually for a narrowboat, there's no internal route from the front to the back: you can't walk through it as you can on most boats. Instead, you have to clamber along the gunnels – the narrow ledge barely wider than your foot – that run along the outside of the boat. It's precarious at the best of times, but in the freezing wet darkness it was treacherous. I clung to the boat so tightly that the muscles of my wrist cramped up. Step by step I shuffled along the gunnels in dread, while beneath me the furious waters of the river writhed and twisted at my feet. Yet loosening the ropes this once wasn't the end of the problem. At the rate the river was swelling, they'd need loosening regularly throughout the night. We'd have to keep constant watch. There could be no question of sleep.

By 3am, the position had worsened. Outside on the deck again, a violent storm raged around us, the rain driving horizontally and the tumultuous river thundering by even faster than before, carrying with it the shadowy shapes of trees and bushes torn from banks further up. The sound of the water was deafening. It crashed by us and collided against the abutments of Lendal Bridge with the roar of waves smashing against a cliff. Occasionally, it surged unpredictably, sending us grinding against the concrete of the banking. We were rocked around violently and could hardly stand straight. We couldn't hear ourselves talk. Once again, I made my way fearfully along the gunnels, but before I could slacken the rope at the stern I saw with horror that the bow was spinning towards the centre of the river, dragging the anchor with it. It came to an uncertain halt facing downstream, tossed about by the flow of the river. Immediately, I realised what had happened. In an attempt at loosening the bow rope the force of the swollen current had proved too much for Em and it had wrenched the rope from her hand. For the rest of the night we were dependent on a single rope, which I couldn't bring myself to think about. Over the years, I had tied and retied that rope a thousand times. Too many times over too many years. It was old and should have been replaced long ago. I knew every fray of its weave, every weakness of its twist.

Now, it seemed, our lives depended on it.

The darkest hour, they say, is just before dawn, but for us the last hour of that night was characterised by a mounting sense of relief. We counted down the minutes, knowing that it couldn't be long before the appearance of a wan light in the sky in the east would signal the end of the nightmare through which we'd been living. When morning finally arrived, it mercifully coincided with a change in the condition of the river. It wasn't that the water level was dropping, more that we could see it wasn't rising any longer. Eventually, we screwed our courage to the sticking point and cast off for a new mooring against a large tug tied up nearby that had recently been doing bank repairs. It was only about a hundred yards or so upriver but making headway against the fierce flow was a gruelling task that challenged our engine to its limits. Afterwards, at least we could change ropes and tie on both lines again. Being so much bigger and heavier than us, the tug secured us more firmly against movement of the river. More importantly, it was moored against a jetty and by using a couple of scaffolding planks we found on board we could get to dry land.

In all, we stayed there four days before the river fell sufficiently for us to move again. It was a terrible time, but though we didn't know it, things were going to get a good deal worse. This flood was the first of six we were to experience that visit to York.

This one was the most docile of the lot.

8

Holed up in Naburn

We left Museum Gardens and moved further down the York riverside to King's Staith, where the moorings were safer and where we were close to the floating landing stages used by the trip boats that ply the Ouse. Visitors inundate York by the thousand, as much in winter as summer, and they all seem to count a river cruise as an indispensable component of their stay. The boats tried to keep operating as best they could but eventually even they had to give up and halt services. Their engines were big enough to deal with the powerful flow, but the river had risen so much that their high superstructures couldn't get under bridges. This bad luck for them was good news for us. While they were laid up, it gave us the chance to talk to the crews about how to deal with the predicament we were in, and it was one of them who alerted us to the Environment Agency (EA) website, where there was a mine of information about the River Ouse and the tributaries that fed it. Using this, we could at least keep track of the way the river was rising and falling.

King's Staith is a different kettle of fish to Museum Gardens. Rather than a stepped embankment, it's a high, straight-sided wharf that, in normal conditions, would have towered so far above *Justice* we'd have had to make use of a ladder set into the wall to climb up to the cobbled square bordering it. However, with the river as high as it was, we could easily step from boat to bank, and as a result we felt more a part of York than we had at Museum Gardens, which empties at twilight and can feel eerie and severed from the city after dark. There's a completely different feel to York at King's Staith. A couple of pubs nearby mean there's always a constant stream of people milling about, either customers or people simply drawn to the river, as people are always drawn to rivers at all times of day and night, especially when they're in flood. In the mornings – for some reason – there always seemed to be parties of grave-faced Chinese tourists around, nodding studiously at whatever their guide was telling them. By lunchtime, these had been replaced by office workers eating their sandwiches on benches nearby. The weather appeared to make no difference to them. Even when it was hammering down, they'd still be in their usual places, the only difference being that they'd cower under umbrellas looking for all the world like campers trapped in a storm on a Welsh hillside. By evening, the square became a stage for courting couples, their shared umbrellas lending them an air of intimacy as they strolled arm in arm though the twilight or canoodled in dark corners away from street lights. By night, the place was different again and became the haunt of drunken groups of young men on stag nights or works outings, completely indifferent to the weather and horsing about boisterously, shouting at each other in the thickening gloom.

On the run-in to Halloween there were ghost tours every night, too, with guides recounting grisly tales of York's history to a script which altered so little, that by the end of our stay, I'd heard it so often that I could have given the talk myself.

After two or three days, the river began to drop and the trip boats resumed service. With the Ouse apparently behaving itself now, we risked another trip to Ripon, an outing that confirmed our status on the Timothy West/Prunella Scales end of the boaters' spectrum. Like them, we can sometimes be – how shall I put this to be kind to us all? – a little 'distracted' when we're boating. Will that do? Pru and Tim demonstrate it in their TV series *Great Canal Journeys* with steering that sometimes verges on the happy-go-lucky. We demonstrated it that day by casting off without pulling up our anchor. I could feel something was wrong as soon as I engaged the throttle. We didn't seem to be going anywhere...

A couple of days later and with the same carelessness, I did a reprise performance, running *Justice* up the slipway of the marina at Boroughbridge so badly that we had to suffer the indignity of being pulled off by a tiny boat powered by an outboard. It was so small you'd have thought it was hardly big enough to pull a toy boat across a village duck pond, let alone drag a grounded 20-ton lump of steel like us back into the water.

Boroughbridge was an ancient settlement even before the Romans arrived there, building roads. Its antecedents go back to the Bronze Age, when three unusual standing stones, the highest nearly 23ft (7m) tall, were erected for reasons that are lost to antiquity. You can see the 'Devil's Arrows', as they're known, on one of a number of well-signposted rambles around the town that take in most of the sights, including the riverside at Milby Lock.

It was there one afternoon that I ran across someone who lived on a boat in a nearby marina. He had been a farmer, it transpired. Since childhood, it had been his ambition to have a farm of his own, but the realities of farming had proved too much, and after years struggling to eke out a living he realised he was never going to make a go of it, however hard he worked. Eventually, reluctantly, he decided he had to give up the life, and a boat was the only financial option open to him.

His was a poignant story that pointed to the variety of reasons people find themselves on the waterways. Of course, large numbers are attracted to the cut simply because they like boats and the nomadic life boating offers; or – like Em and I – they feel a certain empathy with England and the English countryside, its wildlife, its flora and the fascination of its endlessly changing landscapes.

But many thousands of others – especially over the recent years of austerity – have come to the waterways for different, more prosaic reasons. It's not that they didn't feel the same as Em and I about the delights Britain's canals and rivers offer or, even if such considerations weren't a priority at the beginning, that they didn't eventually come to appreciate those joys. It's just that they got drawn to the waterways initially as a solution to more immediate problems they had on land.

Over the years we've been boating – getting on for half a century now – we've met people who decided to move to a boat not out of choice, but because it was the only way they could afford to live after losing their jobs. Some had been made redundant, others had run businesses that failed. We have known people suffering serious mental illness who gravitated towards the waterways because boats seemed to offer a refuge they couldn't find elsewhere, others who sought the solitude of the canals because they rejected the modern world and were looking for a simpler and less materialistic lifestyle. In the same vein, we have run across scores of people, both men and women, whose marriages failed and whose share of the settlement after break-up or divorce forced them into a poverty from which a boat delivered them – or in some cases, to look at it more positively, allowed them, unshackled, to fulfil a dream they'd always harboured. Some of these people had children with them, some travelled alone, rootless and without friends. Some were contented; some cantankerous and bitter, still nursing deep emotional wounds.

More recently, a new type of boater has begun to appear in numbers on Britain's inland waterways. These are retirees. A few are people like Em and I, suddenly blessed with the time and freedom to explore the waterways, seeking a couple of years of adventure. For others who decide to leave their homes and live full time on a boat, there's often an underlying financial motive to their decision, in that on a boat they're able to fund a more comfortable lifestyle than they could otherwise afford. They supplement their pensions by renting out their houses, as we did, or selling them and living off the proceeds. Some who've never owned a house have nevertheless worked out that they can survive more economically on a boat, perhaps augmenting their retirement income with savings or by doing casual work along the way. This is particularly the case with retirees too young to have pensions who've got so sick of the whole wearisome cycle of work, eat, sleep, repeat, that they've chucked in the job early and downsized to a boat, allowing them to live a different sort of life on the cut, a simpler life, but one far more fulfilling than they'd enjoyed before. And who can blame them? Especially if they'd been in some dead-end job they'd always hated.

One thing's for sure: very few boaters of whatever age ever cut the umbilical cord and move to the waterways without the conviction that they've left land-based life behind them for good, believing that nothing except accident or serious illness will ever force them back again. Sadly, for many it doesn't work out that way and the number of boats for sale advertised as 'ready for liveaboard life' is testimony to the fact that dreams don't always work out.

At the other end of the spectrum to retirees are young people who have chosen to live on the canals. Some – like those I mentioned earlier who shuffle up and down the towpaths of London – are casualties of a housing market which has spun so wildly out of control that settling on the moon would be a more realistic prospect than getting a foot on the property ladder. But it isn't just in London where this is happening: all over the country, communities of boaters, large and small, live along the towpath. There are particularly sizeable clusters around Bath and Oxford, smaller ones in Birmingham, Manchester, Leeds and Liverpool, and smaller ones yet away from the urban centres, where anything from two or three to a dozen boats might gather together semi-permanently in a loose affiliation. And then, of course, there are hundreds of lone boaters who see themselves as part of the waterways' community, yet eschew company to live a more solitary existence.

What links these disparate groups is that the vast majority don't have official permanent moorings. A large number base themselves in a particular area and move short distances up and down the same stretch of canal, which allows them to hold down a job, keep in touch with friends and family or keep their kids in school. But it's a precarious existence that – depending on your perspective – means living just inside the rules, or living completely outside them. Insomuch as there is any accord about the circumstances in which you're allowed to live on a boat without a permanent mooring, there's general agreement that unless marked otherwise, you can stay in any one place for 14 days before you have to move. Without a permanent mooring, you become what's known as a 'continuous cruiser' – although the requirements to actually cruise aren't what you'd call onerous, the minimum constraint being that you must travel a minimum of 20 miles (32km) a year.

And this is where the arguments start. Some on the waterways complain that living in this way is not so much staying within the rules as exploiting them to the hilt. Many are angry at the irrationality of 'continuous cruisers' only having to travel in 12 months what most boaters could comfortably achieve in an afternoon. They point out that the waterways' authorities have made it crystal clear that for boats to be considered genuine 'continuous cruisers' they have to be executing a 'bona fide navigation'. In other words, they must be *going* somewhere.

It's an acrimonious and often bitter dispute that shows no sign of abating. And whatever the rights and wrongs of the positions people take, the indisputable truth is that it's a long way from the general image of the canals as places of tranquility and friendliness.

Talking to the retired farmer, I got something more positive than just a tale of woe, for he recommended a pub used a lot by locals where he said the beer was only £1.99 a pint. He wasn't wrong on either count: the beer was the price he said it was and later that evening, the place suddenly filled with the whole of the town council, including the mayor in full robes and regalia. I don't think you can get more local than that.

We cast off the next day and cruised up to Ripon again, where we moored in the basin and where, after a short period — well, 48 hours to be strictly accurate — we were disturbed by someone knocking on the roof of our boat at an excessively early hour of the morning. It was the mooring warden, the same one we'd met on our previous visit, right down to the clipboard and the perma-smirk, which was still fastened to her face as if by superglue.

'I'm sorry to disturb you so early,' said she, which was not a good start to our conversation since far from being at all sorry, the characteristic set of her mouth betrayed that she was actually thrilled to find someone she could pester on her stretch of the waterways when every other canal and river in the area was virtually bereft of boats. 'It's just I can't help but notice that you've been here your allotted time, which you'll see from that nearby sign is 48 hours.' She pointed to the sign. 'I was wondering when you were planning on leaving.'

I got out of the boat and walked over to the sign, making a great pretence of adjusting my glasses to read it. 'Yes, yes, you're right,' I reassured her. 'There's no denying it: the sign does seem to indicate that mooring time is restricted in this location.' After a brief pause I added, 'It's my birthday this month, did you know that?'

I was delighted to see that this sudden change of topic threw her, as I'd hoped it would. 'I ... er ... well ... er ... congratulations,' she blurted. 'But what's that got to do with it?'

'I rarely forget my birthday,' I continued. 'It tends to occur in November at the same time most years. It is November, isn't it? I haven't got that wrong, have I?'

'No, it *is* November,' she replied suspiciously, glancing at her clipboard as if to check this basic fact 'November 1st, to be exact.'

'Mmmm, that puzzles me then,' I said. 'Because I thought that during the winter, most short-stay moorings revert to 14 days unless signed otherwise. From November 1st, unless my memory fails me.' I looked at the sign and then back at her in ostensible confusion. 'But I can't see that it's signed otherwise. Is it signed otherwise? Can you see any signs?'

Her perma-smile hardened, the edges of her mouth started twitching with the effort needed to maintain it. It quickly became less a smile, more a sort of tortured rictus. 'Well, we'll have to see about that,' she said abruptly. And at that, she span on her heel and left.

I watched her disappear up the towpath, a smirk appearing on my face now. I don't often get the opportunity, but sometimes it's such pleasure to be a smug bastard.

Not that all this entertainment made a lot of difference to how long we stayed in Ripon. While I'd been outside dealing with the bureaucratic side of boating, Em had been inside the cabin checking the EA website for the latest news on river levels. It wasn't good. In fact, it couldn't have been worse. At the rate the tributaries were rising it was only a matter of hours before the Ouse and any waterway connected to it, including the canal at Ripon, was going to be in flood. We needed to get back to York as soon as possible; at least it was familiar to us. I opened up the throttle for what I anticipated would be a nervy trip back, though in the event it wasn't the return journey that caused our anxiety levels to hit top register, but our arrival. For when we got back to the King's Staith mooring, water was already lapping over the quayside and beginning to flood the square, the river much higher than we'd experienced so far.

We'd talked about this scenario once or twice, and we'd decided that if conditions made it impossible to moor in York then we'd go back to Naburn, where we'd discovered there was a floating pontoon next to the lock at which we could claim safe haven. The journey downriver to get there was like an adventure park flume ride. The river was surging furiously and in order to keep any control of the boat we had to keep our engine at full tilt so that it powered us faster than the flow. At that speed, the banks flashed by in a blur, so that by the time we got to the cut leading off the main river to the lock – just before the river goes crashing over the weir – we were travelling at a rate of knots that made stopping difficult. Narrowboats aren't cars. They haven't got brakes. The best you can do in an emergency is go into reverse gear. But reverse gear doesn't stop you dead. Especially when you weigh 20 tons and you're hurtling at full speed towards a lock gate...

Luckily, the lock cut at Naburn is a couple of hundred yards long, and by slamming *Justice* into reverse and using the approach to the lock as an airline pilot might use a long runway to decelerate after landing, we were able to bring her under control before any collision. But it was a close-run thing, and believe me, I've had nightmares since in which I've relived the sight of those looming lock gates getting closer and closer while the sound of the engine has punctuated my sleep, screaming as it struggled to bring us to a halt.

My anxiety over the whole procedure was heightened by the fact that while coming down the lock cut I'd been aware of the lock keeper, Ken, watching us every foot of the way. Whether he'd coincidentally been outside when he'd seen us coming or, as I suspect, he was waiting for us because someone from York had called to alert him to our arrival, I don't know. But he was there in his waders to take a rope and, more crucially, connect

127

our water hose to a nearby tap. This was a lifeline because before evening fell, the tap was submerged by the rising flood and so thanks to Ken's quick thinking we at least had a supply of fresh drinking water.

The floating jetty on which we were marooned was about 100ft (30.5m) long and built to allow boats to wait briefly for the correct tide conditions to be able to pass through the lock. It felt unstable in the increased flow of the flood, shifting and wobbling whenever either of us walked across it. It moved vertically, too, as the river rose and fell, sliding up and down on risers – steel tubes set into the canal bed. It was an unsettling experience seeing the water getting higher and higher around you, first covering the lock surrounds, then the beams and finally the paddles so that before long the lock had all but disappeared completely, the tops of a couple of rickety old latticed swing bridges the only reminder that there'd ever been a lock at all. What made it more alarming was that you could see that the risers had not been high enough when they'd first been installed, and that they'd had to have extensions welded on to them. Which was just as well because otherwise we and the jetty would already have been flushed down the river to the sea and halfway to Zeebrugge.

Overnight, the water kept rising. The 1920s semis I'd noticed on the way up – one of which was where Ken lived – were built on a rise. Now they looked as if they were on an island. Ken, we learned later, had already moved his furniture upstairs, anticipating more floods and further rises in the water level, which had already reached the windowsills of the old Victorian workshops opposite. The odd banqueting hall was cut off, too, the river having swollen around it to form a moat.

The sense of all this water isolating us, bearing down on us, threatening to overwhelm us, was sobering. A couple of days later, the levels had risen further yet. We felt totally trapped.

In the York direction, the lock cut had disappeared completely and was now absorbed into the river. Looking in the other direction it was like a coastal swamp and all we could see was water: one massive silver lake, rippling in the breeze and punctuated only by the bare black treetops of occasional copses and woods. Since the flood had enveloped the adjacent weir, what was once a background soundtrack of roaring water was now muted in a way that was eerie, like a voice heard from the depths. Eeriest of all, though, was the movement of the water. Tidal locks mark the division of tidal reaches from the still waters above, but when the water gets so high that it breaches the lock, that division ceases to exist. As a result, *Justice* started to go up and down with the tide twice a day. The same as if she'd been moored off Plymouth, or Whitby or any other coastal port. This is not something you expect 50 miles (80km) inland.

But my, was it sometimes stunningly beautiful. Between the periods of rain there were days when the sky was such a uniform azure blue, with barely a cloud in evidence, that but for the occasional icy winds we could have been on the beach of some Greek island. And the sunsets, oh, the sunsets! Some evenings, it was if someone had slashed the grey sky with a razor, like Tudor men used to slash their doublets, revealing beneath the vivid scarlets of satin, some deep and intense, some muted and washed, some so pale they were more pink than red. The colours flamed across the horizon, reflecting in the flood waters beneath so that some evenings the whole world seemed incarnadine, as if bathed in blood, a wounded landscape ebbing only as the sun set and darkness descended.

It was a couple of weeks before the water began to drop enough for us to get off the jetty – just in time, as it happened, because humankind can live for only so long on as diet of tomato-based pastas and tinned fish past its sell-by date. We'd long since eaten the last wilted remnants of our vegetable box. At the rate things were shaping up, we'd soon forget what a vegetable looked like. Imagine, then, our delight when we discovered the Brunswick Organic Nursery in Bishopthorpe, just outside of York. We stumbled across the place after we'd taken to our bikes and ridden along partly submerged roads to the cycle path that connects Naburn to the city along the old route of the East Coast Main Line, where express trains once thundered between King's Cross and Edinburgh. Seeing the nursery for the first time had something of the quality of a mirage about it, except that rather than being an illusion we knew couldn't be real, it was actually a reality that seemed like a hallucination. A nursery. Selling not just vegetables, but organic vegetables, and not just organic vegetables, but organic vegetables produced by a charity that was set up to provide work and training for people with learning disabilities. The produce was first class, the prices not much more than you'd pay at your local greengrocers. We went back to the boat laden with swedes, celeriac, leeks, winter chard and even lettuces and salad leaves. What was more, by dint of simply buying food we'd garnered levels of virtue that will stand us in good stead when eventually we're required to account for the good we've done in the world.

At length, the river did get back to a stable state, and with my birthday approaching we decided to go ahead with plans we'd made for a couple of friends to visit for the afternoon. One of them has a birthday the day before mine, so presents were exchanged and a convivial time was had by all. Well, it was until one of us happened to glance out of the porthole window and noticed water lapping over the wall adjacent to the jetty, flooding the yard underneath. Our visitors beat a hasty retreat, as well they might since within the hour the river had risen so high they'd have been cut off from their car and trapped on the boat with us.

The River Ouse, it seemed, was getting nasty again. This time, it was going to get nastier than ever.

9

From York ... to Africa

Christmas was getting close. We weren't particularly aware of it stuck on the floating pontoon at Naburn, but on those occasions when the floods receded and we could cycle to York it was as if we were plunged into a different world entirely. York is pretty at any time of the year, but at Christmas it becomes enchanting. Its famous Minster is floodlit as always, but it seems somehow brighter than normal in midwinter, its highest tower – the Lantern Tower – dominating the city like the Star of Bethlehem dominates a Christmas tree. Around it, the narrow medieval streets are decked with a thousand fairy lights strung between shops, along the branches of trees and the facades of buildings.

In December, the whole city seems to turn into a market, resonating with carol singers and brass bands, heady with aromas of the season: cinnamon punch and ginger cake and spiced candles on sale at the chalet stalls that seem to appear overnight along streets and in squares. We wandered about entranced by it all, exploring not just the markets, but the craft shops and the department stores, too. What they were selling didn't interest us that much, but we were drawn to them for what they were: beacons of brightness, citadels of warmth and comfort, places where normal life continued predictably without the constant threat of being swept away by an angry river.

Our biggest concern was what we were going to do for Christmas itself. We'd accepted an invitation from the family in

Leicester, but come the critical moment, how could we be sure we'd even be able to get off the boat to get there? I had visions of our festive dinner being a can of beans and a spoonful of tinned carrots. We left it as long as we could, but with a week to go, when it was apparent water was gathering in the tributaries once more in advance of another offensive against York, we quickly packed a couple of bags, grabbed the cat and abandoned ship, leaving *Justice* under Ken's watchful eye.

It turned out to be the most sensible thing we could have done. On Boxing Day, York suffered its worst flooding in a generation, the Ouse peaking at 17ft (5.2m) above its normal summer level, marginally short of its all-time high. The figures don't tell the whole story, however. Although lower than in the record-breaking year, the effects of the flood that winter were significantly worse. This was because EA staff took what at the time seemed a crazy decision to open a flood barrier that would normally be kept closed in these conditions. The Foss Barrier, as it's called, lies at the confluence of the River Foss with the Ouse, just south of Clifford's Tower, a remnant of the castle commissioned by Henry III in the middle of the 13th century that is one of York's familiar landmarks.

Built much more recently in 1988, the Foss Barrier is essentially a lift gate used when high water levels on the Ouse block water trying to get out from the tributary, effectively damming it and preventing it from draining normally. This used to happen regularly before the barrier was built, and as a consequence the Foss backed up, causing untold damage upstream. Now, when the Ouse is badly in spate – as it was the year we were in York – the gate is dropped and eight high-capacity pumps redirect water from the tributary straight into the bigger river.

Except that on Boxing Day, without any warning whatsoever, EA staff turned off these pumps and lifted the gate. At the time, what they'd done seemed inexplicable. Parts of York along the Ouse riverside are used to flooding – they've always flooded, they've been flooding for centuries. Now, however, a further 600 properties bordering the Foss found themselves suddenly under water, too.

Yet senseless as it at first seemed, the EA acted entirely rationally. Exceptional floods had led to water leaking into the control room of the barrier, and staff were afraid that before long the fuses might blow and interrupt the power supply. If this had happened then not only would the pumps have stopped working, but the gate would have been locked in the closed position. This would have led to the Foss backing up worse than it ever had, causing much greater flooding than if the gate had just been opened and the river left to its own devices.

The decision to open the gate was a tough call, and you can imagine how difficult a dilemma it was for the EA. Indeed, until the full details of why the decision was made became clear, the agency took a lot of stick for what it had done.

We sat in Leicester watching in horror as the full extent of this latest flood unfolded on television, where it was a lead story on the main news broadcasts. One thing was clear: with the local emergency services at full stretch, York was no place to be for a couple of elderly adventurers on a narrowboat. The family, of course, offered to put us up for the duration, but we'd already talked about a Plan B so as soon as the seasonal festivities were over I phoned a travel agent to make a provisional booking somewhere. 'Somewhere?' the travel agent asked, a note of misgiving in his voice, as if he was talking to some kid involved in a schoolboy jape. 'Where exactly do you want to go?'

'That's a difficult question.' I replied. 'The truth is, I don't rightly know. Somewhere you can get us a flight to before the end of the week. Somewhere warm. What can you offer?'

We decided on Cape Town. But there was one small problem – our passports. The ones we hadn't got with us. The ones that were on the boat. The ones we would need in order to go anywhere abroad, Cape Town or Florida's Cape Canaveral. Reluctant though we were to return to York when the city was in such chaos, there was no alternative. We *had* to go back. Yet how was that going to help us? Naburn Lock was totally cut off by road. The only way we had of getting back to *Justice* was … well, by water. When we stepped on to the train at Leicester to return north we hadn't much idea of how we were going to square that circle.

Our only plan – if you could call it a plan – was to try to make contact with the skipper of a cruiser who lived on the river and whom we'd become acquainted with when he stopped briefly on the jetty to fill up his freshwater tank. He was an eccentric-looking guy, well into his 60s, with flyaway grey hair and a devil-may-care attitude to risk – evidenced by the fact that despite the perilous conditions, his was the only boat still moving on the Ouse when anyone with any sense had long since tied up somewhere safe. On the sea, you'd probably have called him an old salt, but on the inland waterways we don't have a term for these sorts of folk. The best we can muster by way of an equivalent is Charlie Allnut, the character played by Humphrey Bogart in the classic 1951 movie *The African Queen* who spent his life bumming about on the water, making a living as best he could.

Unsurprisingly, our lock keeper Ken knew the man and gave us his name, and after some detective work we managed to track him down. All we had to do now was to persuade him to take us to *Justice*. I thought this was going to be a pushover, given that we were willing to pay him serious money for his time and trouble. I was sadly mistaken. At first he claimed the river conditions were too bad, even for him. Then one of his engines needed work. Then he was too busy... On and on it went, each apparently intractable problem melting away as I increased what I was willing to pay him for the job. I began to wonder whether the only way to arrive at any sort of deal with him was by chopping off my right arm and presenting him with that on a platter. Finally, however, we did arrive at an arrangement suitable to us both. We shook hands and agreed to meet the following day at a nearby marina, which he assured us we'd be able to get to – although, he added as a parting shot, it might involve us paddling through a foot or two of water...

That night, we stayed with friends in York who'd been very welcoming and supportive to us during our sojourn in the city. But it was a strange city to be in at that time; I'd never seen anything like it. Whole areas of the centre were submerged, shops and houses deluged and cars bobbing around like abandoned rowing boats. I remember looking down from one vantage point at a stationers and watching as firefighters in waders walked past, causing a wash that slopped under the door, sending loose reams of sodden typing paper slapping against the inside of the plate glass front window. On one street corner, we chanced upon a small group of people held up at a police road block and sheltering patiently as best they could in the driving rain, waiting to be allowed back to their homes. The whole city stank of river water. There was a sinister silence in the streets. A penetrating chill in the air. As dusk fell, the atmosphere became more creepy yet. Street lights cast a strange and ethereal glow across a scene so desolate it was like something from a half-remembered nightmare. We take civilisation and the sanctuary it affords us too much for granted. When it is stripped away by natural events, we realise how thin the veneer that separates us from chaos really is.

The next morning, we met up as arranged with the skipper of the cruiser, who was now gung-ho about the job he'd agreed to do, a change of attitude I put down to the thick wad of notes that I was compelled to hand over and that he insisted on counting out one by one before securing them in his back pocket. I can't say we felt the same enthusiasm for the trip. One look at his boat was enough to get us worried. It really *did* look like the *African Queen*. Its once-white hull and superstructure had long since turned green with algae, and as we clambered aboard we stepped across old engine parts, offcuts of wood, and overflowing rubbish bags strewn across the deck. Our confidence in the craft wasn't greatly increased when the skipper started his engines and a thick plume of black exhaust fumes puthered across the river like storm clouds careering across the sky.

From the boatyard to the jetty where we were moored was only a short journey around a couple of bends in the river, but it's not a trip I'll forget in a hurry. Once he'd cast off and manoeuvred the boat into the central channel of the river, it was clear the skipper had underestimated how bad conditions were. The boat, which was surprisingly light despite its size, was tossed about in the swollen current like a bumblebee in a gale. It was sucked into the flows and eddies of the water, turned this way and that, drawn into the troughs of waves and then thrown high on their crests in a way that would have flung us overboard if we hadn't been hanging on for dear life. Meanwhile, the skipper wrestled with his wheel in an attempt to bring the boat under control. At last, much to our relief, he managed to dock alongside *Justice* and we scrambled on board. We had only ten minutes to grab our passports and stuff a couple of bags with anything we thought we might need for a month-long trip to Africa.

We were still cramming clothes into the bags when he started banging on our roof shouting to us. There was no mistaking the alarm in his voice. 'We have to go now,' he bellowed. 'Now! This river's getting higher as I'm watching it. Quick, we have to leave or we'll be stranded...'

A month later, after we'd got back from Africa, I went through a period of having strange and disturbing dreams. That I should be plagued like this is hardly surprising, for this was just after our return to the jetty at Naburn and we'd flown straight from Cape Town to Heathrow and from there gone immediately to York. Confusing the present and the recent past was surely the most natural thing in the world. After all, the South African sun was still burning the back of our necks, the pungent dust of the veldt still scouring our throats. On *Justice*, though, it was as if nothing had changed. With the fire unlit for a month it was cold and a little damper than it had been; and the cabin was in chaos, scattered with clothes from our hurried departure. Outside, it was still raining, as it had been on the day we'd left. Indeed, if it hadn't been for the fact that the floods had eased and the river had almost reverted to normal, we could have been forgiven for suspecting it had been raining the whole time we'd been away.

But the familiar pattern resumed soon enough. It rained in the Yorkshire Dales, the tributaries swelled, and within days Naburn was flooded yet again. A week later it had drained, a week after that it flooded again. It was never-ending, it was Groundhog Day, it was incessant. When the floods receded they left a huge amount of residual flood water in the fields, but at least we could sometimes get off the boat and walk along the muddy dyke littered with driftwood that borders the river, or up towards a nearby caravan park, where the track dipped into what had once been the old course of the Ouse before they altered it as part of the construction of the lock and the lock cut. During periods of flooding, however, there was so much water the river resumed its original course as well as flowing down its new one, so that you could find yourself on an island as it were, the Ouse surging on either side of you, front and behind.

We took bike rides to York when conditions allowed, and we spent long evenings watching box sets of DVDs we'd bought from the HMV shop there, which at least prevented us from going round the bend. This is what they don't tell you about narrowboat adventures: sometimes they can be excruciatingly tedious. A day or two stuck in floods is just about bearable, a week or two even. But when the weeks turn into a month, and one month becomes two and then three... Well, trust me, nothing prepares you for the way your head reacts to this sort of isolation, as many people discovered for themselves during the lockdowns of the Covid-19 pandemic. We found ourselves spending long periods simply pacing up and down our jetty, scouring the horizon for something on which to focus, or gazing at the sky, where spotter planes and helicopters flew overhead, presumably keeping an eye out for anyone in distress.

Eventually, on a day not noticeably different from the one preceding it, or from dozens of others that had gone before that during our stay in Naburn, Ken ambled over in his waders to see how we were, which is what he usually did in the morning when the water was low enough. On this occasion, his visit was more than just a courtesy call. He was the bearer of unexpected and welcome news. The lock at Selby was open for business, he told us. It had been repaired and the powers that be were pretty confident the worst of the flooding was over. He rang his boss, and then rang the lock at Selby before finalising a leaving date with us. Once he'd gone, we sat in the cabin staring at each other speechlessly. After being holed up for so long, we could scarcely believe we were on the verge of breaking away. We were heady with anticipation at our impending release, like prisoners coming to the end of their sentences. The following morning, as a sort of celebratory jaunt, we decided to visit York on what would be our final trip. This time, we would take the boat rather than cycle. It would be a farewell cruise.

Apart from the poor devils who'd copped it in the Boxing Day floods and were still counting the cost of what had happened, York seemed to have returned to normality remarkably quickly. At King's Staith, the local council had cleared up the mud that's invariably deposited in the streets after floods. The tourists were back, too – as attracted to the river as ever despite its recent shenanigans. There were even one or two trip boats, which had chanced their arms and started operating a limited service now they could get under bridges again. However, the biggest indicator that things were back to normal on the river was the fact that there was another narrowboat, crewed by a guy on his own, which pulled up next to us. It had come up from Selby – the first boat to have passed through the lock for almost six months. Its appearance added to our sense of emerging from a dark place into light, from winter into spring. Whether it was the bulbs breaking the soil's surface in the parks or the occasional bursts of sunshine appearing through the clouds, it was clear there was change in the air. It felt as if our months of internment would soon be a distant memory.

But then, on the *very* day we were scheduled to leave, we came back from doing some last-minute shopping to find the river was up to its old tricks again, and this time with a vengeance. It was rising so fast you could yet again watch it going up minute by minute.

The newly arrived boat was already casting off in panic, but in his haste the skipper had untied his bow line without first untying his centre rope. The current, which had become rapidly more powerful, surged between him and the bank, sweeping him out into the river and tightening the centre rope too much for him to unknot. Meanwhile, the river continued to rise and as it did, the boat was starting to tilt precariously.

I saw the danger straight off. 'You'll have to cut it,' I shouted. 'The current's tipping you over.'

For some reason, he didn't seem to grasp the gravity of his situation. He began mumbling something or another about the rope. From what I could make out above the noise of the river, he didn't want to damage it because – of all things – it was new! I shouted again with more urgency. 'Look mate, if you don't cut your rope you're going to lose your boat and probably drown yourself. Do you understand? Look how far you're listing!'

At that, the scales abruptly dropped from his eyes and he began feverishly sawing at the rope. But either the knife he was using was too blunt, or in his anxiety he'd lost his rag completely and wasn't able to function well enough to use it properly. Either way, the river was still going up and he was tipping ever more precipitously. In a minute or two, the water would be over his gunnels and he'd sink like a stone. Em, who'd been watching the unfolding crisis with growing concern, suddenly slapped the sharpest of our kitchen knives from *Justice* into my hand. I immediately started cutting the rope from the bollard on the bank to which it was secured. Mercifully, the knife went through it like butter. The stricken boat bobbed upright and was swept away downstream, until the skipper was able to engage his engine with sufficient power to bring it under control.

We breathed a sigh of relief at his narrow escape – but it was short-lived. When we turned back to *Justice* it was only to discover with horror that it was tipping, too, except it wasn't held by a centre rope but by a centre chain, which we'd been advised to use at night in York in case drunks turning out from pubs attempted to unmoor us – something of a hazard for boaters in big cities everywhere. I hopped on board to fetch the key to the padlock that secured it but when I tried it in the lock I felt a chill of alarm when for some reason it wouldn't work. My first thought was that I had the wrong key. I started to try others on the same key ring, the beginnings of panic now mounting in my gut. The river was still going up and we were tipping now, leaning at enough of an angle that the taut chain was beginning to grate against the paintwork on the edge of the roof.

Suddenly it struck me what was happening. The tension in the chain was putting stress on the padlock. That was why the key wouldn't work. If it had been a rope, I'd have cut through it in a trice. But this wasn't a rope, this was a hardened Grade A steel chain. How long would it take to cut through that? How long had I got? I was in a state of full panic now, but I kept telling myself that in an emergency, panic was destructive, and that if we were going to get out of this crisis with a boat that was still floating I would have to stay calm. I jumped into the engine room and made straight for the box where I keep power tools. This was no job for a manual hacksaw, I had too little time. I grabbed an electric saw. But where the hell was the blade for it? I needed a hacksaw blade, but I only had one hacksaw blade. I'd used it just recently. Only a couple of days before. But it wasn't where I normally kept it.

I started opening toolboxes and storage tins at random, throwing chisels, screwdrivers, nuts, bolts and drill bits across the floor until it looked as if the engine had exploded. But I suddenly pulled myself up short, paralysed by my own stupidity. The bloody blade was already on the saw, wasn't it? It had been there all along. It was where I'd last left it. I scuttled back to the wharf and with the saw on full power it took me just moments to cut through the chain. *Justice* lurched upright, free of her shackles, held now only by her bow and stern ropes, which Em had been loosening while I'd been below decks.

We both breathed a sigh of relief. But just as we began to think that it couldn't get worse, of all things it started snowing. And not just a light dusting of snow, but a blanket of thick, heavy snow, a complete whiteout that covered the boat in no time and reduced visibility to such an extent you could barely see your hand in front of your face. What was so surprising was there hadn't been the least sign of its approach. Exactly the opposite, in fact. It had been a clear, rather beautiful morning while we were shopping, sun shining and not a cloud in the sky. Now, it was an impenetrable blizzard.

Em brought me back to the task in hand. The question she wanted answering was now that we hadn't sunk, what were we going to do next with this Arctic blizzard raging? Staying put and chancing it with the river wasn't an option. We had to somehow get back to Naburn, where we were at least safe from what looked as if it was going to be another bumper flood. At this stage, the idea that we might be going to Selby that day was the last thing on our minds. It simply wasn't feasible in these conditions. Yet, as we cast off into the river, hardly able to see where we were going, the storm began to abate and by the time we passed the ancient frontage of Bishopthorpe Palace, traditional home of the Archbishops of York, it had stopped completely. When we finally arrived at Naburn there was no sign we'd ever been in a snowstorm. Not only had the snow on the boat melted but the boat itself had dried out completely and was gleaming in bright sunlight, which had appeared abruptly as if to mock us by adding another far-fetched element to the day's weather. Even so, it had been such a traumatic day we'd had enough of it. We decided to moor and not go any further.

Ken, however, had different ideas. He'd seen us approaching and opened the lock gates, unaware of any change in our plans. For some reason, we felt ourselves drawn to go into the lock. Perhaps we were thinking it might be a convenient place for us to explain to him that we'd changed our minds? Or perhaps we hadn't changed our minds? Perhaps we were just thinking that we'd come so far we might as well get it over with and get to Selby while we could? Either way, it looked as if we'd somehow embarked on a course of action, if not exactly made a decision to pursue it.

As soon as he'd closed the lock gates behind us, Ken hurried over with another man, who from his dress and demeanour you'd have known was an office wallah even if he hadn't been introduced to us as The Boss. 'We'll have you through in no time,' he said. 'Though it'll be a bit sad to see you go. After so long, you've become part of the attraction of the lock.'

We laughed politely. Ken was more serious. 'The water's running a bit fresher today than we expected so it could be a bumpy ride,' he said as he lifted the paddles to empty the lock

We surveyed the tidal river downstream. It was not a reassuring sight. The water seemed to be flowing even faster on that side than it was on ours. But what could we do? We were committed now. And what was the alternative anyhow? Staying another week or two, maybe a couple more months, going stir crazy at Naburn? More waiting? More Groundhog Days?

'Just watch yourself when you turn into Selby Lock, it's bad enough at the best of times,' The Boss said. 'With the speed of the current today it's going to be a good deal worse. Just remember to start turning as soon as you pass under the railway bridge. And keep away from the bank under the trees on the left just as you go into the lock. If you get stuck there you'll be on a mudbank and we can't help you.'

'Good luck,' he shouted down to us as Ken opened the gates to let us out.

Viewed from this lower level, the tidal river looked far worse than it did from the top. What from the lock seemed just a series of gentle eddies and decorative whorls of water were – once you were actually on them – powerful whirlpools, vortexes that I could feel through the tiller. They were constantly pulling the boat to places I didn't want it to go. I had to struggle continually to keep control, wrenching and heaving the tiller to force it to bend to my will. Normally, the process of steering is a leisurely, gentle one. Now, it was more like a stiff workout on a cross-trainer at the gym. The current was far faster than it looked as well. Just beyond Naburn, there's the first of a series of S-bends that characterise this part of the Ouse. At that stage I hadn't registered the speed at which we were travelling and I took the wrong course. As a result, we were swept so close to the bank it was a wonder we weren't washed up on it.

The only reassurance of the terrifying trip was that at least we could keep in touch through a VHF radio that we'd bought in York a short while before, in anticipation of this part of the voyage. This was critically important since we needed to maintain contact with the bridge keepers responsible for the swing bridges between Naburn and Selby. Because the river was running so far above its normal levels they were concerned we might be so high in the water we'd collide with the bridges while trying to get under them. They therefore needed to know whether to open them to let us pass.

The bridge where we had to begin our turn into Selby Lock – the Ousegate Railway Swing Bridge, to give it its full name – posed the biggest challenge. Apart from its navigational demands, it's the lowest bridge on this stretch of the river and if you need it open, it's the one that requires the earliest notification. It's a railway bridge, after all. You can't open a railway bridge in the face of an oncoming train without adequate warning. I'd measured the height of *Justice*'s superstructure above the waterline time and time again, and I'd spoken to the bridge keeper, who'd confirmed we'd get underneath safely. All the same, I was still worried about it. Had I measured incorrectly? Had the bridge keeper miscalculated? I could imagine running into the bridge full tilt. At the speed we were travelling, it could be carnage. It might seriously weaken the structure of the bridge. A passenger train might be passing overhead. It might go plunging into the icy water...

The thought of these potential catastrophes fazed me. I was so anxious about it that it was only after we'd passed under the bridge safely, and with so much room to spare Em and I could have danced a *pas de deux* on the roof, that I realised I should have already started turning into the lock as we'd been instructed to do. My delay was only a short one but it was critical. As I swung the tiller, the full force of the swollen river hit us broadside and immediately swept us sideways. I saw us pass the lock where the gates were already open in anticipation of our arrival. Two men on the side were waving their arms to get us to straighten up. But I couldn't straighten up. Not without powering the boat towards the bank and the trees that I'd been warned to keep away from. Yet there was no other way to turn except by heading for the bank...

The low branches of the trees swept across the top of the boat, which lurched as it hit the mud bar we'd been warned against. I swung the tiller again and wound the speed wheel on the engine to full power in the same way I had on the Ribble Link when we'd been in trouble. Thick black smoke billowed from the exhaust pipe on the roof. The engine coughed and faltered but it didn't stop. It ploughed through the silt. It seemed to relish the effort. It was like one of those nightmares in which you're mired in sludge and can only move in slow motion. Inch by excruciating inch, *Justice* edged forwards until at last her bow was parallel with the mouth of the lock and I was able to swing the tiller round into open water, and finally into the lock itself.

It was then I realised that one of the men I'd seen waving earlier was The Boss, who'd driven down from Naburn. He'd only just arrived, he told us. 'You nearly beat me,' he added. 'You must have been travelling at a hell of a lick.'

A short while afterwards, we were moored in the canal basin – the first time we'd been on still water for months and the first time I'd felt truly safe for a lot longer.

For the rest of the day, I couldn't stop grinning inanely. Eventually, Em couldn't take it any longer. 'Why have you got that idiotic smirk pasted on your face,' she said. 'What is it, relief?'

I shook my head. 'No, I was thinking of that dreadful moorings warden in Ripon, the one who kept hassling us because she said we were overstaying on a 48-hour mooring.'

'So why is that so funny?'

'I was just thinking what she'd say now. You see, it struck me leaving Naburn that we'd spent the better part of six months on a mooring restricted to a couple of hours...'

10

Goole, Doncaster and Sheffield

We woke before dark to catch the early tide, and so we didn't realise how misty a morning it was till it was light. When the sun rose, burning its way through the haze, it smouldered in the sky with the vivid orange and yellow glow of a Turner painting, illuminating the canal with a subdued flush like a lamp burning beneath the murky surface. There were a couple of sailing barges moored opposite and a seagoing barque, rigging hanging from its masts and its yardarms silhouetted against the sky like crosses on a hill. It seemed an appropriate image at the time. Easter was approaching. Soon it would be Holy Week. Soon Good Friday.

We were in Keadby, where a lock opens on to the tidal River Trent from what is known collectively as the Sheffield and South Yorkshire Navigation, a network of wide industrial canals that until as late as the 1970s were used for regular commercial transport and that still carry occasional cargoes. They aren't pretty, but they are impressive; and for anyone who's interested in waterways and tiring a little of the twee, picture-postcard canals you see so much of on TV, it's a fascinating system, linking some lesser-considered towns and cities that you'd never go out of your way to visit but that still have a lot to offer tourists.

Goole, for instance. I loved Goole. For me, there's something about these inland ports that evoke a lost England, when we traded by sea and considered the oceans our domain. Even though

Goole has declined since its heyday, when it was one of the country's major maritime transshipment ports to and from the inland waterways, it's nevertheless still important, with its annual trade estimated to be worth more than £800 million. It advertises itself as 'the UK's Premier Inland Port' and arriving there on long, straight and wide waterways, through electrically operated locks that are so enormous they're more like lochs, I can believe it. The place is unnerving for a narrowboat, as if you've inadvertently ventured from Toyland into the real world. The docks themselves are a wilderness of transit sheds, hoppers and cranes, secured from the outside world by high security fences and barriers, above which you can occasionally glimpse the soaring superstructure of some Panamanian-registered container vessel or cargo ship. Tucked away among all this are sporadic reminders of Goole's historic past in the shape of still recognisable Georgian warehouses, brick-built with slate roofs, at least one of them still with its original cast-iron casement windows and characteristic Georgian glass panes.

Soaring above the jumble of the docks are a couple of extraordinary water towers, which are local landmarks. They're nicknamed 'Salt and Pepper', although frankly neither of them looks to me particularly like a domestic condiment dispenser. To be blunt, one of them reminds me of a dildo, a brick-built phallic symbol of enormous proportions including – forgive me for even mentioning this – an unmistakable bellend, which Goollyians, or whatever they call themselves, have become so accustomed to they don't notice it anymore, and are offended if you do. The other one is little better, even if it is a little more discreet. Built of concrete, it looks a bit like a gas holder made of stone. Or putting it more kindly, a rather elegant tube draped in a filigree of decorative arches, like a lace coverlet, and to my eye every bit as yonic as the other is phallic. Or perhaps this is just my dirty mind at work.

Surrounded by all this industry you'd think it would be difficult to find a pleasant place to stop, but in fact nothing could be further from the truth. Goole lies at the junction of the rivers Don and Ouse just before it joins the Humber, and a couple of marinas provide moorings for an eclectic mix of boats: motor cruisers, fishing vessels, yachts and narrowboats. We pulled up canalside adjacent to one of them, divided from it by a wide ribbon of well-tended lawn. Nearby was a small but rather lovely museum of Yorkshire's waterways' history, which sadly has since closed down. There were splendid sailing barges of one sort or another all around, their masts towering above us, and in the midst of it all was the North Star Marina Club, which was open to visitors and as friendly a place as you'd find anywhere – although one evening I overheard a group of blokes at an adjoining table having a right barney about the damage that might be done to Goole if we left the EU, which, as referendum day got closer, led me to reflect that the atmosphere might not be quite as sociable in these parts for much longer.

Mind you, even with political arguments raging, I'd have chosen the Marina Club for a night out above any of the local pubs, which were just a step too far away to be comfortable. Even the nearest, *The Vermuyden*, would be a fair walk with a pint or two inside you. Located on a wasteland between a warehouse and the blank brick wall of a dock, it's hardly the most prepossessing place – though it does have a lively clientele who swear by it, and it does serve the function of keeping the name of Vermuyden alive in Goole. Because without him, Goole wouldn't exist.

Cornelius Vermuyden was a Dutch water engineer who came to prominence after draining Canvey Island at the mouth of the River Thames in Essex in the early 17th century. This brought him to the attention of Charles I who, before he lost his head on the scaffold, employed Vermuyden to drain land on a couple of his manors in Hatfield Chase on the Isle of Axholme, a flat and frequently flooded area straddling south Yorkshire and north Lincolnshire. Vermuyden attempted this by altering the course of the Don, which in those days was a sluggish, barely navigable river that meandered to its confluence with the Trent past a succession of small villages notable only as places where local sailors had an inclination to set up home.

The project wasn't a success. Vermuyden badly underestimated the volume of water flowing down the Don and the floods still persisted. Indeed, the 'improvements' made by his team caused more problems than they solved because they led to sediment silting up the river's traditional drainage channels. As well as this, the rerouting of the Don meant that adjoining villages lost their access to the river and, along with it, the salmon that were a traditional bonus of living there. Eventually, simmering local animosity exploded into all-out riots, with feelings running so high that after the Dutch engineers packed up tools and left, locals destroyed the settlement at Sandtoft, where they had established their expat community.

However, all this did eventually have a positive outcome, for in 1633, after legal pressure, Vermuyden was compelled to clear up the mess he'd left by having a second go at drawing water from the Don. This time, he figured that the best way of solving the problem was by digging a new drainage channel to the River Ouse, and for obvious reasons this watercourse soon became known as the 'Dutch River'. Just before the river joined the Ouse, Vermuyden built a simple wooden bridge as a crossing point, and it was around this modest structure that the modern town of Goole grew in the 1820s, when it became the terminus for Yorkshire's industrial canal network.

At one point in its history, Goole was an enormously wealthy town, which you can see reflected today in the splendid entrances to the offices of former shipping companies, adorned with decorative corbels and stone porticos, some of them embossed with romantic depictions of galleons in full sail. Indeed, so affluent was the town, with so much commercial shipping operating out of the place, that it was possible for artists to make a decent living painting ships as keepsakes for the captains who sailed them or for show in the boardrooms of the shipping companies that owned them.

The most famous of these 'portside painters' was Reuben Chappell. Born in 1870 not far from the docks, he won a scholarship to the local grammar school and was afterwards apprenticed to a photographer in the town, where he was employed colour tinting black-and-white photos. Though almost completely self-taught, Chappell clearly had a talent for art and he began drawing boats in his spare time. He sold these occasionally to local newspapers, and afterwards, more significantly for the turn his life was to take, he started to sell sketches of ships to local seaman to keep as souvenirs to remind them of the boats they'd worked on. Before long, he was a regular face at the docks, where he'd meet arriving ships and tout for work. As time went on, he set up a business as an artist selling paintings: 5 shillings (25p) for a watercolour and 30 shillings (£1.50) for one in oils.

It's estimated Chappell painted 12,000 or so pictures of boats over the course of his career, a number of them with familiar nautical landmarks in the background, such as Spurn Point or Flamborough Head. Today, his paintings of the clippers and sloops that sailed out of Goole, and the steamships that in later years began to dominate the seaways, are to be found all over the world, in private collections, museums and galleries. As a result, they're not exactly rare, so if you come across one in the attic it won't make you a millionaire. All the same, they're still worth a bob or two and you'd be advised to think twice before offloading it to a charity shop.

Goole celebrates Chappell in a distinctive way I've never seen before anywhere on my travels, for as you wander around the town there are a dozen or so reproductions of his paintings, complete with decorative frames, mounted on the outside walls of various shops and offices. One even hangs on a set of security palings, although the one that really stands out in my mind is the painting of the *George Kilner*, a topsail schooner named after the Rotherham businessman who invented the glass jars so beloved of generations of Women's Institute jam-makers. Uncharacteristically, Chappell painted it against a grey sky on a thunderously dark and choppy sea, uncannily anticipating its stranding in 1899 off the Caribbean island of St Kitts in a storm, when it was lucky not to sink.

Doncaster, halfway between Leeds and Sheffield, is another town we found more interesting than we thought it would be, although it has to be admitted the place has a bad image problem. I'll tell you how bad an image problem: so bad that not long ago there was a move to step back a couple of thousand years and revert to the name Danum, which is what the place was originally called by the Romans. Whether this attempt to improve its PR was to do with a decision by the government to publicly shame Doncaster by labelling it an antisocial behaviour hot spot, or whether due to the disclosure that it was former *Top Gear* presenter Jeremy Clarkson's home town, I couldn't say. Either way, I still don't understand the negative reaction to the town, and why people living in the place still persist in dissing it in such numbers that it regularly makes the top ten in Britain's 'Crap Town' list. Kids of a certain age obviously loathe the place. 'Doncaster's a shit hole surrounded by other shit holes' one wrote a couple of years back on the web. Another, with more literary aspirations, described a night out in Doncaster with warped eloquence: 'Bums sitting on steps drinking White Lightning near the old strip club or the Jobcentre, and chavettes with near nothing on, looking to volunteer to contribute to Doncaster's rising pregnancy rate.'

We just couldn't see it. The town's got its problems as all big towns have, and I'm sure there are pockets of poverty. All the same, the centre was plainly prosperous, and it felt like a place on the up: lively and safe, even at night, in a way that other bigger and wealthier towns aren't. You want bums and chavettes? You want problems of poverty? You should come round our way, and see what we have to put up with. And we live in central London, which is apparently the epicentre of prosperity in the affluent South East!

Culturally, Doncaster was buzzing. It's top-heavy with cinemas yet a new one was being built next to the Cast theatre and arts complex, which we stumbled across one afternoon. It seemed a huge facility for a town of its size. There's apparently a smaller community theatre as well, and a culture and learning centre is planned, along with a museum and gallery. What impressed us most though, were the amount of flyers in small shops for music gigs, shows and comedy events at pubs and other small venues in the area, a classic indicator of a vibrant cultural life and one I hope won't have evaporated with the coronavirus lockdowns.

If they know anything about the place at all, most people will know that Doncaster has one of the largest racecourses in the country, home to two of the world's oldest horse races, the Doncaster Cup and the St Leger. But we found there was a good deal more to the place than that. Its cathedral-like Minster church of St George, for instance, was designed by the Gothic revivalist architect George Gilbert Scott, whose other work includes the Albert Memorial and the restored Midland Hotel at St Pancras in London. Or at least I think it does. These Gilbert Scotts are a confusing family when it comes to who designed what because they were a dynasty of architects, all of them renowned for something or another. Be that as it may, the church of St George in Doncaster is an impressive building by any measure, yet no one seems particularly proud of it or overly keen to get anyone to visit it. You can't say the same of the town's elegant Georgian Mansion House, which is widely marketed by the council, who own it. One afternoon, Em and I visited and had sandwiches, cake and a pot of Darjeeling in what must be one of the grandest tea rooms in the country. The place is Grade 1 listed and it was heaving; we were lucky to get a table. If all this isn't celebration enough of Doncaster, it's got a terrific fish market, too, though from what I read it's a shadow of what it used to be. There are safe and convenient moorings nearby, as well, which encourage you to linger in the town longer than you might otherwise do.

We were coming back from the market one day, weighed down with slabs of fresh cod and a bag of shimmering bright-eyed sardines, when we found ourselves with a new neighbour just down from where we were tied: a gleaming cruiser, barely out of the boatyard where it was built. Now, everyone has a dream, don't they? Even people like Em and I, who many would think are living a dream already. Our dream is one day to win the lottery and buy a boat exactly like this, a steel-built Dutch boat three stories high and with a bathing platform to boot for those times you find yourselves on the Med. We were standing on the quayside gazing at it in admiration when the owner and his wife, and a woman we later discovered was his mother-in-law, arrived back from their own shopping expedition. Inevitably, we began chatting and before long we'd been invited on board and were drinking tea in their spacious main cabin, dazzled by the sun streaming through the windows, reflecting off the lustrous varnished wooden surfaces and polished brass fittings. The boat was a peach, a thing of beauty, a vessel as big and as well-equipped as a luxury house and with a cruising range enough to take you the length and breadth of Europe. All we could do was wonder at it, gobsmacked with admiration and ill-concealed lust.

'I mean, if you don't mind me asking,' I said, plucking up courage to ask a question that I knew I shouldn't, 'just — roughly, you know — how much would you expect to pay for a boat like this?'

I thought at first it was my imagination, but I could have sworn at that instant I saw the owner glance apprehensively towards his wife and mother-in-law. Then he quoted a price. It was a high price, a very high price indeed, way beyond anything Em and I could hope to pay for any boat. But here's the rub: one evening not long before, we'd been fantasising about the future, surfing the net together looking at how much Dutch coastal cruisers similar to this one cost. And what we discovered was that even from companies not as well regarded as the one that had built this boat — and even buying second-hand — they were still *far* more expensive than what the owner had just said he'd paid for his state-of-the-art vessel, launched no more than a couple of months ago.

'Wow! that seems amazing value,' I blurted out. 'Incredible...' But then I stopped myself in my tracks. It had struck me that there might be more to all this than meets the eye, and that this matter of the price might be more of a tangled web than I could imagine. The awkward moment blew over as quickly as it had blown up and the owner looked over to his wife and mother-in-law once more, this time with a reassuring smile. 'Yes, it's true,' he agreed, 'I did manage to negotiate a ... er ... a rather good deal on it...'

'So what was all that about?' Em asked me later, after we'd got back to the privacy of *Justice*.

'I'm not sure,' I said, lowering my voice so as not to risk being overheard by anyone passing, 'but if you want my hunch, I think there may have been some chicanery surrounding the purchase of that vessel, a smidgeon of deception about what he paid for it.'

'How do you mean?' Em asked.

155

'Well, I can't be certain, but one thing I do know for sure is that whatever he shelled out for that boat, it was a good deal more than he's willing to let on. My guess would be that he wasn't entirely upfront with his wife about how much he'd paid for it.'

Em pondered this for a moment or two before she spoke. 'His mother-in-law seemed to suspect something as well,' she said eventually. 'I mean, I could be wrong too, but I just happened to be looking in her direction when you asked him how much he'd paid and … well…'

'Well what?'

'Well, when he told you, I could swear she smirked. As if she didn't believe it either.'

A few days later, we cast off, heading south-west to Sheffield. This wasn't just a simple matter of starting our engine and engaging gear, since to get to this one-time Steel City you have to arrange matters ahead of time with the lock keeper, who manages all boat traffic. As it happened, there was an expedition from a local club doing the trip at the same time, so our passage was hooked on to the back of theirs.

We tried to give them space and maintain a polite distance between us. However, this soon shrank at the first of a series of locks on the river, which you have to navigate before you branch off to the 4 mile (6.4km)-long Sheffield and Tinsley Canal, where a flight of 11 locks connects to a basin in the centre of the city. There, a sort of controlled chaos ensued with the Boat Club crews running around like headless chickens, no one quite knowing what they were doing. They struck us as a peculiar crowd, mainly because they weren't particularly accomplished at boating, but also because they didn't seem to be enjoying it much either. I put this down to the fact that mooring so close to Sheffield, a club outing to the city wasn't much of a knees-up for them. They seemed a bit like … well, like beginners, actually, too self-conscious about everything they did. Except that beginners who are out for a trip are invariably excited by what they're doing and thrilled at the challenges of cruising. Most of this crowd were grumbling at every opportunity and seemed reluctant to be on the water at all – like people who'd signed up for a package holiday and decided on the first day that it wasn't for them. They seemed a bit apprehensive about the locals, too, and when they all tied up that evening at a recommended mooring spot on the outskirts of Rotherham, they clung together like a wagon train overnighting on the Oregon Trail.

It was a shame they didn't get much pleasure from the cruise because it had been a glorious day for boating. The weather was perfect, unseasonably warm with bright sunshine, and we'd passed through the pleasant wooded sections of the river valley towards Conisborough, where the romantic views of the 12th-century castle inspired Sir Walter Scott to write *Ivanhoe*.

The next day, despite everything we did to avoid it, we somehow found ourselves once more getting increasingly integrated into the club convoy, though I still can't work out how this happened. One moment we were bringing up the rear, the next we were in the middle of the flotilla, being encouraged to move forwards in the queue. At first, this was no inconvenience, but as we began to climb the Tinsley Flight, we felt duty-bound to help, not just the boats trailing along behind us, but the ones in front of us that were flagging and holding everyone up. This made the going a lot harder because despite the best efforts of the lock keeper to get the locks prepared for such an unusually heavy influx of boats, the flight was still a swine: the paddles were stiff, the gates heavy and for some reason the locks themselves filled with logs, as if someone had been cutting down trees and couldn't be bothered to gather what they'd chopped up.

To be fair, there's not usually much traffic to Sheffield by water so the canal can be a bit of a rubbish dump at the best of times. Enclosed by scruffy factories, warehouses and the yards of long-abandoned workshops, it's like canals in towns used to be when we first started boating. That's one reason why there isn't exactly a waiting list to go to Sheffield by canal. The other is that after you've struggled up 11 cussed locks to get to the basin at the top, the canal stops dead in its tracks and there's nowhere else you can go except turn round and come back down again. Canal boaters don't generally like going up dead ends. Generally, we like things more conveniently arranged. We like to cruise 'rings' – that is, routes that allow us to finish up where we started so we don't have to repeat any section. We narrowboaters like to 'do' our waterways – a term you hear whenever a group of us gather in a pub or at a boat rally. It's as though we're marking them off like Americans mark off countries on a tour of Europe, as if we're collecting waterways like kids collect football cards. 'Oh yes, we "did" the so-and-so canal a couple of years ago.' 'Oh, we're planning on "doing" such-and-such canal this summer...' etc. etc.

Travelling the waterways like this has always seemed to me a perfunctory way of exploring the system, which is, after all, one of the glories of the country's heritage, so iconic that today it even features on British passports. It assumes that one trip along a canal is enough to see everything it has to offer in one hit. My view is more old school. I don't think you can even pretend to know a canal until you've travelled along it at least a couple of times in different directions. A single trip simply doesn't give you enough time to explore the canal itself, let alone poke around the villages and towns it passes through along the way. The fact is, canals look different depending on which way you travel along them. They look different for a whole series of other reasons, too. It's extraordinary, for instance, how contrasting a landscape can be at various times of day. Light affects the way we see everything, and it's particularly the case when you're gazing at the countryside from a moving boat. The way the outline of a cloud falls on a hill or a beam of midday sunshine catches a copse can change how you see the whole unfolding vista before you. In the same way, those long evening shadows piercing the fields just prior to sunset can paint the countryside with a totally different palette to the same scene viewed in the morning when sometimes the very earth itself seems to glow with the burnished promise of the new day.

Weather is another variable in this ever-shifting panorama of England: places feel different in the rain, they move differently in the wind, they smell different in the sunshine. Above all else, the seasons transform everything. Exploring England by canal is a passage through the cycle of the year, and a place that in the summer is blissful – perhaps a sun-kissed meadow, thick with buttercups, or a dappled woodland grove tangled with dog roses – can, in winter, when the nights draw in and the damp mists coagulate, be a place of dark menace and threat that arouses deep primeval fears, as uncontrollable as they are inexplicable.

And then there's that fourth dimension of time that changes everything so insidiously we scarcely notice that anything has changed at all. That measured passing of the years during which everything alters so imperceptibly that nothing whatsoever seems to have altered in any way until we wake up one morning and realise with a start that nothing in the world is quite as we remember it. You can't get any sense of that on the canals from a single outing. You can't really understand that until you have been kicking around the waterways for long enough that they've wormed themselves into your psyche in the way they can do if you let them. They're like a drug in that respect. They can exert a pull so intense you feel bereft if you're away from them for long. Those of us who have spent significant time on the waterways all come to feel the same way about them. None of us are immune to their magnetism. Possibly, it's something to do with their place in our culture, which is so tied up with our sense of ourselves that they become inseparable. Or maybe it's because they're a conduit between the past and the present that can transport us almost magically from the heart of our contemporary world into the depths of rural England, an England that appears so locked into another era it's sometimes hard to believe it still exists. Or maybe the attraction is in the solitude canals afford us. In an era when seclusion is such a precious commodity, perhaps it's simply the isolation and privacy we can enjoy on the cut that gives us the space to learn to love ourselves a little, and maybe in loving ourselves we come to love them, too.

In the past – in a forthright 'does-what-it-says-on-the-can' sort of way appropriate to an industrial waterway – the basin at the terminus of the canal in Sheffield used to be called Sheffield Canal Basin. But it's been rechristened, and as part of the inexorable gentrification of the waterways it's known nowadays as Victoria Quays. 'Quay' is one of the current buzzwords of the waterways that architects have discovered is acceptable to the well-off, who wouldn't countenance having to look over something as utilitarian as a 'basin' from the cramped balconies of their executive penthouse flats. Don't ask me why, but they don't mind 'wharfs' either. 'Harbours' are acceptable too, even 'piers'. 'Marinas' are passable as well. 'Dockyard' is an absolute no-no. That would be like living in Factory Street.

Whatever you call it, there was hardly any room to moor because the boat club had commandeered most of the available space. We needn't have worried though because the next morning, before we'd even got out of bed, they'd all gone, vanished into the ether as completely as if they'd never existed.

The exception was one boat owned by a couple of similar age to us whom we'd run into while coming up the locks and who'd given us the impression they were as unhappy as we were at being trapped in the club melee. Her family were seafaring folk from Wells-next-the-Sea in Norfolk, and he was a shipwright by trade, the son of a boatman. As a teenager, he'd frequently accompanied his father on deliveries of grain to Sheffield, so he had a unique perspective on the canal.

Sheffield was a sentimental journey for Em and I because it was here, many years ago, that we'd first met as journalists on a training course. Apart from the Penny Black pub beside the bus station, the city was almost unrecognisable, especially around Kelham Island, which back in the day was one of the centres of steel production in the city, said to be the place where the joists for New York's Brooklyn Bridge were manufactured. Today, it's an interesting mix of museums, restaurants, bars and imaginative housing, much of it fashioned from the imposing offices that had once fronted the steelworks.

We spent a few days taking in several films, a couple of exhibitions and even a show at the Crucible, which is probably less famous nowadays as the theatre we once knew than as the venue for the World Snooker Championship, which it has hosted for more than 30 years. There, we by chance, after a performance we'd all seen, happened to run across our neighbours from the basin, and as so often happens on the cut, we decided to have a quick drink together, which turned out to be neither quick nor single. We were still knocking it back after midnight when we agreed to travel back to Doncaster together the next day. It turned out to be a delightful trip despite our throbbing heads. They were great company and made working the locks seem effortless, in complete contrast to our escorts on the way up.

The play at the Crucible wasn't bad either. Talk about blurring the boundaries of fact and fiction, it was called *The Nap* and

161

was about snooker of all things. Halfway through, the central character is involved in a grudge match at the World Snooker Championship and his opponent – who must have been a real professional player acting the part of one – comes on to make a crucial break. Of course, the balls were pre-placed. Even so, I can genuinely claim to have seen a break of more than a hundred at the Crucible.

11

Cruising back to the past

I can't remember a time when I wasn't aware of waterways. Born in the canal town of Loughborough in Leicestershire, for most of my adolescence I lived in a small village called Rothley on the River Soar, where as a kid my mates and I were always up to some sort of mischief. Messing about on canals for as long as I have, I've seen the system evolve through different stages of its history. In 1962, after a century and more of decline, responsibility for it was transferred to the British Waterways Board (BWB). I can't say I was aware of the change, and if I was it made no impression on me. At that time in my life, if it wasn't pretty and didn't wear a skirt, not much did. However, for campaigners in the early post-war years who'd fought to keep canals open, the development was a glimmer of hope in an otherwise barren landscape. Sadly, any expectations that this transfer of responsibility might signify a new canal age were dashed after The Big Freeze the following year, when those few remaining canal folk who were still living on their boats and managing to eke out a precarious living by sporadic commercial carrying were frozen in by the ice for months on end.

I remember The Big Freeze clearly as anyone who lived through it does. It began in December when an anticyclone formed over Scandinavia, drawing cold air south from the Russian steppes. Before the year was out there were 20ft (6m)-high snowdrifts covering parts of Wales and the South West.

Over the next few months, temperatures plummeted and canals and rivers froze in some of the coldest conditions ever recorded in the UK. Afterwards, BWB decided that there was no future in a transport system so vulnerable to weather conditions and got out of the canal haulage business completely, a move that effectively signalled the end of 200 years of carrying on British canals. This dealt the boatmen and their families a double blow. First, they were told they'd lost their jobs. Then they were told they'd lost their homes, too. BWB owned their boats, you see. They wanted them back.

I remember that winter of 1962/63 for different, less consequential reasons, because for a brief and glorious moment Leicester City Football Club, the team I'd supported since I was a kid, were in serious danger of winning the FA Cup and League double, the first time they'd won anything in their entire history. Of course, being Leicester, they blew it at the final hurdle, losing all but one of their last nine league games and getting torn apart by Manchester United in the FA Cup Final at Wembley, where I stood on the terraces in tears. That season, I avidly followed the 'Ice Kings', as they were dubbed by the press, barely missing a match. Somehow, by first covering the pitch with straw, making it like a farmyard barn, and then enveloping it in a sort of blow-up plastic tent that heated the surface and made it an even worse mud patch than the one they usually played on, City managed to complete matches when nobody else could.

The connection between these two events on the canals and on the football pitch didn't occur to me until years later when we washed up at a place called Charity Dock in Bedworth, just outside Coventry, where we moored for a decade. Nearby, at a small basin at Hawkesbury Junction where three waterways converge, a large number of canal families were trapped that winter before being made homeless. Left destitute by BWB's heartlessness, they were thrown on to the good offices of the local council, who in those days at least had a responsibility to house them, which it's worth mentioning they wouldn't today. Many finished up in the large council estate bordering Charity Dock, which was run by an irascible rogue called Joe Gilbert, a stocky rough diamond of a bloke who was such an out-and-out rascal that I'm told the boat people composed a song they used to sing in the local pub about how he used to rip them off. God knows why he took to us, or why we liked him so much. Our engine broke down as we were passing one year and he took us under his wing, probably because we were mugs enough to pay him mooring fees at a time when nobody else there seemed to pay anyone for anything if they could help it.

Charity Dock is an extraordinary boatyard even now: a study in canalside kitsch. Essentially, it's a messy scrap yard, piled high with wrecked cars, vans and lorries and littered with twisted shopping trolleys, derelict engines and the rusty skeletons of what might have once been motorbikes. Against this backdrop, along a quay that bends sharply to follow the line of the canal, is a row of boats, narrowboats and cruisers, some inhabited, some dilapidated. A few former wooden working boats lie half submerged in the oily water. Behind all this is a display of debris that, depending on your perspective, is either something you'd find at a council recycling depot or an exhibit you'd see at Tate Modern. Mannequins, some salvaged from department stores, dominate the display. They're dressed as clowns, circus performers or pirates. One is done up as a spaceman, another as an army captain in dress uniform, sheltering beneath a camouflaged bivouac behind which hides a female figure in what appears to be khaki hotpants. Another female dummy, a parody of the local icon Lady Godiva perhaps, poses provocatively side saddle on a horse, her short skirt emphasising her slender, stockinged legs as she sits lewdly cradling what seems to be a rolling pin, or maybe a truncheon. Another model of indeterminate gender seems, inexplicably, to have the giant head of a hare transplanted on to its shoulders. Distributed among all this is other decorative detritus: tattered flags, old street signs, collections of watering cans and large numbers of wooden Polynesian fertility masks. There are two or three huge ice cream cones that must have once been used in an advertising promotion. There's a life-sized statue of the Venus de Milo wearing headphones, garden gnomes, rocking horses and a brightly coloured children's climbing frame.

Like it or not – and a lot of people don't like it at all because it's ramshackle and doesn't fit the sanitised image of modern canals – the place has a certain eclectic style to it. It didn't have that when we were there. When we were there, it was just a scrap yard – though one with an impeccable lineage. It was home to rats as big as cats, no doubt the progeny of rats that lived on the site in the 1830s when it was a wharf and basin serving the nearby Charity Colliery and which were doubtless still living on the site a century later when John Griffith established the boatyard.

At the time we washed up in the dock, Joe was still doing intermittent jobs repairing wooden boats. It was his specialism and he was one of the few remaining people in the country who still had the skills and tools to do it. Working for him then were Arthur, whose surname I never knew, and Ted Beck, a short, wiry bloke who'd been a boatman himself but who was now the odd-job man and general factotum. His main area of responsibility seemed to be brewing huge pots of tea made with sickly sweet condensed milk, and tending to the enormous pot-bellied stove in the dock around which we used to sit drinking it. He was a kindly man, though, and I have fond memories of him. In the winter, when we came up from London for the weekend, he used to light our fire for us so that our boat was warmed through when we arrived.

Arthur was a different sort of bloke entirely. For a start, he was a big man, an Oliver Hardy to Ted's Stan Laurel. Of greater consequence was that he'd qualified in the army as a mechanic and was the most technically skilled person at the dock. His face was a map of impetigo from the work he did, a condition not helped by his habit of constantly wiping sweat off his forehead with an oil rag. But he was a genius where anything to do with engines was concerned, a fact we can testify to personally since we bought an old Lister that he managed to tease back from the dead during our time there. He drank heavily, however, starting at lunchtime in a pub in nearby Bulkington, where I'd join him occasionally for a 'pint' that invariably finished up with us having five or six each. Afterwards, I was wiped out for the rest of the day and was good for nothing except sleeping. But you couldn't tell Arthur had been drinking at all. He'd drive back to the dock looking as if he'd just left a Temperance Society meeting hall, and once there he'd put in a full afternoon's graft.

On one occasion Ted joined us in the pub. This was unusual. Ted didn't have the build for booze and didn't seem to have experience of it either. After a couple of pints, he was stumbling around so badly that when he got back to the dock he tripped and dropped a full box of tools into the cut. Joe was incandescent with rage and made him get into the filthy water and fish out every last one of them. Joe was not a man of great compassion when he felt that basic rules of behaviour had been transgressed, although it had to be said he broke enough of them himself. These were the early days of leisure boating and if any hirers went past the dock too fast, he'd ask them politely to slow down. After that, he'd start lobbing bricks at them.

The old boatmen who were now living in Bed'uth 'on the land', as they used to say, couldn't keep away from the dock in those days. Swept from the cut like so much debris, by forces they didn't understand, they were now drawn back to it by a compulsion they didn't grasp either. They used to wander down to the water's edge and stand with glazed eyes staring across the canal, deep in thought, as if they were waiting for boats they knew would never arrive. Who knows what was going through their minds. On the whole, they were stout, taciturn men who, when they spoke at all, spoke in the dialect of the Black Country, where most of them originated from. It was so thick you could have cut it with a knife. Not that they spoke much to us. For years, the best we'd get from them would be a terse nod by way of acknowledgement of our existence. But they must have got used to us eventually, or maybe they'd just got irritated by the things we did because one day while I was painting, or splicing a rope, or something, one shouted over to me 'Yow'm mekkin' a right mess o' that.' It wasn't exactly the start of a close relationship, but afterwards he and others would never visit the dock without asking how we were, and how we were getting on with whatever was our latest project.

The exception was John Saxon, another one-time boatman, who with his wife Phil befriended us from the outset. The Saxons were an old canal family who'd worked the cut for generations, though John had seen the writing on the wall faster than most and had left the cut by the end of the 1950s, after he'd spent three unpaid weeks hanging around waiting for a load for his boats. Canal water ran in his blood though. Eventually he bought *Lion*, an old working boat he converted for pleasure cruising. As he grew older, and new people drawn to the canals for leisure began to get more interested in waterways history, John wrote regularly for canal magazines about his life as a boatman. He even collaborated with the travelling waterways theatre group Mikron on a show for which he wrote a couple of songs.

John's work is invaluable in recording at first hand a past that would have otherwise been lost, but it's also played its part in the growth of a mythology about working boatmen who in some circles are feted today as if they were Heroes of Labour by people who wouldn't dream of doing the same for redundant miners, steelmakers or factory workers.

Nowadays, there are canal enthusiasts who so romanticise the old boatmen and are so desperate to recreate the lost world of the cut that they dress up in outfits purporting to be those that working boatmen at the end of the 19th century might have worn – the women in long dresses, the men in moleskin trousers, waistcoats and red neckerchiefs. What's more, they do this not just in the privacy of their own boats but in public, at boat gatherings and festivals, where even the presence of other enthusiasts as keen as they are on the canals can't entirely shield them from the derision they attract.

As farcical in a different way is that some fanatics with more money than sense acquire original unconverted 70ft (21.3m) working narrowboats and then cram themselves for living space into tiny 8ft (2.4m)-long back cabins, leaving most of what used to be the cargo hold empty but for a picnic table and a couple of bags of coal for their own use. It seems a lot of trouble and expense to play at being an itinerant 19th-century manual labourer, but I guess they do get the added bonus that they can lord it over the rest of us with their authenticity. Though, thinking about it, perhaps that isn't such a high price for the rest of us to pay if it keeps these lumbering old Leviathans out and about on the system, seeing as how they're so wonderful to see and so expensive to maintain.

Mind you, Em and I aren't ones to talk about romanticising the waterways. When we had *Justice* constructed 25 years ago, we had her built with one of these traditional back cabins I'm disparaging. We convinced ourselves it was for practical reasons, which was to some extent true, since when she was alive, Em's mother often used to cruise with us, and the layout gave us all additional privacy. But I'd be kidding myself if I claimed that was all it was. The fact is, there's a bit of me that can't escape the myth, too.

Putting aside for the moment the general tendency of we Brits to do this to our history, this sentimentalisation of the working waterways is going some, even for us. We're in the process of recreating the canals as a linear theme park, a caricature of the real, embellished by brightly painted and brass-covered boats, the only function of which is to provide a *tableau vivant* to the scenery. Anyone still harbouring crazy ideas that the canals are part of the natural countryside will be sadly disappointed. They were never that, even at the outset. They were artificial impositions on the landscape, although there was a point in the 1970s when some were deteriorating to such an extent they were reverting to their natural state. Today, most, but not all, have been saved from obliteration either by regular maintenance or extensive restoration, which continues still.

And a good thing, too. When we started boating, the canals were so shallow that boats used to cruise with grappling hooks and block-and-tackle, so they could haul their way out of trouble when they got stuck in the mud. All boats in those days carried a can of grease and a lump hammer for when the paddle gear at locks was so rusted it was jammed. And a length of plywood on a piece of string, along with a bucket of ashes from the fire, was standard equipment, too. If the locks were leaking badly and you couldn't get them to work, you dropped the ply behind the gate and sealed the seepage with the ashes.

Towpaths were also in a dreadful state and in countless places they were impassable. Some had crumbled away to nothing, collapsing into the water to become part of the canal, sometimes forming sizeable lagoons in the process. It could look pretty but it was far from satisfactory, and it couldn't be allowed to continue. Left to their own devices, it wouldn't have been long before not only the towpaths became impassable, but also the canals themselves.

Today, the wheel has turned full circle. Canals have improved beyond measure, despite the complaints by newer boaters who can't grasp just how shallow and unnavigable many of them used to be. At the same time, the towpaths have undergone an extraordinary transformation. In places, they're now so manicured they feel severed from the very countryside that surrounds them, detached by a policy of excessive husbandry: mowing regimes that take no account of wildflowers and hedge cutting that destroys natural nesting sites. Worse for a boater, it can sometimes feel they've been appropriated. Too many have been metalled and are like little roads, and though this is convenient for ramblers, joggers and dog-walkers – which is no bad thing and not something anyone could reasonably object to – it has had its drawbacks in their increased use by cyclists.

Now, before anyone starts accusing me of being anti-cyclist, let me say that I've cycled towpaths from one end of the country to the other as well as cycling regularly in London before it became as popular as it is now. But the pure volume of cyclists on towpaths in some parts of the country has become a disruptive presence that boaters and pedestrians (and indeed other cyclists) find increasingly menacing. Of course, when I talk about cyclists in this context, I'm not talking about folk pottering along the waterways for a bit of exercise. Or mums and dads out with their kids on a family outing. The cyclists I'm talking about here are the hardcore Lycra brigade who use the towpaths in towns as commuting routes, and in the countryside conscript them for internet time trials, effectively reducing them in some places to racetracks.

I've been carved up myself more than once both as a cyclist and a boater; very few on the canals haven't had problems of one sort or another. The behaviour of cyclists must surely be the most consistent topic of complaint on canal social media groups, where you hear of conduct that makes your blood boil. There have already been too many near misses and a number of accidents, including a serious one in Yorkshire in which an elderly woman had her hip smashed in several places after being hit by a bike at a flight of locks near Bingley. I can't help fretting that there'll be more accidents yet unless someone takes the problem in hand. The growing conflict between different user groups highlights the problems that occur when the demand on a limited resource intensifies without proper regulation in place to manage it. And the Canal and River Trust haven't managed it well. The official line is that those on foot have priority on towpaths. Cyclists are encouraged to dismount and push their bikes along narrow stretches of towpath, or at constricted bridge holes, or where's there's heavy pedestrian traffic. Mmmm… pigs might fly and hell freeze over. Some cyclists can't even be bothered to ring their bells to alert you to their presence. Some don't even have bells. Indeed, a few years back in London the situation had become so much of a problem that CART were handing out bells free of charge to cyclists on the towpath.

The problem of recalcitrant cyclists isn't inconsequential, but if we're comparing canals past and present we shouldn't lose sight of the fact that the old working boatmen had a far more difficult time of it, facing problems on a completely different scale to the ones we grumble about today. Meandering along the canals of England in the summer sunshine as we do as a pastime nowadays is one thing; hacking up and down the Grand Union in the driving rain of winter for 12–15 hours a day to earn enough to eat is something entirely different. And even if we hit a spell of appalling weather, the minor discomforts of contemporary pleasure cruising don't even begin to hint at the everyday hardships endured by working crews. A large number of narrowboats in the past were on regular coal runs, picking up loads at pits and delivering them to wherever they were needed to feed the voracious appetites of the steam engines that powered the Industrial Revolution and the electric generating plants that came later. That coal often had to be shovelled into and out of boats by hand, back-breaking work frequently done by women and children as well as men. Some boats carried oil and tar, others domestic refuse. They were floating refuse trucks, the difference being that families slept and ate on them regardless of the stinking loads in their holds.

It's a fact that most families who lived on boats struggled against the odds to maintain standards of hygiene and decency as they brought up their families in impossibly cramped conditions but – as some of the pictures taken by the renowned waterways photographer Robert Longden in the 1940s and 1950s show – they weren't always successful. For many, it was a mean and brutish life of poverty verging on squalor and often underpinned by violence. Occasionally, evidence of this emerges out of the fog of history, such as the infamous 1839 rape and murder of 37-year-old Christina Collins by boatmen on the Trent and Mersey Canal at Rugeley in Staffordshire – an event on which Colin Dexter based his 1989 Inspector Morse novel *The Wench is Dead*. Improbably, the case appears to have been a factor leading to the setting up of a select committee in 1841 to examine whether canal traffic should be banned on Sundays. In inimitable Victorian fashion, some thought that if they banned canal-carrying on the Sabbath, the morals of the boat people – including, presumably, their penchant for rape and murder – might be improved by churchgoing.

More seriously, I can't help suspecting there was a dark underbelly of violence in the lives of many boat people, as there was, to be fair, in the lives of many working-class people at that time. You glimpse it in the many fights that were reported at locks, during which crews were quick to resort to fists when there were disputes over who had right of way; and in occasional incidents reported by observers, such as George Smith in his book *Canal Adventures by Moonlight* (1881), in which he describes an incident in an adjoining boat when he was moored one night at Rickmansworth on what's now the Grand Union Canal. He depicts a fight in which boots, bricks and even the boat's tiller were used as weapons. I have a sense of the brutality of their lives, too, from various apocryphal stories I've heard over the years about domestic violence on boats, so many that it's hard to believe there isn't at least a grain of truth in them.

I suspect something even darker yet is to be found in the zeal of reformers in the 19th century to improve conditions for boat people. The author George Smith was one. He was the son of a Staffordshire brick-maker, a political activist who cut his teeth crusading for kids employed in brickyards before turning his attention to the canals. In 1873, he launched a campaign in the press to highlight the overcrowded and fetid conditions in which boat people were forced to live. The result of his efforts were the Canal Boats Acts of 1877 and 1884, which set up registration authorities that meant all canal boats used as dwellings had to be listed prior to being issued with certificates specifying the number and sex of who could live aboard. The mixing of the sexes in overcrowded canal boats was one of Smith's concerns – an obsession, you might even say. In one of his pamphlets, he describes a back cabin accommodating 'a man, his wife, six children, one of the girls being 16 years of age, one 14.' He describes how closely together they were forced to sleep, his tactic being, according to an article in the *Victorian Periodicals Review* published by Johns Hopkins University Press, 'to imply that such propinquity led to incest.' Maybe Smith implied it because he knew that incest *was* happening. But how was he going to name such a thing in an era where even piano legs were covered out of a sense of misplaced propriety? How was he going to prove it when we have enough of a problem doing that today?

The Duke of Richmond and Gordon, moving the second reading in the House of Lords for the bill that would eventually become the 1877 Canal Boats Act, knew precisely what he was dealing with. He said the purpose of the bill was 'to prevent or to mitigate the evils which had been found to exist in the condition of that scattered and shifting population which was employed in the navigation of boats and barges upon our canals and rivers.' It was to prevent 'the mischiefs which arose from the dwelling of whole families in the close cabins of these boats, both in a sanitary and moral view.' These, he went on, 'were very great.' One way or another the Canal Boats Acts led to the requirement that in back cabins there was a 'door' between the main bed and the adjoining bench where kids slept, although that soon shrank to become no more than an ineffectual 'modesty flap', which is what it's called today, a throwback to an earlier age. They are popular though, and initially Em and I installed one in *Justice* when we had our back cabin built. Then we found out what it was originally for and took it out again. I mean, who wants reminding of that sort of stuff?

Many of those who used to drink in The Furnace, round the back of Charity Dock during the time we moored there, were sons and daughters of that last generation of boat people. It was a rough hole, long since demolished, although for some reason Em and I never felt uncomfortable there, perhaps because what was seen as our posh accents and odd metropolitan manners marked us out as different and inexplicably endowed us with a sort of immunity to the worst that could happen. It meant that when the fights started – as they frequently did on Saturday nights when the place got a bit lively – we were left as spectators while chairs, tables and people went flying across the room like a scene from a Western movie.

Today, the sentimentalists would have you believe that in canal pubs in the past the boat people sat around in friendly concord, quaffing pints of foaming ale and singing traditional folk songs to the sound of a squeeze box. They'd sing all right, that was true. But the songs were more likely to be contemporary songs culled from the music halls that sprang up all over the country at the beginning of the 19th century. As for drinking, that was always a serious problem for boatmen. They had a reputation for drunkenness, and a level of alcohol-related health problems significantly higher than that of the general population. It was partly to wean boaters off the wickedness of the demon drink that boaters' missions began to grow in such numbers after the first was established in 1846 in a rented room in Worcester Bar in Birmingham. You'd think there wouldn't be enough time for drinking, given that working boats were often underway long before dawn and still moving while there was light to see. But it's easy to forget that there was a lot of time sitting around waiting for work, or waiting for boats to be loaded and unloaded, or waiting for repairs to be done at places like Charity Dock.

It leads me to think that The Furnace on a Saturday night in the 1970s was closer to the model of how things used to be in a real canal pub than we'd like to admit.

12

Up the Trent to the Chesterfield Canal

When the lock keeper at Keadby opened the gates and let us out on to the tidal River Trent, it was a very different River Trent to any I'd travelled on before. The morning fog we'd woken to was still thick, a pea-souper by anyone's measure, yet at the same time the sun was struggling to force its way through the murky morning. It looked like a kitchen light bulb seen through greaseproof paper. On the water, it felt bleak and damp, and visibility was so limited that I could barely make out the massive piles of Keadby Bridge bearing down on us from out of nowhere. It's the first thing you meet as you turn upstream from the lock, but we'd gone under it before we realised. The river is very wide at this point – 655ft (200m), maybe more. In these conditions, when you can't see both banks at the same time, and when the river looks the same behind you as ahead, you lose all sense of space and distance and it's as if you're floating through a vast and hostile void.

We'd come out of the lock with a couple of other boats, which were hurrying upstream to the junction at Torksey where a lock leads from the Trent to the Fossdyke Navigation and on to Lincoln, so we'd lost sight of them almost immediately. Our schedule called for less urgency. We were only heading 15 miles (24km) upriver to West Stockwith, where we'd have to negotiate a lock to take us on to the Chesterfield Canal, but we all faced the same problem. We all needed to time our trips to the tide so there'd be enough water to get over the sills of the respective locks we had to pass through. It meant that whereas they had to travel purposefully, we had to dawdle.

This suited me fine. On the tiller, I could barely see my hand in front of my face and so I'd have been forced to go at a snail's pace anyhow. Caution became my middle name. I steered a course far enough into the river to avoid any obstacles along the bank but not too far that I lost sight of it, since its nebulous outline was the only way I could keep track of where I was in the dense brume. We were travelling on an exceptionally high tide, which would have probably carried us upstream on its own without any engine power, and how wonderfully quiet a way to travel that would have been except, of course, we had to keep the engine running in tickover to be able to steer. Not that it mattered. At such slow revs, the JP3 was so silent you could hardly hear it anyhow. In the sodden atmosphere of the mournful morning it sounded muted, like a sewing machine might sound in a cathedral, its gentle resonance lost in the vastness.

The concentration required to navigate under these conditions is exhausting and nerve-racking. I couldn't help imagining some unexpected obstruction in the river appearing from out of nowhere, or being confronted by a ship suddenly coming at us. I wondered whether I should be sounding our horn to alert others to our presence, although in fog this thick I couldn't see how that would help. What little sound I could discern seemed to distort so that it was impossible to locate where it was coming from. Mercifully, however, conditions were changing as we crept along, though at first we were so focused on navigating that we barely noticed what was happening. The fog gradually became less of a fog and more of a mist, as if we were passing through a cloud. Then, little by little, it turned into a thin haze that swirled above the river before evaporating in curling wisps, like plant tendrils searching out the sunlight.

Before long, it had cleared completely. It was as if some meteorological miracle had taken place because suddenly it was a beautiful morning. Later, it became more beautiful yet as the sun rose higher until, finally, it was blazing with a strength that soon became uncomfortably hot. On the foreshore, swans had appeared and reed buntings were hopping around on bedraggled bulrushes. On one skeleton of a tree overhanging the water, a cormorant stretched out its wings to dry, like the angel of the east country. Everything was still, everything quiet. *Justice* barely ruffled the surface of the river as she progressed.

All this was a novelty to us. When we'd cruised this part of the Trent before it was invariably in bad weather and the water was unpleasantly choppy for a flat-bottomed boat like ours. The views never made you want to reach for the camera, either. This was because we'd always travelled on lower tides, when all you could see of the river this close to the Humber were featureless expanses of mudbanks or piles of rocks dropped apparently randomly to strengthen them. On this trip, with the water at a higher level, it was a delight to be able to see over the river dyke and look down on small villages, such as West Butterworth with its curious onion-shaped windmill, and Owston Ferry, which, as its name suggests, was an important river crossing as late as the 1940s. There's a Dutch feel to this part of Lincolnshire, the Isle of Axholme as it's known. Partly, it's the style of buildings that you glimpse as you pass, a legacy of when that man Cornelius Vermuyden, the Dutch water engineer, was importing Flemish workers in a vain attempt to drain the area by rerouting the River Don. But that aside, the landscape itself in these parts is enough to remind you of the Low Countries as it stretches out to the horizon in a flat and apparently never-ending patchwork of fields.

Yet this is deepest rural England, so locked into its own past that just a couple of miles away from the river is the village of Haxey, where they still retain working vestiges of medieval strip-farming, and where every Twelfth Night they re-enact one of those slightly sinister English rituals in which a 'sway', as it's called (for which read 'football scrum') battles it out in an attempt to get a 'hood' (for which read 'ball', even though it's shaped like a leather tube) into one of whatever of the villages' four pubs they support (for which read piss-up). This practice is said to date from the 14th century when the wife of a local landowner lost her silk riding hood in the wind until it was caught for her by one of a dozen or so farmworkers who'd been scrambling around trying to retrieve it. It's said she was so amused by this show of obsequiousness that she donated land for common use so the chase could be re-enacted on it annually.

You might be inclined to dismiss this whole tale as charming rural folklore, but there are tempting historical hints to suggest it might possibly be rooted in fact. It's certainly the case that the landowner associated with the story, John de Mowbray, the 3rd Baron Mowbray of Axholme, did actually exist, and he definitely had a wife at the time. Records show, too, that in 1659 he gifted land for common use in a way consistent with the story. If true – and I haven't checked the source material, so don't hold me to it – this would make the ritual more than 350 years old and one of the most ancient of England's surviving traditions (for which read forelock-tugging displays of deference to the higher orders).

We relaxed into companionable silence as we enjoyed our slow and idyllic progress upriver. But then something caught my attention and I must have involuntarily cried out because Em said, 'What?' in an irritable voice, as if to rebuke me for disturbing the tranquility of the day.

I shook my head. 'Er, nothing,' I said. 'Nothing. Just a mistake. Forget it, I thought I saw something...'

But a moment or two later, I shouted out again, this time pointing at the river. 'There! There! Look over there!'

'What? I can't see anything.'

'There! There!' I shouted again, becoming irritated at her inability to see what to me was obvious. 'Over there,' I said once more. 'Just to the left of that piece of driftwood.'

'I still can't make out what you're looking at. Where...' But then she stopped dead. 'Oh my God!' she exclaimed.

What she had seen was a porpoise or dolphin about 20ft (6m) or so behind us following in our wake, possibly hoovering up any fish we might have been disturbing. However, if it *was* feeding it didn't seem to be doing it with any great conviction. It seemed to be drifting on the tide, scarcely moving, as if it was just out for the ride and the feeding was only a game it was playing. It was about 5–6ft (1.5–1.8m) long, with a characteristic beak that would have identified it beyond doubt as a dolphin if it hadn't had a characteristic triangular dorsal fin as well, which, confusingly, marked it out as a porpoise. Best perhaps to say we just didn't know what it was, and it wasn't going to help us out, either. A couple of times, as we were straining to get a better view of its fin, it flipped on to its back so we couldn't see it. On other occasions, while we were struggling to see whether it had that distinctive smile typical of dolphins, it swam off in a flurry of spray and we'd lose sight of it until one of us spotted it again bobbing along happily behind us. If you ask me, it knew precisely what we were doing and it wasn't going to play along.

We lost it finally just before Gainsborough when we turned on to the Chesterfield Canal. Our guess was that the water wasn't brackish enough for it that far up, and so it had turned tail and headed back to saltier surroundings nearer the coast. Or maybe it had retreated because the tide was turning and it could travel back where it had come equally effortlessly. Who knows, maybe it had simply got bored with our company and had gone off to find itself another, more interesting boat to play with.

The tide at this period of calm, when it's changing from an incoming, or flood tide, to an outgoing ebb tide, is called slack water. Without too much unpredictable water movement to make life difficult I was able make a perfect entrance into the lock without as much as a touch on the sides. The lock keeper, however, was unimpressed by my steering; and to be fair, why should he have been impressed since taking a rowing boat across a park pond would have presented more challenges than getting *Justice* into the lock on water as still as that? Even so, we were expecting a little more in the way of enthusiasm from him when we told him about our sighting of the dolphin or porpoise, but it made about as much impact on him as my steering skills had. As we waited for the water levels to adjust to let us into the small basin that lies at the start of the canal, he told us that sightings of cetaceans in these parts were commonplace, something mildly interesting but nothing special. But I'm not so certain that can be right for, in the past, sightings on the Trent have merited mention in newsletters of the British Marine Life Study Society, which suggests to me that while we might not have witnessed something unique that day, we certainly saw something out of the ordinary.

We stayed in the basin for two or three days, taking advantage of the weather to carry out some much-needed running repairs. There was a pub so close to where we moored I could have ordered a pint from the deck, and ten minutes' walk away was another that brewed its own beer and did a great line in fish and chips on a Friday night. In addition, there was a yacht club in the basin that was open to the public three evenings a week and Sunday lunchtimes too, apparently. Three drinking establishments in a tiny village like West Stockwith, with its population of barely 300, is not bad going by today's standards, when barely anyone seems to drink out at all because it's too pricey. In the past though, it would have been considered a poor tally, for at one time the place had nearly a dozen pubs, most operating out of people's front rooms, which was the way of things in those days when a public house was exactly that, a house selling beer that was open to the public. But this was back in the late 18th century after the coming of the canal, when West Stockwith was a much larger place, a bustling riverside community with a prosperous shipbuilding industry and all the associated trades that went along with it: ropers, smiths, mast, block and sail makers and the like. Today, exploring West Stockwith's unique lanes, which gave villagers access to the Trent for their domestic water, it's difficult to imagine it ever being busy. Barely a car seems to pass on the road nowadays, and silence seems to envelop the village most of the time.

Mind you, if we thought West Stockwith was quiet, we hadn't seen anything yet, as we discovered when we left. Immediately beyond the basin, the canal heads west to skirt the village of Misterton, which has a population of 2,000 and is a teeming metropolis by comparison. And after that ... well, after that, nothing. Nothing except miles and miles of isolated countryside and deserted canal punctuated by occasional woods, spinneys and the odd lock. Nothing except fields stretching into the flat distance, so far away that they dissolve into the horizon. Nothing but a landscape that often seemed uninhabited except for farmhouses, or the occasional lock cottage or faraway hamlets with squat church towers that on damp mornings seemed to appear out of the misty meadows like vague memories emerging from the past. We loved it. How could we not love it? How could anyone not love an England like this in spring when the hedgerows are heavy with May blossom, and the woods strewn with primroses, wood anemones and bluebells? Everywhere we looked, the natural world was exploding around us, and above it all – a cupola on the world – was such an expanse of wide and endless sky bearing down so heavily we felt it would root us to the soil if we stayed still for too long.

This was our first trip on this canal, and not only was every mile a revelation in the way it used to be when we were young, but after so many years' boating we'd unexpectedly chanced upon one as scenic as any we'd ever visited. It reminded us of the Oxford Canal, or at least that section of the Oxford Canal above Napton on the Hill where you climb a lovely flight of locks to the 11 mile (17.7km)-long summit level. This loops around left and right in a series of agonisingly tight bends through a secluded landscape of fields very similar to the Chesterfield in that both seem unchanged since medieval times.

We've been moored at Banbury for years so we've travelled the Oxford Canal more times than I can remember, and I can tell you there's something about the solitude of the summit that is haunting, especially in what the Scots call the gloaming, when day and night hang in that uncertain balance and it's difficult to say which is most dominant. Scientifically, I know that the reason the world seems to flatten in your perceptions at twilight is because the retinas of your eyes begin to convert from the cone cells that function at higher light levels to the rod cells responsible for night vision. Yes, I know this, but such a dispassionate explanation doesn't do it for me. It seems too clinical and takes no account of how you *feel* at that time of day, especially when you're boating alone, as I've often done, when every movement in the hedges or gust of wind in the trees seems somehow chilling and unearthly, every sound some communication from another world.

The Oxford Canal's meanderings reach their climax at the 400ft (122m)-high Wormleighton Hill, where you'd make quicker progress walking than boating since the canal doubles back on itself, clinging to the contours of the countryside. The result is that you have to cruise half an hour to get to a place you could walk to in five minutes. Wormleighton itself – a tiny settlement a brisk half-mile walk from the canal – was the ancestral home of the Spencer family before they made it big stealing common land and enclosing it for sheep farming, after which they moved to their current, somewhat larger, residence 20 miles (32km) away in Althorp. The most celebrated Spencer of modern times was, of course, Princess Diana, the former Lady Diana Spencer whose son William will one day make it *really* big when he inherits England and moves to a larger dwelling yet, in The Mall in London. And they say crime doesn't pay!

It's no coincidence that these two canals, the Oxford and the Chesterfield, were built around the same time and that they both utilised the skills of the celebrated engineer James Brindley. Brindley had made his reputation a decade or so before when he'd been an engineer on the construction of the Bridgewater Canal in Manchester, the first British canal of modern times and the one that set the ball rolling on the Canal Age and the frenzied mania of building that accompanied it. Brindley's reputation was at its zenith during that period and there wasn't a canal project in England where he didn't somehow manage to get his finger in the pie. The heavy workload wore him down eventually, though. He was caught in a downpour while he was out and about surveying in Staffordshire and developed a chill from which he never recovered, dying at the age of 56 and leaving many of his projects uncompleted. Among them were both the Oxford and the Chesterfield.

But such is the way of things on this small island where someone with skills that are thought to be indispensable will always be in demand. New ideas always tend to burn bright and travel fast in England – and that was especially the case back in the day when the world wasn't as fixed in its ways as it is now and it was easier for individuals or small groups to have an elemental influence on the societies in which they lived. Events intertwined easily and history layers on history, creating the matrix not just of our national narrative, but – as we incessantly feel the need to remind ourselves – the narrative of the world itself. This area Em and I were travelling through, for instance, this flat and scarcely populated landscape of no more than 75 square miles (194 square km) between Doncaster and Gainsborough in the north and Retford and Worksop in the south, was the land from which the Pilgrim Fathers originated before they set out on their 1620 voyage to the New World in the *Mayflower*. There were never many of them, the fanatic religious group from which they sprang perhaps no greater than 300 at its height. Only 35 of them ever settled in what became the United States. But the remoteness of this region where the Midlands' counties of Lincoln and Nottingham fuse allowed them seclusion enough to engage in religious practices that would otherwise have been banned. Its proximity to the Trent helped, too, giving them access to a flow of new ideas from the Continent arriving in books and religious tracts through the ports of Boston and Hull. The Pilgrim Fathers never set out to establish a country any more than James Brindley set out to launch an Industrial Revolution, but in both cases the search for the new, whether technological or spiritual, had consequences beyond those that anyone at the time might have predicted.

Our journey continued to be a delight. The Chesterfield Canal may have been shallow and weed-covered, the towpaths ragged-edged and ruched with the tattered remains of last season's bulrushes, but we rarely saw a boat in either direction and it felt as if we owned it. What was less of a delight was the weather, but what can you expect of England in April? The mornings were sometimes bitterly cold, and one day we woke to a light covering of snow over our roof. Other days, it would rain with that fine mist farmers call growing rain, falling across the countryside like a pall, trapping us in the cabin until we felt we were going round the bend with the claustrophobia of it. At other times, though, we woke to sunshine bathing the countryside in a radiance the colour of a glowing fire, heralding an explosion of birdsong from first light when the wood pigeons were like an irritating alarm clock, to sunset when the querulous mallards packed it up for the day, the drakes finally deciding to give the ducks a rest from their persistent attentions. It was a period of great happiness and contentment for us. But then we got to Worksop. Not that our change of mood was the fault of Worksop, an old mining town that seems to have recovered better than most from pit closures following the 1984 strike. It was because we visited Mr Straw's House, the three-storey Edwardian semi that was once the home of local grocer and tea merchant William Straw and his wife Florence.

The couple moved into the house in 1923, and after their deaths it passed to their sons, and on their decease to the National Trust, which inherited the place along with a sizeable bequest of almost £1.5 million. I confess that though I'm a long-standing member, I'm no great lover of the National Trust, which I think has spent too long pushing a particular vision of Britain's past encapsulated in the lives of a very small number of the country house rich, that *Downton Abbey* world of privilege and entitlement. Or putting it another way, they've created a myth out of the past as part of a process of creating a national narrative. However, credit where it's due, they've recently started taking a broader view of their role, and the lives of those below stairs in the kitchens are now as much a feature of the properties in their care as the lives of those upstairs in the drawing room. And – is this my imagination? – have the volunteers been let off their leash? Nowadays, they're as likely to give you a passionate exposition of how the master of the house made his money by slave-trading as how the mistress managed to get Reynolds to paint her portrait.

The decision to take on the more modest Straw's house was part of this strategy to reflect the lives of more ordinary people, and although the promise of a cash legacy that size can't have blunted its enthusiasm, the main attraction of the endowment was less the house itself than the thousands of objects inside it, which make it a sort of time capsule of its age. It has everything an ordinary home of that period would have had, but it has it in spades because the family was well-off and able to afford to buy anything they wanted. They were hoarders, too, so nothing got thrown away. If they purchased a new vacuum cleaner, the old one was dispatched to the lumber room upstairs, which would have been servants' quarters if they hadn't been too tight to employ servants. Every room is cluttered with furniture, the walls plastered with plates, paintings and sepia family photographs hung on long strings from picture rails. Wardrobes and dressers are crammed with William and Florence's clothes, which their sons couldn't bring themselves to throw away. Some are even laid out across the bed, protected from the light by copies of the local *Worksop Guardian*. Everything from the contents of the larder to the kitchen sink is kept as it was. Everything remains unchanged. This is a house that's not so much preserved as embalmed.

Em and I visited because we were National Trust members and we didn't feel we'd done enough to justify our subs that year. It seemed a pleasant enough way to get off the boat and while away a few hours, so we booked a visit, which you have to do because it's too cramped to accommodate more than a few people at a time. But my goodness, what a depressing experience it was! There was something about the place that was bleak, something that was soulless. At first we put this down to how dark it was, though in fairness this was less to do with the gloomy Edwardian décor of the place than the National Trust keeping it like that to preserve the artefacts inside. Eventually, it struck us that it wasn't the house that was making us feel so wretched as the Straw family itself. When they first moved to the house they were like all couples relocating to a new home and they made changes enthusiastically. Florence, who had a keen eye for contemporary design, decorated it with loving care, ordering wallpapers from Sanderson and an Egyptian-style stair-runner inspired by the discovery of Tutankhamun's tomb, which had happened just a few years before. I can't help wondering what her husband felt about all this. He comes across as an intransigent conformist, the epitome of conventionality. He was the sort of man who, unfailingly, took the family to Scarborough every year for their summer holiday. He was the sort who would walk out of a sermon at his church and not return for years because he took a dislike to the views of the vicar; the sort who would stand for hours at his window watching for kids scrumping from his garden; and the sort who, when he caught them, would insist that the magistrate fine them rather than just reprimand them. He didn't seem to be a man of much warmth. His home didn't seem to be a place of much love.

Despite its name, the Chesterfield Canal doesn't go to Chesterfield. It used to go to Chesterfield, but one of the most significant acts of the BWB after it took over responsibility for the country's canals was to trigger a procedure for closing them. This, I have to say, was precisely what everyone expected to happen. Indeed, most people believed it was the very thing that BWB was established to do. Under the 1968 Transport Act, the country's waterways were classified under three headings. They became commercial waterways, cruising routes or what was termed 'remainder' waterways. This latter definition was the killer. Essentially, stripped of the jargon, it meant that BWB couldn't see any future for them and walked away from any responsibility to maintain them. The Chesterfield Canal partly survived the chop after the section from the Trent to Worksop was designated a cruising route; the rest was 'remaindered', as the phrase was. In other words, it was destined for the scrapheap.

However, regardless of what the apparatchiks thought in their gleaming new offices in Watford, out there in the real world the news didn't go down too well. Half the population of the UK lives within 5 miles (8km) of a canal or river, and people feel personally about them. They walk along them with their dogs, they fish them, they take the kids down to feed the ducks. Canals are part of the landscape of their lives and people don't react favourably to outsiders messing with that sort of stuff. Besides, by the 1960s, canals were getting more popular. They were attracting a whole new generation of people like me, boaters and walkers who'd realised what a resource the waterways were and who were exasperated at seeing them deteriorate into stinking ditches. Local councils were catching on, too, recognising that canals were a valuable community facility. Local amenity groups and boaters' organisations were beginning to get their act together as well. Even English Heritage had woken up to the fact that BWB was responsible for some 2,500 listed structures across the country, the third largest curator of heritage sites after the Church of England and the National Trust.

All over the country, restoration groups grew up. From the Union Canal in Scotland to the Kennet and Avon in the South West, canals that were unnavigable and thought to be beyond repair were brought back into use, often with spectacular results. At Caen Hill, for instance, near Devizes in Wiltshire, a flight of 29 derelict locks went straight up a hill like a steep flight of stairs. Every one of them had to be completely rebuilt. All over the country, other restoration projects were started, some – like the Huddersfield Narrow Canal, which I've mentioned already – were successful beyond anyone's wildest dreams. Others still continue, kept alive by small coteries of devotees and enthusiasts.

The Chesterfield Canal Society, founded in 1976, and the Chesterfield Canal Trust that succeeded it, were part of this movement. As a charitable company run entirely by volunteers, it has managed to restore 12 miles (19.3km) of canal and an astonishing 37 locks and 11 bridges. Today, there are only 9 miles (14.5km) left to complete; and though as I write you can't cruise any further from the east than the 2,893 yard (2,645m)-long Norwood Tunnel that collapsed in 1907, from the west, on the Chesterfield side, some impressive renovation is taking place, with fresh basins being dug and new locks constructed.

We took the boat as far as the tunnel end just to say we'd reached it and from there we cycled the rest of the way into Chesterfield down a flight of ruined locks that used to take the canal to its terminus. I predict some problems restoring these locks. The houses parallel have colonised them, expropriating what they saw only as derelict ponds into their gardens as water features. Some weren't happy about us even passing on the towpath. No telling what they'll think when the restoration gangs move in with cranes and bulldozers in tow.

Before you get to the tunnel from the Worksop direction you ascend a flight of locks that is among the most beautiful in the country, vying for the title with the Marple flight on the Peak Forest Canal near Stockport or the Foxton flight near Market Harborough in Leicestershire. A fascinating mixture of single and staircase locks, it borders extensive bluebell woods near Shireoaks, where we spent some time on the way up. We moored up there a second time on the way back. It was too beautiful to pass by without stopping, especially at that time of year when the woodland floor is so thickly carpeted that looking through our porthole in the sunshine we were confronted by such an intense blue it was as if we were moored in the Mediterranean. We took advantage of the exquisite network of public footpaths that thread through the woods, one of which just happened to take us to the pub in the deliciously named village of Thorpe Salvin, winner of the Britain in Bloom contest on no less than three occasions. The woodland hereabouts is dotted with former quarry workings where stone was lifted to build the locks, and – more impressively – where almost a quarter of a million tons of it were used to rebuild the Houses of Parliament after they burned down in 1834.

It was there one morning, as we sat drinking coffee on the deck, that a wire-haired woman in her 40s rolled up on one of those sit-up-and-beg bicycles so beloved of ex-PM John Major, who associated them with 'old maids cycling to communion'. She'd got a slow puncture and she'd seen our bikes on the towpath and correctly surmised that we might be able the help her out with a repair kit. We'd been surveying the copious covering of flowers opposite, pondering on the curious fact that half the bluebells in the entire world are in England, and that in most countries they're as much a rarity as orchids are to us. But we were happy to be disturbed, especially by someone as cordial and chatty as she was.

'Terrible, though, isn't it?' she said. 'The news this morning, have you heard?'

We'd listened to the news that morning but couldn't imagine what she could be talking about. Nothing we'd heard had been that bad. She soon enlightened us.

'London,' she explained. 'They've just elected a new mayor. A Muslim,' she announced, her voice rising with the horror of it.

Beside me, I could feel Em bristle. 'What's wrong with that?' she asked coldly. 'His father was a London bus driver, he was born in London…'

'Yes, I know all that,' the woman said, dismissing Em with a cheerfulness that I mistook at first for embarrassment but soon realised was pure bigotry. 'Of course, I know what you mean,' she went on. 'Really though, could you see yourself ever voting for someone like that?'

Em stood up stiffly in a way I have seen her do many times before. Her lips had tightened, her jaw had set. Usually this is my signal to put on a hard hat and take to the trenches for what can often be an angry outburst. This time, however, although she may have been furious, she was coldly quiet. There was a look of abhorrence on her face, a look tempered only by pity.

'As a matter of fact we *did* vote for him,' she said, before disappearing below deck into the cabin, 'We're from London. We had a postal vote.'

I was left alone and flustered. I didn't know what to say or do now.

'Let me get you that repair kit,' I spluttered eventually. 'We'll have that puncture fixed in a jiffy…'

But she decided to leave. She'd come to the conclusion that after all it would be as quick to walk home.

We pottered down to Shireoaks, an old colliery village that I knew from my days covering the 1984 Miner's Strike for BBC's *Panorama* when the whole of this area was bitterly divided. However, it made for an interesting take on the dispute, and I came to like the place as much for the market in nearby Shirebrook, where I could buy chitterlings – a Midlands' delicacy unavailable in London – as for the people of the district, who always had time for you and whom you could always count on for a good quote.

The marina used to be the old colliery loading wharf and we moored outside near the entrance, a convenient enough place for a stop-over but with nothing distinctive enough about it to make you think it would burn its way into my memory the way it has. For that night, Chelsea drew with Spurs – Tottenham Hotspur F.C. – in an unexceptional end-of-season Premiership football match that under normal circumstances wouldn't have been of the slightest interest to me as a Leicester City supporter.

However, these weren't normal times because our assortment of veterans, rejects from other clubs and cheaply purchased overseas players no one had ever heard of, had challenged odds of 5,000–1 during an extraordinary season that I'd followed closely from the boat, catching the odd match or two when I was lucky enough to blag a ticket. We'd led the league for the previous four months and the result that night meant our nearest challenger, Spurs, couldn't catch us. Unbelievably, we'd won the competition. It was our first major trophy since our foundation in 1884 and it is still talked of today as a miracle and the biggest-ever upset in sporting history.

I'd been following the match on the radio, but at half-time, with Spurs leading 2–0, hope sprang more bounteously than it ought to have done given the way things were going. I couldn't stand the stress and I went out on the towpath for a walk. It was Em who told me the final result when I returned. Chelsea had pulled back a goal at the beginning of the second half and equalised less than ten minutes before the final whistle. As soon as my brain could absorb what had happened it wasn't elation I felt but deep sadness. I was suddenly a disappointed 14-year-old again on the terraces at Wembley in tears after watching us lose an FA Cup Final everyone expected us to win. I could feel the pain of that result, the fragility of my own childish hopes. It's strange that sport can make you feel like this, but it can. It's about more than simply winning or losing: it's about dreams and ambitions, about the aspirations you dare allow yourself and the potential suffering you risk when you do. Sport is a wager you make with yourself, one where you risk real emotional suffering, gambling hope and expectation for the slim possibility of triumph. It's not a bet you win very often.

'Are you crying?' Em asked me.

'I think I might be,' I said.

13

Down the Fossdyke and Witham to Lincoln and Woodhall Spa

It was strange to be cruising along the Fossdyke Navigation, which is as wide as a river, and flanked by banks like a river, yet isn't a river. It's actually a canal, but not a canal as we know it, Jim. It's virtually without locks, it's deep and wide, and it has long stretches as straight as a Roman road. This isn't surprising because the consensus of opinion is that it was built by the Romans. Contrarians – and this being England, you won't have to look far to find a few of them – say it was built hundreds of years later by Henry II. One way or another, no one as far as I know disputes that it's the oldest artificial waterway still navigable in the UK. Now, I won't say the Fossdyke is an uninteresting canal because no canal should be dismissed out of hand like this, even the Paddington Arm of the Grand Union that leads from Bull's Bridge Junction to Little Venice though the enervating suburbs of West London, or that bit of the Trent and Mersey that you pass on your way from Fradley to Burton-on-Trent where the A38 is so close to the water's edge that in wet weather you get covered by the road spray of passing lorries. No, that would be wrong. No canal should be burdened with the reputation of being dreary and monotonous. They all have something to teach us. They all are part of the rich tapestry that is Britain's diverse canal system.

Even so, cruising along the Fossdyke, Em went down below deck one day while I took over steering and I was so bored I fell asleep at the tiller and ran the boat up against the bank.

She ran back on deck in a panic, wanting to know what on earth was happening.

I waved her away. 'You're always making mountains out of molehills,' I said. 'It was just a … a momentary lapse in concentration. No damage, no casualties…'

We'd arrived on the Fossdyke after leaving the Chesterfield Canal and heading upstream on the Trent to the lock at Torksey, where we diverted towards Lincoln. We were following in the wake of those boats that had come on to the Trent with us that magical foggy morning five or six weeks before – a journey that was fading into memory and already seemed an eternity away.

Given its importance in Britain's canal story, you might wonder at the relative anonymity of the Fossdyke. It's not exactly a canal that springs to mind when you think of Britain's waterways – not even to enthusiasts. But every story has to have a beginning and since the Fossdyke is the oldest canal in Britain, that alone should ensure that it's better known than it is. The problem is that it doesn't quite fit the pattern. It doesn't suit the story. In the same way the National Trust built its myth of England around the lives of the country house rich, the myth we've conscripted to the service of our national narrative about British initiative and resourcefulness doesn't have room for the Fossdyke Navigation and so we've painted it out of the picture.

The story we tell ourselves – the story we teach our kids – is that canal building began in the 18th century with the construction of the Bridgewater Canal, named after Francis Egerton, 3rd Duke of Bridgewater. The tale is that he built it after he was jilted by his fiancée, Elizabeth Gunning, the Dowager

Duchess of Hamilton. According to this version of events, when the engagement went belly-up the brokenhearted Egerton, nursing his unrequited love, went on one of those Grand Tours so beloved of aristocrats of the time. This trek across Europe in search of art, culture and the roots of Western civilisation took him to France, where he saw the Royal Canal in Languedoc in the south. In this account, when he returned to England he gave up on women completely and set his mind to developing his estate, where coal had been found. This, he knew, could be a money-spinner if only he could get it to factories in the growing mill towns nearby that were crying out for the stuff. So with memories of Languedoc in his mind, and his trusted agent John Gilbert at his side, he commissioned James Brindley to build him a canal to Manchester from his mines in Worsley. Despite a series of challenging obstacles and setbacks they brought the project to a triumphant conclusion, making Bridgewater the richest aristocrat in England and ensuring his place in history as 'the father of inland waterways'.

Well, that's the story, at least. And – hands up here – it's a story I've peddled myself in the past too, before I knew better. That's because it's such a compelling tale. History reduced to personalities. A radical new system of transportation, a completely new supply line for raw materials, an Industrial Revolution, no less. All British. And all on the back of a failed love affair. Oh, what untold consequences can result from trifling human affairs!

The trouble is, the story's got a couple of glaring holes in it, which you've probably noticed yourself by now. The Fossdyke Navigation, for a start. Where does that fit into this narrative? Doesn't it count? And what about that French canal Bridgewater saw on his Grand Tour, the one we now call the Canal du Midi? The one opened in 1681, nearly a hundred years before he saw it? The one built with broad, stone bridges to accommodate wide barges as opposed to the piddly little ditch Brindley eventually

197

finished up building, designed for the narrow underground tunnels of his Grace's coal mines – a pattern that has hindered the growth of a viable system of industrial water transport in Britain up to the present day?

Blimey, the Canal du Midi left me astonished when I saw it in the 21st century; it must have left Bridgewater gobsmacked in the 18th. But there's no sense of this in the story we're told.

Even the account of the break-up with Elizabeth is a deception, since the truth is almost certainly not that she jilted him but that he jilted her. She was a society beauty from Ireland with dreamy blue-grey eyes, so drop-dead gorgeous she was celebrated by every contemporary portrait painter of the age, from Joshua Reynolds down. Egerton, by way of comparison, was a bit of a dog. A very rich dog, true, but a dog all the same. A relief made at the time of him as a young man shows him even then with a thick bottom lip, a prominent nose and heavy bags developing under his eyes. But it wasn't his looks that did for the relationship, but the social conventions of the age. Elizabeth had a disreputable sister, Maria, Countess of Coventry, who was renowned among her other improprieties for having scandalous slanging matches in public with her husband's mistresses in Hyde Park – conduct that Elizabeth refused to censure. The wonder is not that the engagement broke up but that they got engaged at all. It was never going to work; any fool could have told you that.

In building Bridgewater's canal, I grant you Brindley did construct a significant aqueduct at Barton to go over the River Irwell, a project that was considered such a feat of engineering for the time that crowds travelled from all over the country to marvel at it. All the same, don't let's forget that when it was first filled with water it was built so badly the arches buckled and it needed months of botching before it could be used. By way of comparison, on the Canal du Midi those ingenious Gauls had built not one but three aqueducts, one over the Cesse river, a wide and elegant triple-arched structure with a central span of 6oft (18.3m), which is still in use today. What's more, while Brindley avoided building locks like the plague because they cost too much, in France they'd built not just locks but wide locks, including an astonishing staircase of eight of them at Béziers, which makes our staircase of five at Bingley (built a hundred years later and the best we can offer) seem a tad puny.

But you can see what's happened here, can't you? Egerton's come back from his extended travels with this notion in his head of getting his coal from mine to market by canal, and he's employed people to get the scheme off the ground. Except they're not experienced canal builders. In fact they're complete novices. Brindley was a millwright, which wasn't as much of an impediment to this sort of project as you might think since millwrights were the technocrats of their time, experts in what was effectively the science of water-driven energy generation. Even so, he was no civil engineer. And he was illiterate to boot – so illiterate, it's said, that when a Parliamentary committee asked for plans to better understand his design for the aqueduct at Barton, he explained it to them by using a round of cheese cut in half to represent the arches. If his boss, Bridgewater, had been interested in building a proper canal, he'd have done the sensible thing and sent him to France to learn how to do the job the correct way from people who knew how to do it.

But this is the point: Egerton *wasn't* interested in building canals. All he wanted to do was get his coal to Manchester; the means to do it was a secondary consideration. So Brindley was on his own, left to reinvent the wheel. And with no experience to draw on, he played it safe and built the canal to follow the contours of the land, avoiding not just the technological problems of locks that a gradient would have involved, but the significant additional costs it would have incurred, too. Maximising his Grace's profits was the name of the game: earning the greatest financial return in the shortest possible time. Commercially, it was a successful formula – one Brindley used as a basis for other canals he built afterwards. Sadly, it set a pattern for canal construction that even the great Scottish engineer Thomas Telford couldn't entirely break when he turned his hand to building canals 30 years later.

This drive to do it on the cheap was the overriding consideration in Bridgewater's strategy, the one that blinded him to European expertise. He'd seen with his own eyes how canals could be built – how they *should* be built – but he wasn't in the game of building a national infrastructure. We British rarely are – which is why after a period in Victorian times when we were proud of civic construction projects – our railways, our town halls, even our sewers, for God's sake – building cheap for maximum profit is what we've returned to today. It's short-termism, and we British are so wedded to the practice it's become a national characteristic. Worse is that we've compounded it by another article of faith that's become a national characteristic too: the belief we can go it alone and that we don't need any input of ideas from outside, particularly from Europe.

It's only when you get to the top of the cathedral – in what they call the uphill part of the city – that you realise how much Lincoln dominates the surrounding countryside. It's the major city in these parts, the point at which the Fossdyke Navigation meets the River Witham. All around you are the flat and fertile plains of the Fens and the Lincolnshire Wolds, a sea of green stretching into the distance as far as you can see. Compared with a modern building like Canary Wharf in London, the cathedral at 272ft (83m) is a fraction of the height, though for more than 200 years between 1311 and 1548 when its central spire collapsed, it was the tallest building in the world. But where Canary Wharf's built on the flat banks of the River Thames, Lincoln Cathedral is built on a hill 171ft (52m) high. Now, I grant you that as hills go a pitiful pimple like that wouldn't exactly qualify as a Munro, which is the Scottish designation for a mountain higher than 3,000ft (914m), or even a Corbett, which is one with a height of more than 2,500ft (762m). However, if we were to redesignate Corbetts not after J. Rook Corbett, the man who first classified them in the 1920s, but after the diminutive comedian Ronnie Corbett, then the hill on which Lincoln is built might just about make the grade.

One way or another, to get to the cathedral you have to climb up to it first – and it's hard going. The route is up a street called Steep Hill, which is not called that facetiously when it's not really steep at all. No. It's called Steep Hill because it's steep, very steep indeed, the fourth steepest street in England, in fact. It's steeper than the stairs at the Oscars, steeper than the price of a Spurs season ticket, so steep babies have to get out of their buggies and push them up themselves because mum can't manage it. There are occasional seats dotted along the way and a selection of independent tea and coffee shops at regular intervals, where you can take the weight off your feet. And there's an eclectic mix of shops selling all sorts of curios, from bling to arts and crafts, retro fashion to oo-gauge railway models, so you don't have to rush your ascent. When you get to the top – joy of joys – it's not just the cathedral you get to see, but an 11th-century castle as well, with battlements you can walk around, as well as a Victorian prison that has a remarkable chapel, designed so that every prisoner was kept separate in such a way they couldn't see each other but each could see the preacher lecturing them for what must have been no more than minor infringements, since back in those days anything beyond spitting in the street would have merited the death penalty.

Now, Em and I are canal people, which is to say we're more comfortable on the flat and don't really do steep at all, except at the top of flights of locks, and even some of them can make us dizzy. Be that as it may, you can't visit Lincoln without climbing Steep Hill. From up here on this higher, older part of the city you can see the geography of the place laid out before you as if on a map. Like so many of these English 'movie set' locations such as Bath, York or Ely, Lincoln owes its prosperity to the presence of a waterway, although in its earliest days it was the River Witham that was important to its development rather than the Fossdyke Navigation. Of particular consequence was a deep pool, where the river widened and where the remains of an Iron Age settlement were discovered in the 1970s. This pool – Brayford Pool – provided natural moorings, and since it lay at the head of a river connected to the Wash, it attracted not only the Romans – who, as we'd seen, extended it to the Trent through the canal – but also in later years to the Vikings, who re-established the city's prosperity after a period of decline.

Today, most of the banks of Brayford Pool are occupied by pubs, bars, restaurants – and the University of Lincoln, which is growing at such a rate I swear they designed, built and opened another hall of residence during the short time we were there. Most of the water space in the Pool is taken up with a marina and the other space along the banks seemed to be rented out to individual boaters or clubs as permanent moorings. What little remained was only available to crews like us on the move for a maximum 48-hour stay. However, I'd heard on the grapevine that we could get temporary moorings for longer at the marina, and I rang to organise it – though when I went to the office to finalise the paperwork, the man there appeared to know nothing about the arrangement I understood we'd agreed.

'Can't do it,' he said. 'These are all permanent moorings, all spoken for.'

'But *you* told me there'd be a mooring available,' I replied. 'Well, maybe not you personally, but someone who sounded a dead ringer for you. Maybe it was one of your colleagues? Perhaps your brother, maybe. Does he work here?'

The man behind the counter looked me up and down suspiciously as if trying to work out whether I was just winding him up or actually taking the piss. Whatever his conclusion, he decided to ignore me. 'Sorry,' he said. 'It's just not possible. These are all permanent moorings.'

'So what about all those spaces out there?' I asked.

'Spaces? What spaces?' He seemed astonished to hear about them, as if he'd arrived at work that morning at a packed marina only to discover as a result of what I'd said that boats had evaporated.

'All those gaps,' I said. 'Twenty or 30 of them, all over the marina. Is there something wrong with them?'

It turned out these were all leased to boats that were out cruising. They were away for weeks, months, years, for all anyone knew. But he couldn't let us stay in one even for a week. At least not at the moment he couldn't. In a few days things would be different. He would telephone the berth holders and arrange something for me. I didn't like to tell him that this is exactly what he'd promised to do when we'd spoken on the telephone before, so I left it at that, and in the interim Em and I found ourselves a place on one of the 48-hour moorings that would do as a stopgap. A couple of days later, I went back to the boatyard office again.

The man behind the counter was the same one I'd spoken to before; though it was clear he didn't know me from Adam.

'Can't do,' he said, when I asked about a space to stay. 'These are all permanent moorings, all spoken for, sorry.'

'But that's what you said before.'

'That's because they were permanent moorings then, too. They haven't changed.'

'But you said you'd be contacting the berth-holders to arrange something for me...'

'Why would I do that?' he asked, as if this was a completely new idea I'd just come up with off my own bat. 'They're all permanent moorings and you're looking for a temporary one...'

I stood nonplussed for a moment or two, trying to work out the logic of his thinking. Then I began to consider all the witty put-downs I could fire off, and all the complaints I could make about him. I thought about making an official approach to his boss or submitting a formal protest to the local tourist board. For heaven's sake, I'm a journalist; I could contact the local paper and kick up a stink. Or – alternatively – I could just do nothing and walk away. Which is what I did.

Sometimes life's just too short to bother.

'Do you know what cheeses me off most though,' I said to Em that evening as we sat over steaks and glasses of red wine in a very pleasant pub/restaurant. 'Lincoln is one of those must-see places on the waterways that people make the highlight of their holiday. They travel for weeks to get here, yet when they do there's nowhere for them to stay more than a couple of days and that's nowhere near long enough to explore a city like this. The Canal and River Trust is taking money from us for our licences but it can't provide us with adequate temporary mooring because it's renting out the space to other people for permanent ones. Surely there's something wrong here...'

Em shrugged with a couldn't-care-less insouciance. 'It's like you say yourself,' she said, smiling. 'Sometimes life's just too short to bother.'

'But you know we're overstaying where we are now? Breaking the rules?'

'Cheers,' she said, raising her glass.

For those travelling by water, Lincoln reserves one of the jewels in its crown as a farewell for those leaving. Boaters exiting Brayford Pool along the River Witham towards Boston and the sea have to pass under the three-storey, half-timbered house that's built on the top of what's called the High Bridge. On this occasion, a Lincoln place name fails to deliver on its promises because High Bridge isn't particularly high at all. It is, however, the oldest bridge in England that still has houses on it. It lies on the site where the Romans first erected a timber bridge to take Ermine Street from London northwards to York. Today, it's the High Street, with Marks & Spencer looming over it and Primark just a step or two away. The short, crooked archway underneath, through which the Witham passes, is picturesque, and for generations boatmen have known it as the 'Glory Hole' – a reference to the way the sun shines through it, lighting the dust from the busy street above to give the illusion of the beams you see emanating from the halos of saints in medieval paintings. Well, maybe... It's one explanation at least. Another is that it got its name from a couple of angels that are carved in the timbers of the shops above. Yet another is the name has something to do with a chapel that once stood on the east side of the bridge dedicated to the medieval world's favourite rock-star saint Thomas à Becket, who lost his life meddling in politics – a fate that in my unkinder moments I could see myself wishing on other clerics who dabble in things that don't concern them.

But who knows where these names originate? And who knows when and how they change. Apparently, a break in the clouds that the sun penetrates is called a 'glory hole', too. Nowadays, the term is most commonly used as sexual slang, so you better tread carefully in Lincoln if you're asking for directions to find the place.

We pressed on through the town down the Witham, past an attractive modern district where the decorative railings outside

Wilkos are all that separate shoppers from the river, and where two figures sculptured in aluminium and steel stretch out to each other across the water, their arms open wide in greeting like long-lost friends. Soon, we were passing the imposing Victorian brick frontage of Doughty's Oil Mill, where we had to nudge past great flocks of swans that had abandoned their more familiar haunts in Brayford Pool. We blamed it on the university. The poor birds have had their traditional territory commandeered by ever-swelling ranks of academics and students walking to classrooms from town along the narrow spit of greenery adjacent to Brayford Wharf South. They've even had their image appropriated for the university's crest after it junked its traditional one featuring the Roman goddess Minerva. The swans were probably feeling harassed. They probably suspected the modern world had it in for them and they'd made a break for it while they could. If nothing else, they'd have learned from the university's motto *Libertas per Sapientam* – Through Wisdom, Liberty.

Stamp End is officially Lock 1 on the river. It's an electrically operated guillotine lock, which means its top gates, which would normally swing open, have been replaced by a single gate that falls and rises like a guillotine – pretty much how you'd expect a guillotine lock to operate, given its name. Once you're through it, the river widens out and you're suddenly in the countryside again on long, straight stretches of water so like those on the Fossdyke that you'd be hard-pressed to tell the difference between canal and river. We'd been navigating this part of our trip from an outdated guide that mentioned just a couple of mooring spots in the 32 miles (51.5km) between Lincoln and Boston where we were heading, so the large number we actually discovered along the way as we were cruising was an unexpected and pleasant surprise. It meant that every day was an adventure in itself. We'd set off with no idea of where we'd finish up that night, and as a result we chanced upon some delightful spots. There was barely another boat on the river, and what overnight moorings we eventually did tie up at were invariably unoccupied, so we could bask not only in the solitude of the surroundings, but also in the glorious weather that had suddenly sprung up unannounced. It made the clear river waters sparkle in the sunshine. You could see shoals of fish darting between the reeds.

I have fond memories of Fiskerton Fen, where we tied up early after one scorching hot day. That evening, we had a barbecue sitting outside in the balmy air, watching the sun staining the river red as it set. Fiskerton's a bird sanctuary where, according to an information board, linnets, yellowhammers and corn buntings have been sighted, though you'd hardly register them as anything special, so copious is the birdlife in these parts anyhow. For the enthusiasts, they've built a hide near the mooring after the design of an Iron Age hut where you can watch out for rarer birds like bitterns and marsh harriers, which they're hoping to attract by a strategy of reed planting.

One of the continuing delights of Britain's inland waterways is randomly coming across places like this, places you'd never find any other way. Cruising rivers and canals is a constant voyage into the unknown. Beginners – 'newbies' as they're called on the cut – are sometimes so beguiled by the idea of having a boat at all that they tend to spend most of their time dashing about, trying to get as many miles as they can under their belt in the same way they did when they were hiring. Or at least that's what we did. There were times when we covered unspeakable distances in short periods. Rushing didn't even begin to explain it. After two or three years, we calmed down a bit, and after ten, when we were getting the hang of boating, it struck us that constantly pushing on in search of a perfect place to tie up was futile when we were passing dozens of lovely potential moorings on the way.

Canals, as they say, are the quickest way of slowing down. I mean, it's not as if you're going anywhere on a canal, is it? Not anywhere consequential at least. You just have to build in additional time to explore places you invariably stumble across along the way.

This is what happened to Em and I coming down the Witham. We pulled up at the tiny hamlet of Kirkstead Bridge, not because it was pretty, because it wasn't, lying as it does in the shadow of one of those off-the-shelf concrete bridges built in the 1960s to replace an earlier swing bridge. Our waterways' guide wasn't the reason we stopped either because it made nothing of the place beyond mentioning that the remains of Kirkstead Abbey – founded, incidentally, by monks from Fountains in Yorkshire – were nearby. No, what made us stop was the presence of a pub. We'd been in the middle of nowhere for too long. We fancied finding somewhere we could socialise in the company of other people. What we found, though, was more than just a pub. A mile or so up the road, buried in the woods, we found the small and matchless town of Woodhall Spa.

The place has a remarkable past. Back in 1811, John Parkinson, steward to the famous botanist Joseph Banks – one of those instrumental in establishing Kew Gardens – was prospecting for coal when he hit a spring. This brought the project to an abrupt halt as water began to rise through the exploratory shaft he'd sunk. There the matter stood for 20 years until the then lord of the manor Thomas Hotchkin had the strong-smelling water analysed and discovered to his delight that it contained high concentrations of iodine and bromine. Whether these substances are in any way beneficial to human well-being is immaterial: the fact is people *thought* they were and Britain has a long history of the so-called 'health' spa stretching back to Roman times. Hotchkin set about in earnest developing his spring as a resort and sank some serious capital into it, surrounding it with baths and building the Victoria Hotel to cater for guests he gambled on the place attracting.

In establishing Woodhall Spa, Hotchkin was helped immeasurably by its location among thick woodland, most of it pine forest. As it developed into a popular Edwardian holiday destination it nevertheless remained small enough that it could grow organically among the trees, giving it a unique ambience that it still retains. Today, wandering around the woods scattered with grand villas, or browsing in the town's craft shops, or tarrying in its tea rooms and ice-cream parlours, the ever-present fragrance of pine sap in the air somehow lifts you even without the need to dose yourself with acrid chemicals. I tried the acrid chemical route years back when we moored in Leamington Spa, drinking water from the tap outside the famous colonnaded Pump Room. Never again. It was so unpalatable I nearly threw up.

The fashion for spas abated early in the 20th century, and when the Victoria Hotel burned down in 1920 it signalled a period of decline for Woodhall Spa, which it emerged from only during the Second World War when an airfield was constructed close to it as a satellite station to nearby RAF Coningsby. Among other units based at the airfield during the Second World War was the famed 617 'Dambusters' Squadron, which relocated there after what is probably the most famous bombing mission in British history, the daring surgical strike against dams in the Ruhr, Germany's industrial heartland. The raid used an extraordinary drum-shaped bouncing bomb, which the engineer Barnes Wallis had invented and developed against the opposition of intransigent officialdom.

Though the 19 Lancaster bombers involved in that raid took off from RAF Scampton, 25 miles (40.2km) away, Woodhall Spa has become the spiritual home of 617 Squadron and you can't walk around the place without being aware of it.

Group Captain Leonard Cheshire became squadron leader after the death of Guy Gibson, who led the Dambusters raid, and he took the title of Baron Cheshire of Woodhall when he was made a life peer in 1991, cementing the relationship between town and squadron. The imposing memorial celebrating those killed in the raid is located at Woodhall Spa on the site of another of the town's former hotels, ironically bombed by the Luftwaffe in 1943. The eccentric Kinema in the Woods, which dates from the 1920s and was used for military briefings, still survives, too. The airmen christened the place 'The Flix in the Sticks' and it still operates a full programme of contemporary films. During our stay, we saw *Eddie the Eagle*, the film about the eccentric British ski jumper Michael Edwards. It seemed curiously apt in a place where so many brave and strong-willed young men like him had thrown themselves through the air in the past.

The most moving place in Woodhall Spa is the Petwood Hotel, which was requisitioned during the war as an officers' mess for the station and where the small squadron bar has been preserved as it was during wartime, with mementos and memorabilia on display. Nothing prepared me for this bar. I wasn't ready for the emotional jolt of being thrown so abruptly back into the past. That black-and-white photograph of the whole squadron, taken like a school photograph in front of a Lancaster bomber, for instance. Five long rows of bright-faced youngsters, most of them in their early 20s, some even younger, so many of whom wouldn't survive the war, scores dying as planes similar to the one behind them became their airborne tombs. The picture in one corner of Gibson with his characteristic cocksure smile caught me unawares, too, when I realised it was taken on the hotel terrace, just yards from where I was standing. Even the framed mission briefings on the wall threw me. They were surprisingly complex yet the whole aircrew had to commit them to memory for recall in the heat of battle as their planes were being shot at both from the air and the ground. How could crews do that under fire? How could they concentrate knowing that they were an instant from death?

What it came down to was that I couldn't come to terms with the raw bravery of what these young men did when it must have been apparent to all of them as they prepared for the raid that they might not make it back alive. And it wasn't just the Dambusters raid, either. 617 Squadron operated out of Woodhall until the end of the war, destroying V-1 launch sites, U-boat pens and – in another famous sortie – helping to sink the feared German battleship *Tirpitz*. The last raid from Woodhall was an attack on Hitler's mountain retreat, the Berghof near Berchtesgaden.

The burden of their sacrifice hung heavy on me. I felt inspired by their bravery and yet embarrassed to be the beneficiary of it, a cosseted child of the post-war years. It struck me that I was the future they'd been fighting for.

Eventually it all became too much and I had to leave.

14

To Boston and the Wash

Maybe it was because I was a post-war baby that Woodhall Spa made such an impression on me. When I was a kid, the war was too close for me to be interested. It bored me. It was the stuff my dad went on and on about incessantly until I could have screamed. Like many of his generation, he'd served in the forces; he'd had no choice in the matter. He was a hosiery mechanic, dragged from the small Leicestershire village where he'd been born and brought up and conscripted into the REMEs, the Royal Electrical and Mechanical Engineers. For six years, he went on his own sort of Grand Tour with Montgomery's Eighth Army across North Africa and Italy. Two of his three brothers fought in and survived the war too, ostensibly uninjured, though both suffered severe mental problems afterwards – today we'd call it post-traumatic stress disorder (PTSD). Denis, the youngest, was abandoned by his officers during the Dunkirk retreat and told to make his own way back to Blighty. His sense of betrayal and the terror that followed it was still capable of reducing him to tears 50 years later. After his discharge, Reg, the eldest, had what they called in those days 'a nervous breakdown'. Before he was called up he'd been a cabinet maker and he built beautiful furniture, including the inlaid drop-down desk I did my homework on as a kid. After the war, he never touched his tools again. He became a dustman, but turned down every

213

promotion they offered him to lead his own team as a driver. He'd had enough of driving. Driving was what caused his problems. He'd been a driver during the Italian campaign and had to transport ordnance under fire and in darkness on the precipitous mountain roads of Monte Cassino.

Nowadays, people are obsessed with the war. If we're not commemorating VE or D-Day, then it's the Battle of Britain or Dunkirk. I found myself at a *Celebration of the 40s* festival in Sandwich on the Kent coast a few years back; the whole place was given over to a sentimental tribute to the wartime years with Spam sandwiches, jitterbugging to big band music and half the town in military dress and the rest in those dreadfully cut 'demob' suits they used to give troops on their discharge. It's as if we can't forget those years. As if there was something we had then that we've lost now. After Woodhall Spa I couldn't help agonising about what that might be and why what we'd lost should be so important to us. It was the details of Woodhall Spa, you see. They played on my mind long after we'd untied and cast off for Boston, the next stop on our trip. That roller parked on the lawn of the Petwood Hotel, for instance, which wasn't a roller at all but the shell of one of Barnes Wallis' bouncing bombs, a killing machine reduced to a garden ornament. Or those bullet-scarred statues in the grounds, testimony to some shooting contest after a drunken dinner in the mess. Chris, Em's mother, had talked of this sort of exuberance among air crews. She'd been in the WAAF – the Women's Auxiliary Air Force, attached to Bomber Command. She knew pubs around Newmarket that had all but been ripped apart by high-spirited airmen on beer-fuelled binges. The Ministry just paid for the damage, no questions asked. What else could they have done? Court-martialled them?

'It was important not to break their spirit. After all, they didn't know if they'd be alive the next day,' Chris explained.

Perhaps my perspective of Woodhall Spa and 617 Squadron was shaped as much by personal experience as anything, for as a youngster just out of university and in my first job, I worked as a reporter for the Kentish Times (KT) group based in South East London; and it was from there, after years of churning out obituaries, wedding reports and accounts of local council planning meetings, I was sent on a plum job to Germany to cover a town-twinning conference. The KT newspapers circulated across Bexley borough, part of which is Crayford, a down-at-heel suburb that had at one time been the site of a major Vickers-Armstrongs armaments factory employing at its height some 15,000 men and women. Barnes Wallis worked for Vickers-Armstrongs at the time he developed his bouncing bomb and it was partly for that reason that after the war Bexley twinned with the small towns of Neheim and Hüsten, which cling to the valley of the Ruhr as it winds towards the Netherlands and the North Sea. The town-twinning movement was launched in the wake of the war in a spirit of reconciliation and determination that Europe should never again be torn apart by conflict. The union between Bexley and Neheim-Hüsten was a particularly poignant one in that respect because the German towns had both suffered badly from the tsunami that swamped the valley after the Dambusters raid, which breached the nearby Möhne dam.

The casualties among 617 Squadron as a result of the raid were bad enough – though par for the course under gung-ho 'Bomber' Harris, who headed Bomber Command. Out of the 133 airmen who started the raid, 53 were killed, a fatality rate of almost 50 per cent when you take into account that three of the 19 planes that started the raid had to turn back for one reason or another and got nowhere near the action. However, on the ground, the situation was of a different magnitude entirely: 1,500 were killed, most drowned. At the time, it was the highest number of casualties Bomber Command had ever inflicted in a single raid. Two-thirds of the casualties weren't even German but Polish and Russian women abducted from their homes to work for the Reich – essentially slave labourers. Neheim and Hüsten suffered particularly high casualties in this regard since of the 800 or so killed that night, more than 500 were Russian women held in a forced labour camp close by.

Even the squadron commanding officer, Guy Gibson, questioned the moral justification of the raid. In his memoir *Enemy Coast Ahead*, written not long before his death on active service in 1944, he wrote: 'The fact that they might drown had not occurred to us... Nobody liked mass slaughter, and we did not like being the authors of it. Besides, it brought us in line with Himmler and his boys.'

Despite the controversy that still surrounds the effectiveness of the raid, it remains the case that most of the structural damage caused by the bombing was repaired within a month or two. Its biggest – and most incontrovertible – achievement was in creating another of the mythologies that have become part of our national narrative. This one at least had purpose in that it bolstered the morale of the British public during the dark days of war. With the handsome, devil-may-care Gibson as its figurehead, the raid became a classic fable of how stiff-lipped derring-do coupled with world-beating British invention and ingenuity could triumph over the sterile constraints of leaden officialdom. You have to smile at the irony. According to the last surviving Dambuster, George 'Johnny' Johnson, Gibson was the epitome of officialdom. He described Gibson as bombastic, autocratic and a strict disciplinarian. 'The basic problem was that he was unable to bring himself down to mix and talk with lower ranks.'

Even so, it was a message that played well, not just during the war but into the 1950s when *The Dam Busters* movie was made and when demobbed servicemen like my father were looking for confirmation of the value of what they'd been fighting for. The message that Britain was a first-class world power, unsurpassed in so many areas, struck a chord that made the sacrifice of struggle worthwhile. It still does, even now, though more recent appeals to British primacy are increasingly less credible, born more out of political expediency than veracity.

All these notions about Britain's relationship with itself and Europe were passing through my mind as Em and I cruised down the River Witham towards Boston. The Brexit debate was reaching a climax and it was turning nastier by the day. On social media, it had become so caustic that reasoned debate was impossible. Fostered by a series of fictitious claims and counter-claims without any evidential foundation, it had reached the point where families were rupturing and lifelong friendships were being torn apart. Meeting people casually, face to face, was a risky business. You never knew whether an offhand comment in a shop or a pub could turn nasty. There was hatefulness in the air. There was a sense of the truth crumbling so that you lost sight of what was genuine. There was violence simmering under the surface, too many reports of casual and overt racism, too many accounts of people seen as 'foreign' – some of them just tourists – gratuitously attacked on the streets.

Then one Thursday, a Thursday much like any other, by which I mean a typical English June Thursday with kids playing in the park and the sun poking intermittently through the clouds, the lunchtime news broadcasts carried the first reports of the fatal attack on a young MP called Jo Cox. A mother of two, she had been shot and stabbed multiple times as she made her way to a routine constituency surgery in Birstall West Yorkshire. Her assailant, a Nazi-loving white supremacist, had shouted 'This is for Britain', 'Keep Britain independent' and 'Britain First', as he'd killed her.

There can't be a better way of approaching Boston than from the river. You turn a gentle bend and there before you, at the end of a wide straight, standing out like the launch pad at Cape Canaveral, is the extraordinary church of St Botolph, which, without a spire, looks like a rocket without a nose cone. However, it has to be said that without it, splendid though the building is, it looks a bit, well, stumpy – hence the nickname by which it's more generally known: 'The Stump'. You need to get used to The Stump when you arrive in Boston since you'll be seeing a lot of it during your stay. In fact, you can't get away from it even if you wanted to. It's more than 270ft (82m) high and it dominates not just the town – where you keep catching sight of it unawares around every street corner – but also the Wash beyond, where sailors still use it as a navigational landmark. We were thinking a lot about the Wash at that time because although our original plan had been to turn around at Boston and come back up the Witham again to the Trent, where we could cruise to Nottingham, we'd been idly kicking around the idea of returning to the Midlands by another route. Perhaps – if we had the bottle for it – we could go across the Wash to join the River Nene and from there cruise up to Northampton?

There were a few drawbacks to this plan, however – the first being that though, strictly speaking, the Wash is a 'bay' in the North Sea, it's a very big bay – 185 square miles (more than 479 square km). In other words, it's the sea. That creates a few problems for *Justice* because she's not a boat built for the sea but for inland waterways. She has a flat bottom and rolls alarmingly in even a gentle swell. When she pitches it's even worse. Her bow burrows into the water so deeply that from the stern you're never quite sure it'll come up again. Some 20 years ago, before it was common for narrowboats to make the trip, we'd travelled down the Severn Estuary from Sharpness to Bristol by way of Avonmouth. That had been no picnic, I can tell you. The tide fall in the Estuary can be more than 45ft (13.7m), the second highest in the world; and it's such a maze of shifting sands and fierce currents that it can put the fear of God into round-the-world sailors let alone ditch-crawlers like us. We weren't exactly champing at the bit to get out on the briny again. Besides, we'd be foolish to do the trip without a professional pilot and they didn't run cheap. We put the idea to the back of our minds and focused on Boston.

The town is immediately welcoming to anyone arriving by water. There's a surplus of clearly marked, well-appointed moorings on rising jetties, similar to the one we'd spent so long on at Naburn. A ten-minute walk away is The Stump and the fine cobbled market square where there's a busy food market twice a week, and a bric-a-brac bazaar and auction stalls at other times. With a bagful of freshly caught cod and locally grown veg, we couldn't help but warm to the place. The market square is lined with some wonderful buildings, and though they vary in period from Georgian to modern day and everything in-between, they hang together in a harmonious whole that is very pleasing to the eye. Every now and again, a street or enticing alleyway branches off, drawing you into different parts of the town where, if sightseeing's your bag, there's the charming old 14th-century Guildhall and museum to explore and, further out, the seven-storey Maud Foster windmill, which still grinds corn and which, with its billowing five sails slowly turning in the wind, has to be among the most impressive surviving mills in the country.

This period on the run-in to the Brexit vote was an odd time to visit because beneath its sleepy, market town exterior, Boston was seething politically. Not that you could see it on the streets. There weren't riots or outbreaks of mob violence. There weren't fights in the street. Even so, you didn't have to be in the place long before you could pick up a sense of simmering resentment and division. Journalists had got wind of it, too, and there were so many stories about Boston in the national newspapers and on TV that sooner or later I was sure I'd run into a former colleague knocking off another opinion piece on the basis of an hour's walk around the centre. In that respect, we at least were different. We were in it for the long haul. Some friends, Sue and Quentin, who overwintered with us in Wales the previous year, had arrived at the moorings and as soon as we mentioned that we were thinking about crossing the Wash, they were up for the idea too, deriding our reservations as the anxieties of a couple of namby-pamby southern wusses – which wouldn't have been so bad except they were southern wusses themselves too. At least with a couple of boats making the trip it would halve the cost of the pilot, though when we contacted him to make the booking, which he was happy to accept, he warned us we could be hanging around for weeks before the weather was safe enough for him to even think about taking us over.

It was a fascinating period to be in the town. Although local people said there were other issues at stake in the referendum apart from just immigration, when you got them going it was only immigration they really wanted to talk about. It was understandable and I wasn't unsympathetic. Between 2004 and 2014, the town's migrant population grew by 460 per cent. The proportion of Boston residents born elsewhere in the EU now stands at around 13 per cent – largely immigrants from accession countries such as Lithuania, Poland and Latvia. According to the 2011 census, Boston had the largest population of Eastern European immigrants in the UK; and this was clearly a significant factor in the way people voted in the referendum, for when the result was counted more than three-quarters of Boston residents voted to leave the EU, a higher proportion than anywhere else in the country.

From what I could make out, their suspicions about what one man described to me as 'colonisation' wasn't based so much on unadulterated racism — that is, the hatred of individuals based on their ethnic origin. I think they'd have reacted the same if there'd been major immigration from Tyneside or Surrey. At root, it seemed to me, was fear of change and the threat of cultural alienation newcomers might pose. No one had prepared them for the influx. No one had told them what would happen. No one had funnelled any resources their way to offset the inevitable strain the newcomers would place on local health, education and housing services. People felt that immigrants had been dumped on them by the government, and they were angry that farmers and major food producers who'd benefitted from the influx hadn't been asked to step up to the plate and take some responsibility for assimilating the new communities.

On a human, one-to-one level I lost count of the people who complained about the number of Eastern Europeans in town, but made an exception for their workmates, or the bloke who saw them right for their weekly meat order, or Tad a few doors down who was the nicest bloke you could wish to have as a neighbour and would always be there to help you out. I don't want to paint over the other reality I experienced in Boston at that period, for I can't deny there was a lot of mindless prejudice, too, based on difference and nothing else. People would complain that immigrants were coming to the UK attracted by state benefits, and then in the next breath they'd protest about them taking jobs from local people. They'd talk about the town being in decline at the same time as they'd complain about the immigrants opening new shops. I was advised more than once to 'go down to West Street' to see what 'they' had done to the place. When I did, as a resident of multicultural London, I found it unremarkable, disappointingly so. Away from the picture-postcard centre, this part of town had obviously seen better days — but then so have cities from one end of the country to the other. The one or two Eastern European food shops and a Brazilian grocer and bar I found didn't seem to me so much blighting the area as improving it. But it was as futile to point out the contradiction in attitude to certain people, as it was to start quoting statistics. They just didn't want to hear that Boston was actually quite a prosperous town with an unemployment rate far below the national average. They didn't want to know that all small towns across the country were taking a battering as patterns of shopping were changing, more and more of it being done on the internet. Facts like this weren't what the referendum was about – a reality that the Vote Leave campaign realised much sooner than Remainers. The people turning their back on Europe weren't actually complaining about the present but yearning for the past, a lost past, a mythical golden age in which the uncertainties of the contemporary world could be disregarded in favour of an earlier era that was known and therefore less threatening.

It's a shame Boston should have rejected Europe so comprehensively because originally, when it was the second most important port in the country, its links with the Continent exporting wool, salt and grain were precisely what made it prosperous. Later – you have to laugh, don't you? – its most significant export was people; for in the same way that in the 21st century Eastern European émigrés came to Boston to make a better life for themselves, so in the 17th century for that self-same reason there was an exodus of people from Boston to what eventually became the United States. And here I'm not just talking about the Pilgrim Fathers. They're the local celebrities, the luminaries of this story, but they were the extremists – the Talibanistas of Puritanism, zealous and self-righteously convinced of their own entitlement in the eyes of God. More relevant to Boston, Lincolnshire, is the later exodus of people from the town, estimated to be as many as 10 per cent of the population, which was facilitated to a large extent by John Cotton, the minister of St Botolph's. This 'Great Migration', as it's called, led to the foundation of the Massachusetts Bay colony and its capital city, which, of course, was named after the birthplace of its founders. A stone plaque in the church today commemorates the astonishing number of five men associated with Boston, Lincolnshire, who went on to become governors of Massachusetts.

Matt was heading for the States too. He's an American friend of ours, a lawyer who'd just completed a contract in Cambodia working for the UN-backed tribunal prosecuting war crimes under the Khmer Rouge. A self-confessed Anglophile, he'd flown into Heathrow and decided that rather than take a plane straight back home, where he was scheduled to take up another post in Washington, DC, he'd take a couple of weeks' holiday. He arrived by train in Boston in what, after the bright lights of London, must have seemed to him like the dead of night. I met him at the station and his first words to me as I led him back to the boat through the narrow, empty streets echoing in the gloom to the rumbling of his suitcase wheels was, 'Where the hell are you taking me, Steve?'

As an outsider, it had been interesting surveying the town anonymously, melting into the place unnoticed without any obligation to give myself away until I opened my mouth and my accent betrayed me. Matt, however, is black. He carries his difference visibly, without my advantage of being able to disappear into the woodwork by simply saying nothing. In a place that was rich with immigrants, yet unremittingly white, he stood out like a sore thumb; and despite the fact he'd travelled the world, it was an uncomfortable experience for him in a country that he'd thought more racially integrated than it actually is. English politeness is one of our most endearing qualities, but it can be deceptive. The formalities of good manners can often mask hostility. I had felt it myself as we'd travelled around on this odyssey of ours, during which Em and I had been compelled

223

to come to terms with our status as perpetual outsiders. It is the constant complaint of travellers the world over: the contradiction of feeling you belong everywhere you lay your hat, but at the same time aware you belong nowhere at all. Matt, I know, was feeling it badly after so long in South East Asia. I suspect he thought that by taking a brief break in the UK before going back home that he was back in his own culture again. This fractious country, suspicious of outsiders and squabbling among itself about them, wasn't what he expected from somewhere that prides itself as the cradle of democracy. But who can blame him for the mistake? Before Brexit, I wouldn't have expected it either.

Even so, he was dismissive of our mounting apprehension that the UK would actually take the plunge and vote to leave the EU. 'It won't happen,' he said with the reassuring confidence that lawyers bring to bear with anxious clients. 'It's not worth worrying about.'

And as for Em's concern that the TV reality star Donald Trump would get elected President of the United States, he launched off on a closely argued, psephological analysis of swing states and voter intentions that would have had my head spinning even if I hadn't been on my third whisky of the night.

'Rest assured,' he concluded finally, 'there will be no President Trump...'

A few days after Matt had returned to London to catch his flight to Washington we got an early morning telephone call. It was the long-anticipated alert from our pilot Daryl. The weather was looking good for Tuesday, he said. Could we be at the Grand Sluice Lock, the start of the tidal stretch of the river, by 8.30am? Our flotilla had now swollen to four boats, with not only Sue and Quentin joining us, but also a couple of mysterious newcomers who'd arrived at Boston more recently and had decided to tag along. We were up at the crack of dawn that morning, doing last-minute engine checks, securing our breakables, and tying up cupboards and drawers to prevent them flying open in the event of a rough crossing. By the appointed hour, we had all assembled at the lock, bright-eyed, bushy tailed and ready for the off.

As it transpired, one of the mystery boats failed to show, but of more concern was that so had Daryl. By 9am, we were all beginning to doubt ourselves. Had he actually said we were crossing today? Had we got the time wrong? Had the weather changed and there'd been a change of plan? Our doubts evaporated with the welcome sight of him appearing around the corner of the adjacent wharf on his motorbike. Within moments, all three boats were in the lock and dropping down on to the tidal river, which at low water isn't the prettiest of waterways you'll ever see, lined as it is by high industrial corrugated-steel banks, and with mud flats along its edge and even the wreck of an old wooden barge to remind you how risky these waters can be.

Daryl had chosen to travel on our boat. This, I fear, was less a comment on how safe he felt it was for a trip like this, and more that we'd let it slip we had bacon on board and were planning butties for breakfast. The industrial part of the river further out of Boston still functions as a port, and though it's small, it nevertheless continues to accommodate some sizeable seagoing ships, which dwarfed us ominously. The bridge of the Rotterdam-registered *Beaumonde* was like a block of flats towering above us, yet another indicator of how mismatched we were in these waters, like a kiddy car trying to play grown-ups with the traffic on the M6.

Eventually, the river widens as it leaves the town, the banks flattening steadily until 6 miles (9.7km) or so out of Boston you finally pass a light buoy marking the transition to the estuary and what is unmistakably the sea. We could smell it before we saw it, and it wasn't long afterwards that we could feel it, too in the way the swell lifted us and the way *Justice* surged forwards in the deep water, released from the restrictions of the canal and riverbanks that normally constrain her. Around us were one or two small fishing boats out for the day, with men sporting rods from their stern decks. In the far distance were tankers and service ships laying cables to nearby wind farms. And then there were the seals, lots and lots of them, some following our progress in the water, others barking at us from sandbanks that became more visible with the falling tide. It is difficult to describe the feeling you get as someone accustomed to the confines of the canals to be suddenly presented with what appears to be a limitless expanse of water stretching out before you as far as the eye can see. Imagine someone with a fear of heights suddenly finding themselves on the edge of a cliff. Or, as must have happened when the railways started spreading across the country, someone who had never travelled faster than the speed of a carthorse suddenly finding themselves surveying the world at what must have seemed exhilarating speeds.

It was terrifying yet intoxicating. It made your blood move faster. It was our boat, but at the same time it wasn't a boat with which we were familiar, not a boat we'd ever experienced in these conditions. I felt as you sometimes do looking at a painting that depicts familiar subjects in such a singular way it changes your perspective on the world. Like a van Gogh chair, or a Turner seascape.

For a while, Daryl was guided by bobbing green marker buoys, but once we were far enough from land that it had reduced to just a distant outline of the coast, Hunstanton a silhouette on the horizon, he suddenly directed us to swing to starboard. The other two boats snaking behind us followed obediently. Within moments, we were all three of us beached on one of those sandbanks, where seals had congregated. They were like a line of elderly parishioners at a Christmas pantomime asked to move seats in the church hall to make a space for latecomers, disgruntledly chuntering as they shuffled position to accommodate us.

This 'beaching' manoeuvre was one we were ready for; we knew it was going to happen. The problem going across the Wash is that you can't do it in a single stab. You have to leave Boston on one tide and then beach your boat for as long as it takes for the next to rise high enough for you to be able to get into the River Nene. This is a wait that at certain times of the year can sometimes be as long as two or three hours. Some boaters doing the crossing fill the time by playing cricket on the beach. Others take the opportunity to give their dogs a run. None of us did any of this. We didn't need to entertain ourselves. We were entertained by noisy RAF jets on a training exercise. They'd clearly earmarked our boats as notional targets and were screaming across the flat landscape towards us at what seemed just above our heads. Trust me, this didn't make for a quiet afternoon. We weren't exactly going to stretch out on a towel sunbathing, though the seals who were only feet away from us at first seemed blasé about the whole thing. Perhaps they were used to it. Or maybe they were just relieved to have company with the planes screaming over us. They were huge creatures, even the young ones, fat and blubbery like wriggling bags of lard. They yawned a lot of whiskery yawns, they grunted, they rolled on their backs, and from time to time they rubbed their rheumy eyes with their flippers, all of which made us gradually realise it wasn't the ear-splitting planes overhead that troubled them most but the three boats bigger than they were that had suddenly appeared, colonising their territory.

I felt much the same way about the seals. I didn't mind the aeronautics, but they troubled me. Don't get me wrong, I'm as much a wildlife enthusiast as the next man; but they don't tell you everything about seals on the natural history programmes. They don't tell you how much they smell, for example. And boy, do they smell! Not to make too fine a point of it, when you get close, they stink to high heaven. They stink worse than an army sock after boot camp. Worse than the London Tube on a sweaty afternoon. Worse than rotten fish. Believe me, their breath could kill at 20 paces. I was as relieved to get away from them as they must have been to see the back of me, even though when we set off again conditions had become much choppier. It hadn't been a bad day, clouds scouring the sky but still and windless on the water with long bursts of sunshine to cheer us on our way. Now, it darkened, and the sea started cutting up rough and choppy with white horses foaming up ahead of us and angry waves slapping against our hull as if desperate to get in. The wind had started to blow up, too. Quentin lost his rude boy hat he'd been wearing all day and, as we discovered later, the women on the other boat were relieved they'd taken their seasickness pills.

In the event, it wasn't the weather that posed the biggest danger of the crossing but three boats in convoy, which suddenly appeared from out of nowhere on full throttle, hurtling out to sea and leaving a wave behind them you could have surfed on. We had just turned into the River Nene, past the twin lighthouses on either bank built by the renowned Scottish engineer John Rennie, the one on the east bank once the home of conservationist, artist and early canal campaigner Sir Peter Scott. When the wash from the boats hit her, *Justice* bucked, lurched and did a stomach-churning corkscrew in the water. Even Daryl looked alarmed, though he'd recovered by the time we got into Wisbech, where he lashed us all together and did a clever bit of boat handling to bring us all safely into our moorings.

15

On to the Middle Level to March

I was at university in Norwich and during my first year I felt
uncomfortable with East Anglia. Coming from where I did,
I was hardly a child of the mountains. Leicestershire isn't the
Lake District or the Highlands. Even so, the incessant flatlands
of Norfolk and Suffolk intimidated me, particularly those huge
skies, which set it apart from other areas of England. In the
first winter after I arrived, on nights when it was clear, I took
a masochistic delight in lying on the ground to survey the vast
star-speckled dome above me that was the roof to our world. It
wasn't that I got much in the way of pleasure from the experience.
How could I? Metaphysically speaking, the experience was like
bungee jumping. It was terrifying: a great rush of adrenalin as
I realised that all those myriad stars at which I was gazing were
suns like our own sun, each with its own planetary system. What
I was looking at was just our own galaxy, the Milky Way. Beyond
that was the Andromeda galaxy, the nearest to us, and beyond
that in an eternity of time and distance were millions of other
galaxies, trillions of them, so many it rendered the process of
numbering them futile. I was scared stiff but strangely inspired
to recognise myself as just a tiny speck in this infinity, supremely
important to myself but completely insignificant in the overall
pattern of things.

How could that be pleasurable for a young man
hesitantly taking the first independent steps on life's journey?

Particularly on those occasions when the ground was damp (which it usually was) and the winds were blowing from the Russian steppes (as they seemed to do all the time in Norwich). On nights like that, I'd frequently have to walk home with ice crystallising on my bum.

Gradually, as I became more accustomed to East Anglia and more familiar with its unique ambience, I began to feel increasingly bereft if I was away from it for long. Something of the landscape, the people and the culture had got into my blood, and I think it must still be there, for whenever I get close to these flatlands again I find something stirring inside me. Wisbech – which bills itself the capital of the Fens – is in Cambridgeshire, bordering Norfolk, part of the old kingdom of East Anglia that emerged after the Romans left Britain; and though it's 20 miles (32km) from the sea, it still has something of an East Anglian coastal town about it, with a small yacht harbour and berths for bigger ships, which still do considerable trade importing timber from the Baltic.

After our taxing day on the Wash, we stayed over to explore the place, which turned out to be a more productive exercise than we could have imagined. We had no guidebook and hadn't done any research so it was fun to discover the town for ourselves. We stumbled across a wonderful Georgian crescent opposite the old castle. Unsurprisingly, it was called The Crescent – though we can forgive the lack of imagination in naming the place for the wonderful skills of the architects in designing it. As impressive in a different way are The Brinks, the roads on either side of the river where, when Wisbech was a prosperous port, wealthy 18th-century merchants built their homes. One of them on the South Brink was the birthplace of Octavia Hill, the eighth daughter of a local banker who was an early social reformer working with the London poor, although she's best known today as one of the three founders of the National Trust.

On the other side of the river, almost directly opposite, is Peckover House, named after another local banker. Working in the same business, the two families must have known each other. Everyone of any note in Wisbech probably knew one another then. They probably still do. In 2019, a record-breaking total of 12 Conservative councillors were elected for Fenland District Council without a single vote being cast when they were all returned unopposed. I bet they all knew each other.

As bankers, the Peckovers were considerably more successful than the Hills, who were left in straitened circumstances after the family firm went bankrupt – a concept that takes a bit of grasping nowadays when everyone in the finance industry seems to finish up with a multi-million pound pension regardless of how their company performs. By comparison, the Peckover's bank prospered and in 1869 it was one of 19 other private banks that amalgamated to form Barclays. Looking at the family house through the high wrought-iron railings that separate it from the street it looked predictably grand, though unwelcoming. However, in one of those ironic twists history sometimes throws up, the property's now owned and administered by the National Trust. We thought that in Wisbech of all places it would be impolite not to visit. Actually, once inside, it's an essay in elegant Georgian living with beautifully proportioned rooms, sweeping staircases and stylish arched Palladian windows that overlook a croquet lawn and gardens that alone would merit a visit.

We left for Peterborough the next day, though we weren't exactly heading for Peterborough. The city was only an access point to the 120 miles (193km) of canals, rivers and drainage channels called the Middle Level that stretch like a spider's web across the Cambridgeshire and Norfolk fens. Some 70 miles (113km) of them are navigable, and after years of dragging her feet, I'd finally persuaded Em to agree to venture on to them with the promise that they led to the River Great Ouse and Ely, both renowned for their outstanding attractiveness.

Wisbech and Peterborough are about 20 miles (32km) apart, a journey of about five hours by water under normal conditions. Except that the day we travelled conditions weren't normal and we battled a relentless headwind on a long, wide and straight river that at times seemed endless, stretching to a point on the horizon where it disappeared to nothing. The trip was made no easier by the fact we were travelling in convoy with the two boats we'd crossed the Wash with, and we had to coordinate so as to arrive at the tidal lock on the route at exactly the same time so that we could all go through together. The reason for this became apparent as we approached the structure that goes by the extraordinary name of Dog in a Doublet. It stands in the middle of nowhere and it's less the sort of twee, chocolate-box lock that those intimate with the Midlands canals might be familiar with, more a huge industrial structure supported by a gantry the size of a house. It's a guillotine lock, and imposing enough, but what makes it more impressive yet are a couple of equally enormous sluices attached to it so that as you're approaching it's difficult to work out which of the three enormous gates barring your way you should be heading for. This is a lock, but not a lock as we commonly know it. It's a lock in the same way that a Cessna and a Jumbo jet are both planes, the same as a kid's train set and the Great Western are both railways.

But what about that intriguingly odd name the lock has? It's been filched from a nearby pub, once an old coaching inn; and improbable though it seems, it's a matter of record that a few years back that pub was runner-up for the Most Creative Name Award held at the glitzy Café de Paris in London's Piccadilly. I'm intrigued to know who'd have received the award if the pub had won it. After all, this was an award for creativity, yet the name Dog in a Doublet doesn't seem to have been the result of anyone sitting down and inventing it, creatively or otherwise. The story goes that it got its name years ago when a small terrier belonging to the landlady fell in the river and for some totally unexplained reason lost its coat. She, for equally unexplained reasons, is said to have knitted it a doublet – the name for a sort of gilet or jerkin common in England until the 17th century. The trouble is there's not the slightest shred of hard evidence that the episode actually happened, though this hasn't stopped the story becoming folklore in these parts.

Frankly, I find it more credible that someone *did* invent the name. Maybe it was that landlady all those years ago, sitting in front of the fire one evening with her husband, her dog at her feet, complaining how business wasn't as good as it used to be and wondering whether there was some idea they could come up with for improving trade. Perhaps a new name, for instance? Something that would make an impression. Something bizarre that would stick in people's minds.

It was probably at that point they noticed that the dog was looking a bit mangy...

You access the Middle Level round the back of suburban Stanground, where the rear gardens of a modern estate stretch down to the water's edge. Stanground Lock is like a border post. You don't exactly have to show your passport but it feels like you ought to. Instead, you have to book your passage in advance and buy a special windlass and key to get access to water and sewerage disposal facilities. In reality, the lock's probably more accurately described as a sluice since its primary function is to control water levels, boating being a secondary consideration on these waterways, which were built over the centuries first and foremost to protect agricultural land reclaimed from marshy bogs – fens as we know them.

The name Middle Level has a Tolkienesque ring to it with its suggestion of strange, mystical underworlds and hobbit houses in the Shires. Sadly, the truth is more prosaic. There are three levels on the Fens, divided and named for purely administrative purposes. The fact is whatever you call them they're all drainage ditches and once you know that, they're never going to sound very romantic however you try to sell them. The problem is image – one shared by another network of waterways built for drainage that we'd passed earlier on our trip off the River Witham near Boston. These are in even more desperate need of rebranding since in characteristically blunt fashion boaters actually call them drains. Their proper name is the *Witham* Drains if you want to be geographically precise, the Witham *Navigable* Drains if you want to be reminded that even though there's barely a town, village or hamlet along the length of them, you can actually cruise them in a boat if you're at a loss for anything else to do with your life.

Until recently, the Middle Level was the only waterways system in the country where you could cruise without a licence. However, as the costs of boating escalated they began to attract craft on the lookout for cheap moorings in numbers that the Middle Level commissioners who administer it couldn't manage under their existing powers. Since our visit, legislation has been passed to bring the system into line with other waterways. Boaters will soon have to pay to use them and they'll have to have insurance and safety certificates like we do on the rest of the waterways. No doubt there'll be more constraints on already restricted mooring, limited stop times and probably patrol officers with powers to fine you or tow you away if you don't stick to the rules. It's harsh but it has to be done, I guess. I don't like excessive regulation any more than the next man but the fact is, a small number of people have been abusing the system, taking it for what they can. Even so, the passing of this last redoubt of liberty on the waterways makes me want to weep. It's the end of an era, the final curtain on what once had been. When Em and I first started boating, canals and rivers were one of the few places in the country where you could escape the heavy hand of bureaucracy and wander off-grid, footloose and fancy-free, without anyone knowing or caring where you were or what you were doing.

People don't believe it now, but in those days boats didn't have the number plates they do now. For years, we had a boat we never even graced with a name. Or at least not one we were willing to publicise to the world by painting it on the side. We felt it was an impertinence to require us to identify ourselves. We felt it was an imposition on our freedom. Well, something like that... Closer to the truth was that we were hippies at heart and wanted to play our music loudly and experiment with questionable substances without anyone knowing who and where we were. And we had a good run of it, too. In those days, there were so few craft on the system you could go away for a couple of weeks and barely pass another boat. You felt like an adventurer. Even canals that today are major cruising routes were then so infrequently used they were overgrown and reverting to their natural state. I remember the Shropshire Union Canal particularly. Running as straight as a die from Wolverhampton to Chester, it occasionally passes through deep cuttings that at that time trailed with thick foliage from the arching trees overhead so that it was more like navigating the Amazon than any English waterway. The Leicester Section of the Grand Union was the same, except there the reed beds had completely spread across the canal so that it was like taking a boat across an overgrown garden. I loved this part of the canal in those days. Hidden behind the Watford Gap services on the M1, just beyond a flight of seven locks, you suddenly entered a world that seemed so remote it was as if it was trapped in the

19th century. Believe me, this is not me being sentimental, nor is it my memory playing tricks on me. I'll tell you how remote it was. It was so remote that once cruising on that stretch we passed though the half-mile long Saddington Tunnel at twilight. So little used was the canal that we disturbed a colony of bats that had set up home in it. Even now, I can feel them flying around me, kissing my hair as they passed.

It couldn't go on. There was no way this centuries' old system could be maintained for a handful of hippies and a few enthusiasts. There was no way it could sidestep contemporary culture. We're talking about the late 20th century, after all. Everything had to pay for itself – people, places, even ideas. One day, we got an odd-shaped package through the post. It was about the size of a large letter box, flat and flexible. It was our first registration plate. I felt like screaming the way Patrick McGoohan did in that iconic TV series *The Prisoner*: 'I am not a number; I am a free man.' Not that that sort of tantrum would get you very far these days. Nowadays, the Canal and River Trust would be down on you like a ton of bricks if you didn't follow the rules. They'd tow your boat away and crush it if you didn't fall into line.

And do you know what? Despite at first being horrified by their attitude, I'm now behind them every inch of the way. Because I'd come down hard on those who prioritise their own interests over the interests of the wider waterways' community – people with no tolerance of others who refuse to observe basic rules and so leave the boating authorities with no option but to bring in all these regulations in the first place.

Tell me I'm getting old. Accuse me of turning into a despot. But rules don't always have to equate to authoritarianism. Perhaps I've just got more open-minded with the passing years. More willing to accept that if we're going to preserve the heritage of the canals then there's going to have to be fresh thinking about their future. Of course, it's important that people are free to use the waterways; it's only by their accessibility that they justify their existence. Yet it's a very old and fragile system that can't be left to its own devices any more than, say, Stonehenge, which would be overrun and destroyed if it weren't carefully managed. Our canals and rivers have to be carefully managed, too, and in order to conserve their crumbling infrastructure we may have to consider the possibility of regulating not just the practices of the people who use them, but possibly even the numbers of those who are allowed to cruise them as well. It's not feasible to keep overloading the waterways with more and more boats without any regard to numbers. You can't just keep licensing them willy-nilly as the boating authorities are currently doing simply because it's a way of raising money when they're having trouble making ends meet. Already in the summer season on the most popular canals there are pinch points at locks and aqueducts where you can be hanging around for hours. Already there are stretches of canal where you have trouble finding a mooring at any time of the year. Places where the joy of mooring outside a canal pub for a pint is a thing of the past since boats – many of them empty, just using the towpath as cheap mooring – are moored for miles on either side. People come to the canals to get away from this sort of congestion; they come for peace and quiet, to escape the 21st century as far as they can. Currently, it's an astonishing fact there are already more boats on Britain's canals than at the height of the Industrial Revolution. It can't go on. Eventually, by cramming boats on to canals we'll destroy their peace and solitude, which is what we most value in them.

Perhaps we should be thinking of approaching the problem the other way round. Maybe we could start by investigating how many boats the system can reasonably accommodate given that there will always be limited funds to maintain it. With a more sophisticated appreciation of the damage overuse causes, we could avoid stressing it further – a process that only leads to further damage yet, and so on in a vicious circle that may be impossible to reverse if we don't act soon. Already the Oxford Canal – the second busiest cruising canal in the country, popular with boatowners and hirers alike – is reverting to the state it was in during the 1970s as a result of poor maintenance. Other canals like the Huddersfield Narrow, which weren't even around in the 1970s because they've only been recently restored, have fared worse and are currently barely navigable as a result of recurrent water shortages. Every year, the system's plagued by what seems like an increasing number of emergency stoppages. Most of them happen because of minor problems – a lock jams or a bridge is in danger of collapse. Others are more serious engineering failures, such as embankments slipping or reservoirs on the verge of breaching. Either way, the result is the same. Hire boat companies struggling to make a living in a competitive world are inconvenienced, holidaymakers fed on a diet of fantasy by celebrity TV programmes become disillusioned, and boatowners become frustrated as the dream they were sold turns sour.

Despite her reluctance to cruise the Middle Level at all, Em soon began to change her tune. In one of the early entries in the boat log she admitted that they were far prettier than she had imagined. A few days later, she wrote that they were more interesting than she'd expected, too. Gradually, she began to emerge from the despair she felt as a consequence of the narrow, but completely unexpected, referendum victory for those who wanted to leave the EU, the result of which had been announced as we'd left Peterborough. She talked of going through stages of grief, so many of them she couldn't remember whether there were six or seven. Shock, denial, anger, desolation, despair… She ran out of words to describe them.

I was more phlegmatic. I can't claim I'd predicted what would happen, or that I felt any happier than she did about the consequences I feared the result might have for the future of the country; but I'd seen enough of England over our previous four years' travelling to sense the temperature of the place, and in particular the underlying resentment felt in certain regions that they'd been disregarded by a London-based political class who were contemptuous of them.

We holed up for a couple of days to get our bearings at the apparently unremarkable town of Whittlesey, which turned out not to be unremarkable at all. It has an extraordinary past, since before the Fens were drained it was an island, the site of a substantial Bronze Age community. At nearby Flag Fen are the remains of a wooden causeway made of 60,000 tree trunks, which the archaeologist Francis Pryor literally stumbled across in 1982 when he tripped on a piece of wood at the bottom of a ditch. Subsequent investigation concluded that it was built about 3,500 years ago, along with an island constructed partway along, which it's thought was used for religious purposes. There's a visitors' centre there now and reconstructions of a couple of Bronze Age roundhouses as well as one from the later Iron Age. At Must Farm quarry, another nearby site, a complete settlement has been discovered containing what's been described as 'the best-preserved Bronze Age dwellings ever found'. Among swords, boats and fish traps excavated are pots still containing food and – extraordinarily – a wheel, the most complete of its type ever discovered in Britain. It may be something of an exaggeration to say it, but you can understand why the site is being marketed as 'Britain's Pompeii'.

I love this about England: that being so small and having a climate that over the centuries has been amenable to settlement, wherever you walk, history is layered on history that is layered on further history so that you always walk in the footsteps of those who've lived before. We will all at one stage be part of this, our individual pasts as transitory as footsteps in the sand, the cultures of which we've been a part, a bedrock for the generations that will follow us.

It's difficult to describe the Middle Level succinctly. In places, it incorporates the old course of the River Nene, which is like a river you'd see anywhere, reed-lined and shaded by willows, with banks no higher than you'd find cruising through farmland all over England. In places, it twists and turns like any watercourse, sometimes quite severely. Outside Whittlesey, for instance, just beyond Ashline Lock, is a savage bend on a narrow section of a dyke that threatened to put an early end to our Fenland explorations. It needed dredging badly and the only course we could navigate took us through thick mud, where we stuck fast and spent the afternoon poling ourselves out, inch by torturous inch.

The artificial cuts are very different and on maps they look like long, straight lines scoured across the landscape. Which is exactly what they are when you get on them, some sections direct and undeviating for mile after isolated mile. You couldn't be anywhere else except the Fens. In places, you become aware that the water course you're travelling on is actually higher than the surrounding countryside so that it's like cruising along an embankment. This is because over the years, the surrounding land has dried out and shrunk. Being high up like this makes you more vulnerable to those East Anglian winds that are no less biting now than when I first experienced them as a student. Now, though, they've been harnessed and you won't cruise for long in these parts without getting close to a wind farm, even if you don't actually pass through one, surrounded on all sides by turbines, their scarcely moving blades broody against the menacing skies, their generators moaning softly as if in the agonies of a death throe.

Occasionally, when you can see over the banks and get a fix on where you are, you're confronted by agricultural prairies, huge fields of wheat and barley stretching out before you as far as the eye can see. Occasionally, the vista is punctuated by odd lines of pylons or the faraway outline of a copse or spinney on the horizon. Now and again you might even see a farm in the distance, though they're rare among all this industrial agriculture. Towns are few and far between, too, bridges infrequent and low, and as likely as not, built of ugly and ungenerous grey concrete, which is about as far removed as its possible to get from the pretty brick bridges that characterise most other waterways.

Coming under a particularly low one connecting the twin hamlets of Outwell and Upwell, just beyond Marmont Priory Lock – where there once, indeed, had been a priory – Em and I were so deep in conversation with each other that neither of us noticed we hadn't taken the chimney off the roof, which is something you have to do all the time in these parts. We watched with horror as it hit the bridge, buckled and scraped the underside with a sound that set your teeth on edge. It was irksome but I can't say it was a catastrophe. We're experts at this. We've scraped chimneys on bridges from one end of the country to the other. All it takes is ten minutes with a hammer to straighten them out and another ten with a paintbrush to make them presentable again. However, as we emerged from the bridge we could see that this time the chimney had not just been disfigured but loosened from its mounting, too. For a second or two we watched it teeter provocatively until eventually it tumbled from the roof and hit the water with a splash. But even this wasn't something that was going to ruin our day. We've dropped stuff in the cut all over England, from Lancaster to Bristol. Over the years, we've lost so many bits and bobs that we eventually bought a magnet with a line attached for salvaging them. And you'd be surprised how much needs salvaging on a boat, from odd forks thrown out in washing-up bowls to spanners that go astray after being balanced precariously on the gunnels during engine maintenance. Believe me, on a boat, stuff just finds its way into the water. It's attracted to it. It's drawn to it.

The trouble is that although magnets are very efficient at retrieving iron and steel objects, they're useless for other metals. I lost a new box of high-quality brass screws near Stafford once, which had me cussing that I hadn't bought cheaper ones. On another occasion I lost a ring of great sentimental value in Whixall Marina on the Prees Branch of the Llangollen Canal. It had been given to me by my father as a teenager, and it somehow slipped off my finger as I was craning out of a side hatch in the engine room, rinsing my hands with Swarfega after an oil change. The Prees Branch never reached Prees but it did nevertheless prove invaluable since a mile or so from the junction with the main line, the builders discovered a rich vein of clay that until relatively recently was used to 'puddle' or line local canals. Whixall Marina is sited on those former clay pits and the water there is very deep indeed, too deep to recover a ring you'd have thought. Except that I *did* recover it. And not *just* recover it, either. No doubt used to trawling for things they'd lost, the marina had a child's fishing net on a pole 15ft (4.6m) or so long. I borrowed it and on my very first dip I brought up a netful of mud, in the centre of which, glistening at me, was the ring. Now, what would be the odds against that – 5,000:1? Maybe even more?

Small magnets are about as useless as a chocolate poker for recovering heavier objects, too. Though a boat chimney isn't particularly heavy of itself, it is when it's immersed in water and stuck in the mud underneath a bridge. I guessed that getting it out would be a long job but I didn't anticipate exactly how long. The problem wasn't that the magnet was too weak to lift the chimney but that I couldn't locate the chimney at all. At first I fished about at random, but then when that was unsuccessful I drew a mental map and went about the job more methodically. But wherever I threw the magnet, even far out from the bridge, and however many times I dragged it along the bottom, I couldn't find the damned thing. I didn't even get close. Instead, I brought up so many rusted screws and so many shards of unidentifiable metal fragments that I should have saved them and offloaded them to a scrap yard. Half an hour passed, maybe longer. It's a good job that there isn't much traffic on the Middle Level or we'd have been a couple of very unpopular boaters. As it was, we provided an afternoon's entertainment for the village. A couple of elderly ladies emerged from the small shop above the bridge and stood watching us. Later, they were joined by a younger woman, and then an older man. We were obviously far more interesting than *Escape to the Country*, which I suppose everyone around here's done anyhow.

Eventually I got impatient. 'I'm fed up messing about like this, I'm going in,' I said to Em, stripping off down to my underwear. 'The cursed thing's got to be *somewhere* round here. It can't just have disappeared.'

Even up to my neck in the cold waters of the Middle Level, I could sense a change of mood among my audience. At the time I thought it was concern for my safety. Looking back, I think it was probably outrage at my underwear. Well, not my underwear as such. That was perfectly decorous Marks & Spencer stock. I think it was the idea of wearing it publicly that offended them. Even half submerged, I could sense eyebrows rising, even those of the older man, who seemed scandalised by my behavior, too.

I must have been at least another half hour dancing around the bottom in bare feet, hoping I could find the chimney before the sharp end of one of those rusty screws found me. I widened my search. I attempted it first from side to side, and then afterwards I did it lengthways, venturing so far from the bridge

I was in danger of finding myself back in Whittlesey again. It had become a battle of wills now, me against the chimney, man against material object. But could I find the chimney? Could I hell. At last, shivering and defeated, I ran up the white flag.

'Let's leave the sodding thing,' I said to Em with some frustration. 'It's not worth the trouble.'

Even so, it galled me I hadn't been able to recover it. It still does. I loved that chimney. Me and it had been through some good times together. Even now in my quiet moments I sometimes find myself thinking about it, wondering why our relationship had soured and puzzling what I had done to make it so heartlessly determined to leave me. I can't help blaming myself. It must have been something I said or did. One way or another, if anyone in those parts happens to come across it sometime, perhaps they'd be kind enough to contact me?

16

Past Denver Sluice to the Great Ouse

We stopped in March for a while, a place that like all these Fenland settlements once stood on an island surrounded by marshland. Today, it's a pleasant but unremarkable town, though it's got a church everyone's very proud of with an unusual double hammerbeam roof, which the poet John Betjeman said was 'worth cycling 40 miles [64km] in a head wind to see.' I'm not certain I'd go that far myself. In fact, I'm not certain I'd go any distance at all to see a double hammerbeam roof. But that's as much due to my general antipathy to church architecture as not having a blind idea of what a double hammerbeam roof actually is, let alone how it differs from a single hammerbeam roof, which I wouldn't recognise either, even if it was to fall on my head.

More to my taste in March is a glorious art nouveau cinema and one-time music hall called the Hippodrome, which after several unsuccessful attempts to return it to its original function has become a Wetherspoons pub. I don't mind this too much despite my aversion to the founder Tim Martin, whose views on Brexit offend me less than his hairstyle, which seems to me to get longer at the back the more it recedes at the front. That aside, Wetherspoons has refurbished the Hippodrome beautifully and it's worth a stroll to the top end of town to look at it. You won't see a hammerbeam roof but you can get a drink and sit facing the old proscenium arch of the stage in front of which is a splendid mural celebrating Fenland life.

March owes a lot to its position on the Nene, though the river's now reduced to a narrow ribbon winding through the town. This is confusing if you've only recently come up the Nene from Wisbech as we'd done, since that bit of the river is so straight and wide it seems a different waterway entirely. That's because it *is* a different waterway. Though they share the same name, the river Nene has effectively split in two, a result of countless water management schemes over the centuries designed to prevent flooding. Today, the waterway that flows between Peterborough and Wisbech into the Wash beyond the lighthouses at Guy's Head – the route along which we'd travelled – is the main course of the Nene. The section that goes through March, joins the River Great Ouse at Denver Sluice and exits to the Wash beyond King's Lynn, is what used to be the main course, but is now called the old course.

The fact is, people have been fiddling around with waterways on the Fens since Roman times, though it wasn't until the 17th century that engineers set about them with serious intent, totally changing the landscape in the process. They connected the Nene to the Great Ouse and altered their outfalls to the sea, they diverted waters between them and built the system of drains, dykes and completely new tidal rivers that we've inherited today.

They were the new technocrats, these people: scientific men with confidence to change the world they lived in. Among them was, predictably, that man Cornelius Vermuyden in whose wake Em and I had been travelling since we arrived in Goole months before. After his less than sparkling success draining Hadfield Chase, which caused so much unrest on the Isle of Axholme, Vermuyden got drawn into work on the Fens where they really didn't need him to upset the locals because they were

PAST DENVER SLUICE TO THE GREAT OUSE

upset enough as it was. All this talk of drainage riled them. It threatened their traditional lifestyle based on the old ways: wild fowling, eel catching and reed cutting. Surveying the prospect of the Fens as agricultural farmland, they feared for their future – and in this they weren't wrong. Historian Eric Ash of Wayne State University in Detroit has written a book on the draining of the Fens and he makes the point that though powerful monarchs and statesmen, such as King Charles I, Oliver Cromwell and the Earl of Bedford, all claimed that in draining the Fens they were undertaking a project for the benefit of the entire English commonwealth, the fact is they all had extensive estates in the Fens and stood to gain a great deal from draining and enclosing common grazing areas.

Foremost in the fight against Vermuyden's plans was a resistance group known as the 'Fen Tigers', who opposed the work by a guerrilla campaign of tearing down the sluices and dykes and sabotaging the windmills that drained them. Nowadays, Fenlanders seem to have forgotten this part of their history in anything but name only. Today, they're more concerned with sightings of a tiger of the big cat variety that is said to stalk the region during quiet news periods, of which there are many in this part of the world. The label Fen Tigers has been appropriated by speedway and football teams, so at least its use in this context is a concession to the idea that there's combat associated with it. I don't know if you can say the same for the positioning of a couple of tigers either side of the official arms of Fenland District Council though, an irony if ever I've seen one. After all, it was establishment lackeys like councils that the Fen Tigers were fighting.

Restless natives weren't the only challenge faced by Vermuyden and other engineers. Their main difficulty was they didn't understand the ecology of the terrain they were excavating. Land that was drained early in the 17th century was under water again by the beginning of the 18th as all the culverts, ditches and new rivers that were dug to drain the area had the unintended consequence of drying it out. This led to the whole of the Fenlands shrinking – increasing the risk of flooding rather than mitigating it. Soon, more and more pumps were needed to keep the land workable but this, in turn, dried it out more. This catch-22 situation in which the construction of new drainage systems led to the need for ever-more sophisticated methods of extracting water continued until Victorian times, by which time the land was sinking at the extraordinary rate of 2in (5cm) a year. The invention of steam engines sufficiently reliable to keep pumps going day and night kept flooding in check for a while, but the problem of how to manage huge volumes of water flowing through the Fens when conditions were extreme wasn't solved until modern times. Many would say that with global warming and rising sea levels it's tempting fate to believe that it's solved even now...

All the same, approaching March by boat you can't help but be struck by the way that some gardens along the water's edge have been embellished in a distinctly maritime way, harking back to the time when the river was more important and shipping was part of its stock-in-trade. Thick nautical ropes line the bank in some places as decoration; ornamental lifebuoys hang on trees. An old rowing boat has been cut in half and upended to make an outdoor washroom, complete with a tap and sink.

People's back gardens say so much about them, and travelling along rivers and canals you get privileged views of intimate spaces that aren't designed to be seen publicly. It's as if you're sitting in the stalls of somewhere like the Hippodrome in the old days, looking at an empty stage. From time to time actors stumble into view and you catch them unawares and unprepared. Sometimes they're in an embarrassing state. If you'll excuse the French in describing this most English of tendencies, they are déshabillé, just out of the shower or worse, completely au naturel. Sometimes they are scratching places they shouldn't be scratching, picking at bits of them they should leave alone. You catch them having cross words, and sometimes you disturb them in the middle of furious rows. Occasionally, they are being more intimate than is seemly for the time of day. It's almost as if they consider the short length of waterway in front of them as a screen. Almost as if it never occurs to them that there might be boats passing and that they might be seen.

On the posh bits of the River Thames, you cruise so far back from houses you don't threaten the privacy of the residents. The people who live in these mansion-type homes are hidden behind gardens the size of parks, with swimming pools and outbuildings you just know are purpose-built gyms or fully equipped home cinemas. One in Goring has a box made completely of glass as a summer dining room. It sits on stanchions at tree level overhanging the water. Houses like this frequently have their own boathouses built over inlets from the river. Some of these boathouses are as big as real houses. Some of them *are* real houses. But even if finances only run to more modest properties, we Brits love our gardens and we let our imaginations run riot in them, untrammelled by any concerns of fashion or taste. I've seen the backyards of two-up, two-down terraces decked out like a Spanish bar, I've seen them like rooms in the British Museum, sporting rows of classical Greek statues. Others proudly display rampant lions on pedestals that wouldn't be out of place on the parapet of a country house. There are Buddhas by the shovelful, the occasional Ganesh and other strange shrines to gods I've never even heard of.

Some gardens are luxuriant with flowers, carefully tended vegetable patches and sheds doubling as summer houses; others are bare, composed in the main of stone chippings designed to be low-maintenance. Some really are low-maintenance.

They're neglected and overrun with weeds, or in the case of one I passed a few years back, overwhelmed with a single enormous rhubarb plant, the biggest I have even seen. Having successfully taken over the garden, you could see it was now eyeing up the house in anticipation of colonising the kitchen, which was the next step in its tyrannical dreams of world domination.

The worst are those forsaken gardens that sadden your heart with the spirit of what they'd once been. Perhaps abandoned after the death or ill-health of those who loved them, they've returned to nature and become a wilderness, flower beds choked with brambles and greenhouses left to become derelict. In one garden that particularly sticks in my mind, a wooden table and chairs had been left rotting for years on what had once been a lawn. On the table, as if they'd just been left for a moment or two while the people who put them there popped back to the house, were a couple of wine glasses green with algae and a Burgundy bottle that had lost its label over the years in the rain. The whole vignette was a sad and eerie reminder of some long-forgotten summer day an eternity ago when the world was a happier place.

One of Em's university friends lived close to March and one evening we met up with her and her husband at a small Thai cafe/restaurant that turned out to be surprisingly serendipitous. First off, I discovered that he, like me, was a Leicester City supporter; second, the cafe had a poster of our Premiership-winning team on the wall. It had us both swelling with pride. 'My husband,' the woman cooking and serving from canteen-sized trays explained in her hesitant English. 'He big fan.'

I was soon her big fan. I lived in Thailand for a while and believe me, the food she prepared was terrific, the sort of authentic home cooking that would cost you an arm and a leg in posher places. This infusion of internationalism into such an apparently sequestered environment as March where you could judge the prevailing political climate by how many Leave posters were still proudly on display in house windows, meant the recent referendum was one of the main subjects of conversation between us. This was particularly the case since Em's friend and her husband are both from farming families, he a former Conservative Party councilor, too – one of that old-school breed of One Nation Tories who was as pro-Europe as us and troubled as much as we were by the implications of the decision. How typical he was of Conservatives living locally I can't say, though I expect not much, since a few years after this the local MP was appointed Brexit secretary. All the same, it was an agreeable evening that even then seemed redolent of a different, gentler age when rational people could discuss politics without searching for some excuse to insult each other when their views diverged.

All this talk of Fenland towns shouldn't blind you to how wreathed in solitude these waters of the Middle Level are. Since arriving on them we'd been travelling along what's usually called the Nene/Ouse Link for the obvious reason that linking the rivers Nene and Great Ouse is exactly what this miscellany of rivers, canals and dykes actually does. These waterways are probably the most used of those in the Middle Level, though that isn't to say they're used much compared to traffic on the main parts of the system. If you didn't dawdle too much, you could probably cruise comfortably from one end to the other in about 12 hours, since by water Whittlesey's not much more than 10 miles (16km) from March, and March is only another 8 or 9 miles (12.9–14.5km) from Outwell.

Between these places, however, the canal penetrates remote areas that – if you're like us and fond of mooring in the middle of nowhere – make you marvel that such places still exist in England. Places where at night you're in almost complete blackness but for the moon, the firmament above, or the puny lights of your boat, which barely penetrate the tenebrous world around you. Places where the silence seems bottomless, deep and profound; for what roads there are crossing these flat lands are little used in the hours of darkness and you're less likely to be aware of cars by their sound than by their headlights sweeping the landscape like searchlights.

Even in the day, the Fens have their own particular quality of silence, which like all silences isn't silent at all. You hear the wind turbines if they're close, of course. And you might even hear a combine harvester at work in a faraway field, or even a light aircraft crop-spraying, its engine like a chainsaw buzzing away in the distance. But underlying this there's a dead silence, an eerie lack of sound. No human voices, barely any insects, few trees through which to hear the wind play. Even the birds seem muted here, reluctant to draw too much attention to themselves among these agricultural wastes.

Yet there are even more remote parts of the Middle Level still to be explored if you're so minded. Just outside Whittlesey, the Whittlesey Dyke cuts across the long, straight stretch created when Bevills Leam joins the Twenty Foot River. This stretches so far into the distance it seems a study in perspective, designed to demonstrate how parallel lines appear to merge at infinity. You get a similar sense of an unending void looking south-east down the Sixteen Foot drain from the hamlet of Three Holes, a tiny settlement of just a handful of houses. Given a couple of gentle bends at either end, which aren't really bends at all but slight corrections in course that you don't notice anyway, this is a waterway that is not just totally flat, and straight as a ruler, but one that is 10 miles (16km) long, too. Ten miles! And not a lock on its length, traffic passing on the busy Chatteris road alongside the only distraction to break the monotony of your journey.

I've never experienced waterways in England like it, though they're not uncommon in these parts. Of course, they're not on the same scale, and they weren't built for the same reasons, but these East Anglian waterways have more in common with the industrial canals of Germany than any in Britain. Even so, regardless of where you are, travelling distances like this on a boat, along canals this straight, is an ordeal. They'd challenge the concentration of a flying crow. It certainly challenges any intrepid canal explorer whose main problem is likely to be maintaining concentration for the hours it takes to travel along them.

In the past, there was at least a reason for doing this because there used to be a back way to the River Great Ouse and Ely by way of Welches Dam Lock, which fell into disrepair but was restored in 1991 with the assistance of the Inland Waterways Association. This organisation – a charity run entirely by members – has been campaigning for the conservation, restoration and maintenance of Britain's waterways since 1946 and it's no exaggeration to say that without it the canals of Britain would not have survived in anything like the numbers they have. It now works closely (some would say too closely) with the Canal and River Trust, the official body that runs the bulk of the waterways in England. However, its relationship with the other body responsible for most of the rest – the government's Environment Agency (EA) – is problematic.

In 2006, in a devious move that wouldn't have shamed Machiavelli, the EA closed the recently restored Welches Dam Lock, blocking it with piles and taking it out of service. At the time, it said this was 'temporary' to 'avoid water loss' from the lock gate, which it claimed had started to leak. Regardless of the truth or otherwise of this, the result was to breach rights of navigation enshrined in law. Some people are under the impression that all that's required to run a public body today is the ability to tell lies easily and without blushing. This is a mistake. It helps, too, if you've got a brass neck. The EA are certainly not short on that score and in 2017, after pressure from local boaters, the requisite closure notice was finally issued. It was 11 years late.

The lock is still closed, and recently the EA has gone further and has been denying it even has responsibility for it – and not just the lock, but a couple of miles of canal beyond, known locally as the 'Horseway Channel', which is silted up with sludge and rubbish. The EA says that too few people use the lock to justify the expense of maintaining it, and you can't fault it for inaccuracy on that score since the reason so few people use the lock is because ... well, it's closed. Like, you can't get through it. It is shut. It is impassable. To use it in the condition it is would require some heavy plant machinery. Cranes to lift your boat, for instance. Bulldozers and dredgers to clear your passage.

However, the EA's reference to the expense of maintaining it does at least hint at the truth of the matter. For the fact is, our waterways aren't exactly top priority for government spending and over the years they have been starved of cash. So I have a certain degree of sympathy for the EA, given that its budget has been cut to the bone over the years by successive governments. Even so, that's no excuse for it to avoid its statutory responsibilities. The problem is, though, how do you hold it to account? Indeed, how do you hold any public body to account in today's world where money will always talk louder than any conservation group? Perhaps we need a few more tigers on the Fens. And a few more prowling in other places, too.

We pushed on towards the Great Ouse by the more orthodox route through the tidal lock at Salters Lode where the lock keeper has a model railway running around his garden. Suddenly, the constricted channels of the Middle Level widen and you're on a broad and open river heading for the extraordinary Denver Sluice, which is less a single structure, more an intricate hydrological engineering complex designed to prevent flooding – that ever-present curse of the Fens. It does this in two ways: first, by acting as a defence to high surge tides from the sea, and second, by managing water coming downstream from the Great Ouse and its tributaries after periods of exceptional rainfall. The site's an ingenious system of locks, sluices and connecting canals that can manage water by diverting it into relief channels, which become temporary reservoirs, or by allowing it to back up to wetlands at Welney 20 miles (32km) upstream to what are called the Ouse Washes. These are an internationally important ecological and bird sanctuary.

Everywhere you look at Denver there are sluices. They're all over the place. There's the Residual Flow Sluice, the Impounding Sluice, the Diversion Sluice, the John Martin Sluice, the Welmore Lake Sluice – though these last two may be different names for the same one. I can't remember; my mind had addled trying to get to grips with it all. I may even have lost a sluice, too. I was wandering around for hours trying to find something called the Tail Sluice until I discovered it was 10 miles (16km) away.

Overall, I thought the most interesting was the AG Wright Sluice, built in 1957 – the Head Sluice as it's sometimes called, since it seems every sluice has to have at least two names round here. It reminds me vaguely of the Brandenburg Gate in Berlin, except that whereas the Brandenburg Gate is all fluted columns topped by Prussian imperial frippery, the AG Wright Sluice at Denver consists of four Brutalist pillars, one of them a tower that could easily pass as a look-out at a Soviet prison camp. All the same, it does have a certain raw architectural style to it that I'm not alone in finding attractive. Where it scores over Brandenburg is that it really is a fully operational gate. Well, actually three gates. Huge things that depending on conditions can be lifted to release water into a Relief Channel, which takes it downriver towards King's Lynn where that Tail Sluice is. From here, it can be allowed to flow away harmlessly into the Wash on low tides, or contained temporarily if that's not possible. The Relief Channel is essentially an emergency drain, with a function not unlike the overflow pipe on your sink, except that whereas that prevents your kitchen flooding and avoids the cost of getting in the decorators, this contributes to allaying the effects of disasters such as the one in 1953 when, in the worst natural catastrophe Britain experienced during the 20th century, more than 300 were killed and 40,000 left homeless after a huge tidal surge devastated the east coast.

The Cut-off Channel, just a step or two away, is an equally impressive piece of design and construction, more so in its own way. Planned to prevent the Southern Level of the Fens from flooding, it sweeps to Denver in a 28-mile (45km) loop from Barton Mills, north-west of Bury St Edmunds in Suffolk, along a course that is so gently inclined it's virtually level. On its way, it draws water from the headwaters of the rivers Lark, the Little Ouse and the Wissey where 40 per cent of the Great Ouse comes from. In times of potential flood, this in turn can be diverted at Denver into the Relief Channel.

Oddly enough this idea of a sort of 'ring road' of water to take the strain off the River Great Ouse was first mooted by Cornelius Vermuyden in 1639. Later, in the early 1800s when the eminent Scottish engineer John Rennie was asked to look at the problem of continual flooding in the area, he came up with a virtually identical solution. On both occasions, the cost of the project was considered too high. By the time the scheme was eventually agreed and completed it was 1964; Harold Wilson was prime minister and the Beatles had just released 'A Hard Day's Night'. By this time, government studies were warning of water shortages in Essex and so engineers decided to make use of the gentle fall of the Cut-off Channel by using it for a secondary purpose. They designed a scheme through which, by raising water levels at Denver high enough, they could make water in it run *backwards* into East Cambridgeshire, where it could be pumped to a tributary of the River Stour and extracted into a couple of reservoirs downstream. All in all, this is a heck of a piece of engineering just to ensure people can get a glass of water out of their tap. I hope they appreciate it.

The Denver Sluice complex is not the prettiest bit of engineering you'll see on the waterways, but it has to be among the most impressive, equal in its own way to Thomas Telford's masterful Pontcysyllte Aqueduct at Trevor near Wrexham on the border of Wales, which towers nearly 130ft (40m) above the River Dee on 18 precipitous stone piers and today is lauded as the jewel in the crown of the British canal system. It's so famous it's everywhere; you can't get away from it. It features in films and on TV programmes, in adverts and in books. It's even been promoted on a stamp. The 1,000ft (305m)-long aqueduct was completed in 1805, the year of the Battle of Trafalgar, and I wouldn't want to play down its glorious history, and how technologically advanced it was for its time, let alone how elegant, stylish and graceful it is. Neither would I want to put off anyone who's planning to go and see it. All I'd say is that before they do, they should know that for all its Grade 1 listing and its razzmatazz status as a World Heritage Site, it's the most overhyped and wasteful engineering project since HS2. The fact is, it took ten years to plan and build and it cost unspeakable amounts of money; yet it finished up being a white elephant, an aqueduct to nowhere, like those roads to nowhere abandoned because of lack of money that you used to see all over communist Eastern Europe.

The aqueduct was originally scheduled to be part of a much bigger project, a canal that would connect the rivers Severn and Mersey by way of Chester, Wrexham and Shrewsbury. Sadly, by the time Telford finished it the cash had run out, so the link was never completed. Meanwhile, the year before in 1804, at the Penydarren Ironworks near Merthyr Tydfil in South Wales, a newfangled machine powered by steam had been successfully hauling carriages along a tramway, essentially signalling the beginning of the end of commercial water transport in Britain.

The poor old Pontcysyllte was left with no function other than as feeder to carry water from the River Dee at the top end of nearby Llangollen to the sections of canal that had been completed. It was a humiliating end to such an aspirational project, which had once celebrated new boundaries of human achievement. In a way, that humiliation continues still, for what was once to have been the keystone of a major industrial thoroughfare has finished up carrying pleasure boats for holiday trips and being gawped at by tourists.

At least the Denver Sluice complex has been doing what it was designed to do in one form or another for close on 400 years. Paradoxically, for somewhere so unashamedly functional, it's a remarkably attractive place to stop, too, with well-tended moorings around the grassy banks of a river which at that point is so wide, and with so many arms connecting to it, that it's like a lagoon. There's a lovely pub nearby as well, with a highly rated restaurant, and an attractive parasol-covered veranda with fine views over the water. While we were there, the weather was sunny and hot; and it seemed there was barely another boat on the water even though by now we were well into summer. We took the opportunity of making expeditions from the place and we explored the River Wissey, one of the tributaries of the Great Ouse, the most celebrated of which is the River Cam from which Cambridge takes its name. We also made a short trip in the opposite direction along the Relief Channel to Downham Market. Imagine my surprise walking around the place to find a blue plaque of the sort usually celebrating some association with someone famous from the past. This one, however, was on a self-effacing modern bungalow. It was headed Leicestershire Heritage and had obviously been erected by a Leicester supporter like me. It read: 'On this site in 2016 we witnessed the fairytale become reality.' I said to Em that we should get one for *Justice*. She wasn't impressed by the idea.

The Wissey is an odd river. For most of its 10-mile (16km) length to Stoke Ferry it's as bucolic and isolated a waterway as you'd find anywhere, reed-lined and occasionally carpeted with lawns of vibrant yellow water lilies so thick they threaten to snag your propeller and prevent you getting through. But around what used to be the village of Wissington – a place that now doesn't exist any more except in folk memory – the river suddenly breaks up into a baffling series of lakes and pools connected by a confusion of winding streams. Suddenly, out of a patchwork of fields emerge the tanks, pipework and smoking chimneys of a British Sugar PLC beet-processing plant. It's not just any old beet-processing plant either, but the biggest beet-processing plant in Europe. It's an immense industrial unit that has grown so huge that it begs the question why was it built in such an out-of-the-way location in the first place. Originally, in 1925, there wasn't even any road access to it, and it could only be reached overland by a light railway that had been constructed for a few local farms. Apart from that, the river was its main transport link and three tugs and a fleet of 24 barges used to operate between here and King's Lynn, bringing back coal on their return journeys.

They needed coal because you need a lot of heat to process sugar beet. That's the reason subsidiary industries tend to develop around sugar beet factories using the heat and the carbon dioxide produced as by-products to grow other crops. Until recently, for instance, Wissington produced 70 million tomatoes a year, which is a lot of passata by anyone's standards.

Recently, it's switched production to medicinal cannabis, which after a long battle by campaigners has now been authorised by government for pain relief and the treatment of epilepsy. This is serious stuff and why I absolutely refuse to take any cheap pot shots at the work being done, let alone make any cracks at the expense of the stony East Anglian soil.

17

To Ely

I don't know if I'd go as far as the 19th-century American
Henry David Thoreau, who wrote that most of us lead lives
of quiet desperation. Even so, I can see what he was getting at.
There's a sense in which we all have to lead our lives bound by
the limitations of the everyday. We've all got responsibilities to
other people, friends, family and loved ones. We all have to eat
and sleep and keep ourselves and our clothes clean. We all have
to work and however interesting our jobs and however much we
love them, there's always going to be the tedious stuff to deal
with. This, after all, is what living's all about. It is, at its basic
level, what life *is*.

And that's where canals come in. For me, canals have offered
an escape route from the humdrum, a way of balancing the
banalities of everyday routine. They've given me a free pass to
a more exhilarating and unpredictable world where you can't
count on anything except that every day will be different to the
one before. In this sense, exploring them has been an ongoing
adventure – though maybe 'adventure' is pitching it a bit strong
since I've rarely set out on a boat intending to do much that was
daring or unusual. On the few occasions I have – such as going
down the Bristol Channel, or more recently crossing the Wash
– it's not been because I've been testing myself, but because
I've simply wanted to get from one part of the system to the
other. I've never been one of those boaters who need to take

their narrowboats across Europe to the Black Sea, or along the rivers of America to prove some point to themselves. Boating in England was more than enough of a challenge for me.

Sometimes the challenge was physical, such as when I took the crazy decision to cruise from Manchester across the newly restored Huddersfield Narrow Canal soon after it reopened following a 57-year closure. OK, my trip wasn't on a par with Fitzcarraldo taking a boat across the Andes, but at least he had people to help him. I was single-handed and had to drag mine along a canal with barely any water in it – a canal that isn't even a canal really, but two endless lock flights divided by a pig of a tunnel. That journey changed my life. Before it, I thought I'd be boating until they nailed me down in a coffin. Afterwards, I realised I was kidding myself.

When I wanted challenges – as I did when I was younger – I set them myself. Even now I can't believe the distances I sometimes travelled. Can it be true, as the logbook tells me, that one year, travelling single-handed again, I went from the basin in Stratford-upon-Avon to Leamington Spa in a single day? That's a journey of 24 miles (39km), which is seven or eight hours' cruising on its own. But there are 56 locks to negotiate too, 21 of them the Hatton Flight – the '21 Steps to Heaven', as the old boatmen used to call them. Or in my case, the 21 Steps to Hell, since I was travelling downhill and the log tells me that I didn't meet another boat in either direction and so had to manhandle these brutes with their ruinous hydraulic paddles entirely on my own. I must have been bananas.

Canals posed challenges of other sorts, as well. To be frank, there were times when they led me into situations that put the fear of God in me. Like that occasion on the Rochdale Canal just outside Oldham when I passed an estate where a riot was taking place – yes, really, a riot, a genuine riot. It was late evening, almost dark, and a thin line of trees was the only thing that separated me from the uproar. I heard the sirens and saw the pulsing blue lights of police cars. The canal echoed to the sound of a mob howling and every now and again a petrol bomb exploded, momentarily lighting up the scene with a blast of blinding brightness like a light bulb bursting. I wondered what chance I'd have if the rioters noticed me trying to slip by unobtrusively in a boat the size of a whale that couldn't have been more of a target unless it had a bull's-eye painted on the roof.

And then there was that time I was cruising with my longtime friend Dave heading for the Caldon Canal when we found ourselves suddenly under fire just outside Stoke-on-Trent. A group of youngsters had got hold of a length of industrial elastic, which they'd strung between two trees. They were using it to launch half-bricks from a railway embankment bordering an estate a full quarter of a mile from the canal. The bricks were flying through the air and landing around us like bombs, shattering as they landed. Any one of them could have taken our heads off. We took shelter under a bridge, and so dangerous was our situation that when we rang the police they were there in minutes and caught the perpetrators red-handed. A week later, they telephoned to say that in view of the circumstances they were exploring whether they could charge them under the provisions of the Firearms Act!

You have to deal with these situations. They're unusual, but they're part of the package. Travelling canals is a constant voyage of discovery and sometimes you have to find resources in yourself you never knew were there. Of course, more literally, it's a geographical voyage of discovery too – a voyage that takes you to the parts of the country you never knew existed and that you would never find any other way. For me, that has been inspirational. It's broadened my horizons as much as travelling abroad ever did. It's changed my perspective on life and made me realise that seeing a lot of the world doesn't necessarily mean you understand it any better. Canals may only be an infinitesimal part of the universe we inhabit but there's a lot to be learned from focusing on the small-scale things of life, as any scientist examining a slide under a microscope will tell you.

I remember that very first canal trip on the hire boat with Dave. We'd pulled up briefly at Trent Junction, a complex interchange on the borders of Derbyshire, Leicestershire and Nottinghamshire, where a couple of rivers and two canals meet. There are pubs there and a tea shop, and it's a popular spot for a picnic – a place where on summer afternoons you can sit on the grass overlooking what's almost a wide lake. In front of you, boats converge from all points of the compass mixing it with paddleboards, canoes and rented rowing boats splashing about in the water. Back in the day, it was nowhere near as busy, and it certainly wasn't busy that bleak and deserted autumn when we washed up there. Fortuitously, though, there was a boat moored along the bank with the owner perched on deck, warming his hands on a mug of tea. We pulled up alongside to talk to him. The fact was, the yard from which we'd rented our boat hadn't provided any maps and so we hadn't the first idea where we were, let alone where we were going.

'Where do all these lead?' I asked, somewhat pitifully, it having just dawned on me that this boating lark might not be the straightforward linear progression I'd thought. I don't know what I expected from the guy on deck but what I got was a gazetteer with a heartbeat. I stood gobsmacked as he explained that this canal over here went to Liverpool from where you could get to Leeds; and that river over there went to Leicester, which led to London; and that one to East Anglia and the sea. He left us reeling at how extensive the system was. It seemed that these twisting watercourses and sluggish ditches could take you pretty well anywhere in the country, with no restrictions on your movement. On a boat, it appeared you could enjoy the sort of freedom that neither of us had ever experienced before. You could go where you wanted and stop where you wanted and stay for as long as you wanted. You had a bed on which to lay your head at night, you had a sink where you could shave and a cooker where you could fix yourself a buttie. What more could a heart desire?

We soon discovered that the icing on the cake was the people you met along the way. Boat people were unfailingly convivial and – importantly – there weren't so many of them in those days that you ever felt cramped by their presence. The canal wasn't just an open road, but a road open to everyone; yet you were only ever reminded that there were other people on it in the evenings when you moored at pubs, as we invariably did – even though these were the days of Watney's Red Barrel and the standard of beer was dreadful. In the bar you could pick out boaters a mile off by their grubby clothes and the miasma of stale canal water and engine oil that clung to them. Boat life wasn't exactly sanitary then. Hire boats had running water and basic showers fed from integral tanks, and some privately owned craft had a rudimentary system for pumping water to taps from containers stored under their decks, often manually. But they were thought wusses for having it. Most people just kept their water in containers – old 5.5-gallon (25-litre) industrial distilled water bottles were favourite. Or they kept it on their roof as the old boat people had, in colourfully decorated water containers called Buckby cans. Boaters like us hiring from the nascent companies that were just beginning to spring up soon got into the swing of life on the canals. We didn't worry too much about water and barely washed at all. After a week or so we looked and smelled as if we'd been born to the cut.

Boats in those days were all very different to each other; there was nothing you could say was typical. There were the odd one or two brand-new, snow-white cruisers driven by blokes who wore captain's caps like the character played by Eric Sykes in that classic (and still funny) Harry H Corbett waterways film *The Bargee*. Most were older craft though. There were a lot of cut-down wooden working boats, as well as a number of full-sized steel ones that had been decommissioned from industrial use and adapted for leisure. Beyond that, pretty well everything went: if it floated that was good enough. There were old lifeboats or beat-up coastal cruisers, dinghies, skiffs and even the odd algae-covered inflatable. Some scarcely warranted the name 'boat' at all. They were rafts with outboard engines, or they were industrial 'flats' – platforms used for bank work with sheds built on top. Some were home-built like the first boat Em and I bought, thrown together by amateurs who knew less about boatbuilding than they did about cellular biology.

Boaters themselves were an equally disparate bunch, too. By day, they could be toolmakers or turf accountants, surveyors or bricklayers, architects or teachers; but come the weekend they all became boaters and what they did for a living was immaterial. Their only common feature was that they were all unconventional types who weren't going to get too hot under the collar because someone's hair was too long or their language too ripe. They all set great store by self-reliance, too. If you had a problem with your engine – and we all did in those days because any old contraption could be adapted to turn a propeller – then they wanted to know that you'd rolled up your sleeves and had a go at repairing it yourself before they offered to help.

It was the breadth of their knowledge that I found most staggering, however. Not only were they familiar with boaty things, like hull protection, insulation or the black art of propeller pitch and size, but they were experts on botany, ornithology and entomology as well. Or that's how it seemed to me since they seemed to be able to name every flower in the hedgerows, every bird in the sky and every arachnid that crawled over your bed at night. Their talk of the cut was esoteric – cabalistic, almost – peppered by abstruse references to chines and sacrificial anodes, cutters and dollies, loobies and joshers. Or to far-flung places like The Twenty One, the Mile Straight, the Oozell Loop or the Curly Wurly.

It seemed astonishing to me that by the simple expedient of just hiring a boat for a couple of weeks you gained privileged access to this new and strange world, a world that was similar enough to your own to be recognisable, but so different from it that it was almost otherworldly, a realm of the peculiar where bizarre eccentrics roamed. I fell in love with it instantly.

For most of my life, I worked as a television producer, where we had a mantra we always repeated when we just couldn't see a way of fitting in a crucial point we wanted to make or a key interviewee we felt should be heard. We'd reassure ourselves that the viewers would never know what they'd missed. How could they know, we told ourselves. No one can miss what they've never been aware of.

I feel the same way about new people coming to the canals today. I welcome them wholeheartedly. No one could fail to be impressed with their enthusiasm for the cut and everything to do with it; no one could wish them anything except joy of it in the future. But I feel regretful for them at the same time, too. Of course, they'll never know what they've missed but there was a time – and a time not so very long ago at that – when travelling the canals was a totally different experience to today, a far richer experience in many ways. The fabric of the canals certainly wasn't better then because as you quickly became aware, the system was falling apart. However, because it was so run-down it meant that we lucky few who had the privilege of enjoying it at that time had the canals more or less to ourselves. The upside of them not being maintained was that they weren't policed either. For many boaters of that era, this just meant they never paid their licence fee. For us, it was the heady liberation this unregulated environment offered which we valued most. In that sense, we were like settlers pushing back the boundaries of the American frontier in the days of the Wild West. We were pioneers. Every new canal could surprise you with something startling; every twist and turn held the promise of a new discovery and the threat of perils, too, whether lengths of canal you had to haul yourself across because they were so silted, locks that you had to repair on the hoof, or just bands of local kids who hadn't seen boats on the canal for so long the only use they could see for them was target practice.

All respect to the founding fathers of the immediate post-war generation, people like Tom Rolt, Robert Aickman and Charles Hadfield, who'd launched the Inland Waterways Association and ensured the survival of the waterways. But their exploration of the system was necessarily limited; it was we of the generation after theirs who were left to push back the boundaries further in ways that would herald a leisure age of the cut when the canals would become widely accessible to all.

The trouble was, we hadn't thought through the implications of what we were doing. We evangelised about canals, arguing that they could be a major tourist attraction or the basis of regeneration in run-down industrial areas. But we had no grasp of what that would ultimately entail. We'd forgotten the centuries-old lesson of Aesop's fable about being careful what you wish for.

Today, no one on a boat would find themselves without a map and lost, as Dave and I were at Trent Lock on that first hire boat we rented. Quite apart from the fact that no decent hire boat company would think of sending customers out without a map, the fact is that when you have to pay the sort of money to hire a boat that you do nowadays, you do a bit of research ahead of time. Before even stepping on to a boat, most hirers will pore over the route they're planning to take. And today there's so much information available about the canal system you don't even need a boat to explore it; you can do it from the comfort of your own living room. Go on to the net and you can find everything you want to know about individual canals. You can learn about their history from Wikipedia, and find out about towns and villages you'll pass through from local websites, where you can discover a plethora of information – from the schedule of church services to the opening times of local shops. You can examine places from above through Google Earth and walk around them before you arrive with Google Street View. You can buy DVDs of your route or look at videos of it on YouTube. And if you want more detailed information yet, there's a host of blogs written by people who've done what you're planning to do; and if that's still not enough for you, post a query on Facebook or one of the hundreds of groups that have grown up on social media to meet the seemingly inexhaustible need of boaters to talk to other boaters. Give them your location. Ask them where's the best place to moor. It won't be long before some enthusiast keen to boast of their expertise replies to you telling you it's next to the third oak tree after the bridge opposite the cornfield.

Can you believe that there are even websites nowadays that will work out all of this for you. Input where you want to start and where you want to go. Tell them how many hours a day you want to travel. They'll do the rest, including telling you where you need to stop at nights and how fast you need to go.

It's all very convenient, I grant you, but where's the sense of adventure here, where's the challenge in it? Today's narrowboats are like motorhomes on water; they're like high-end caravans. They have central heating, baths and wet rooms – even Jacuzzis, can you believe it? They have luxury kitchens with double sinks and freezers and washing machines. Some of them even have Agas. They're floating country cottages. People take them places, moor them up and use them like a hotel. Em and I have done it so I can't take the moral high ground. Even the prospect of an engine breakdown doesn't hold the fears it used to for the unskilled because unless you're on the peripheries of the system where few go, there'll be a boat along soon enough, happy to tow you to the nearest boatyard. Failing that, there's a boat recovery service similar to the AA or the RAC that will come out at any time of day or night and do everything for you, from clearing your propeller to replacing your batteries.

A service like that is easier to run than it ever would have been in the past because boats are much of a muchness today – like cars that, despite all the money the manufacturers spend to tell you how unique they are, all finish up looking alike with more or less the same technology under the bonnet. Boats have to be 6ft 10in (2.07m) wide or less in order to navigate the narrow canals on the system. Most newly built ones are, like *Justice*, around 57–60ft (17.4–18.2m) long. Since locks vary in length, this allows a trade-off between maximum living space and cruising range. Of course – again like cars – there are high-end boats and less-expensive ones, too, but the majority today have proprietary engines and increasingly standard electrical and plumbing systems. The idiosyncratic craft of yesteryear have by and large been culled from the cut by safety regulations that tend to favour the better-off who can afford to maintain their boats regularly rather than the young or impecunious who struggle to stay afloat on the cheap.

Boats have become homogenous, and in my low moments I sometimes feel some of the people who own them have, too. They seem less interested in the culture and the history of the cut; they seem less interested in the old ways. They travel too fast, they jump the queue at locks, some don't even bother waving or nodding to you when they pass, which always used to be one of the endearing customs of the cut. But why should people toe the line, you might ask. What inalienable law says that the conventions I and others of my generation observed should be what new generations of boaters should be compelled to follow? Who's to say that our rules and traditions are worth preserving? Who's to say that things don't need to be done differently?

Except the difficulty is that as canals get more popular and busier, the infrastructure of the waterways is put under increasing strain, and it becomes impossible to preserve it as it should be preserved without accepted codes of behaviour. Cramming more and more boats on the waterways isn't the answer: it merely compounds the problem. The more boats there are on canals, the more maintenance canals need, and the more that puts strain on the budget of the Canal and River Trust whose funding model appears more and more unsustainable with every year that passes. After taking on the mantle of a charity to escape government constraints on investment and fundraising, it's now trying to reposition itself as a charity of 'well-being' in order to attract government funding. So what's been gained, many of us want to know. Except that from being a statutory corporation wholly owned by the government, and as such answerable to the public through Parliament, this national asset is now in the custody of a charity run by a council of 50 members, the overwhelming majority of them unelected. There are nine who are voted in, and of those just four represent the interests of private boaters without which canals will become sterile ribbons of dead water. Is it any wonder that so many of us who spend time on the water feel unhappy at the way the waterways are being developed when it is so difficult to get our voices heard where the real power resides?

Ultimately, the strategy of licensing boats in an unregulated way without regard for the number the system can support will destroy what we value most about the canals, which is the opportunity they afford to escape the tumult of the 21st century. I thought canal rage was a joke when I first heard the term used. Today, it's a commonplace of cruising the cut and I've been guilty of it myself. But you'd have to be a saint not to get frustrated at having to spend your precious holiday queuing at locks or travelling miles beyond where you wanted to stop because you can't find a suitable mooring. And frustration quickly turns to anger.

Em, as so often happens, saw the way things were going long before I did. We'd had a narrowboat then for 13 years and with every month that passed, our private, sequestered world became less private and sequestered to the point where people who had once laughed at me for my enthusiasm were now canvassing me for advice on how to buy a boat of their own.

'I think we may have seen the best of this,' Em said to me one evening getting on for 30 years ago. 'It's not what it used to be any more.'

I seem to remember we were in a pub called The Navigation on the Grand Union, just north of Kingswood Junction in Warwickshire, though I can't be sure. Mind you, these days I can't be sure about much that far back. I have a notion it was the same evening we'd found a couple of hotel boats in the mooring where we were planning to stay for the night and we'd had to tie up over the other side of the canal instead. Whether it was the bizarre notion of a hotel boat, where people had their own cabins and paid for a cruise as if they'd been on an ocean liner, or whether it was because we felt we'd had a mooring we thought was ours stolen from us, I can't say. Either way, we were both feeling testy, as if we'd been cheated out of something that was ours by right. I didn't agree with what she said about having seen the best years, though. Far from it. I was getting restive. I wanted a new boat. A brand-new boat. A boat I could have built from scratch with a vintage engine and without the irritating defects of the one we already had. In the constant war of attrition that is marriage, I finally got my way and we had *Justice* built, and I hope Em will agree with me that neither of us have regretted that decision since, in that over the intervening years we've continued to derive a different sort of joy and delight from boating. Indeed, we can genuinely say we've had the best of both worlds, enjoying the canals as they were and also for what they've become.

But she was right, we *had* seen the best of them, though God knows why we were discussing it at that point in our lives at Kingswood Junction when we were far too young to be grumbling like a couple of old fogies about how the world was changing. That night in the pub, we got talking to the crew of the hotel boats who were our age, and we had a great time with them. We were still drinking and laughing when the landlord kicked us out at closing time, leaving us no option but to retire back to our boat with take-out, where we partied into the early hours.

I must have been thinking about all this as we cast off from Denver Sluice on the River Great Ouse because Em remarked how melancholic I seemed, and how locked into my own head. I shrugged off her kindly meant solicitations. It was a dull, overcast morning with the promise of rain in the air – one of those late-July days that are sent to remind us that summer can't last forever. The sky blackened as we approached Littleport, a small town founded by King Canute, which must be the only place in the country that prides itself on a statue, not of a local dignitary, but of a motorbike. This was erected in 2003 to commemorate William Harley, father of Harley-Davidson's co-founder who was born here before he emigrated to the United States.

As we walked back to the boat after doing some shopping it began to drizzle, and soon afterwards to rain quite heavily; but being so close to Ely, where we were planning to spend a few days, we decided to press on regardless. It was at that point we both registered something we'd forgotten, although it was something we'd talked about only recently: namely that this was the very first time in the many years we'd been boating that we'd ever travelled this way. For reasons of time as much as anything we'd never managed to penetrate the waterways this far into the east country, even though we knew that Ely and Cambridge were jewels of the system.

This was virgin territory. This was new stuff, fresh and exhilarating. It cheered us up despite the weather. We felt better in ourselves. We felt like we were explorers again. We felt like we were young once more.

A headwind suddenly blew up, fierce and purposeful as they are in this part of the world. It stung our cheeks and created wavelets that slapped against our hull and tossed us about, adding to the general catalogue of unpleasantness with which we were burdened on this leg of our journey. But then in the way it often does at the end of the day, the weather changed abruptly. The wind dropped, the waves abated and the river suddenly became millpond calm, glistening like asphalt in a frost. At the same time, the clouds lifted and with it the rain; and the sun appeared low on the horizon, lighting the world with a soft crimson wash. At that point, rising out of the low hill on which it stands, we saw that 'ship of the Fens' that is Ely cathedral and its famous octagonal lantern tower caught in the beams of the setting sun as if fixed in a spotlight beneath the still thunderous clouds above.

The way the light played on it was like that technique Rembrandt uses in his paintings, that startling contrast between light and dark which artists call chiaroscuro. It seemed like a sign. It *was* a sign.

18

To Cambridge and St Ives

Our first summer living on the boat is seared into my memory because it was so wonderful. And yet it started so badly. Leaving home was more harrowing than either of us anticipated. We thought it would be easy, just a simple move to a place that was so familiar to us it was almost like a second home. We'd spent so long on the boat over so many years, you'd have thought we'd have known what we were letting ourselves in for. Except that when we were confronted with the reality of what renting out our house meant we were naively unprepared, and it wasn't until we'd crammed the cat and what belongings we could into the car and left London that the implications fully hit us. After all, we were leaving a home we loved. We were handing it over to other people, strangers we didn't know. There was no going back now; this was a done deal. The cat seemed to know it. She howled the whole way.

The journey to *Justice* was a nightmare. We drove up the M40 in an atrocious storm. Visibility was so restricted that traffic moved at a snail's pace and kept grinding to a halt. If we'd known it was going to be as bad we'd have delayed our departure, except that wasn't an option because we'd signed a legal agreement with the tenants specifying the handover date and they were knocking on the door that morning eager to get in. When we arrived in Banbury, the rain was lashing down and the delays meant it was getting dark, too. We were exhausted. We hadn't got the energy to do more than cart our stuff in a wheelbarrow from the nearby B&Q car park to the boat, where we dumped it on to the deck and threw a tarpaulin over it. We could deal with the problems tomorrow. Tomorrow was a new day.

I find it painful even now recalling the despondency I felt that first night, forlornly surveying those few things we'd brought with us sitting outside in the rain like so much abandoned junk. Inside, the boat was in a dreadful state. Our friend John had been working on it for a couple of weeks, replacing the galley and upgrading some of our facilities; but he'd been running late on the job and we learned later that he'd only finished a couple of hours before we arrived. The place was filled with old screw boxes, spent silicon cartridges and packaging. Wood shavings covered the floor, and sawdust lay in a patina across every surface. We cleaned up the bedroom as best we could and lay that night, the cat at our feet, clutching each other, convulsed by the folly of what we'd done. We'd given up our comfortable London home for this. What on earth were we thinking?

The rain was still lagging down the next day and it didn't let up for the next week as we finalised preparations for our trip. It was still raining when we slipped our moorings and left and still lagging down when we moored up that night. Even inside the cabin of a boat you can never get away from rain. You glimpse it through windows, hitting the canal; you hear it on the roof, hammering down, relentlessly reminding you of its presence. In the middle of winter, when the days are short and the nights long, when the fire is blazing in the hearth and the wind is rocking you gently from side to side like a cradle, this can be comforting. But in the summer, when it's too warm to light the fire and the long days stretch out endlessly, and everything is damp and miserable, including you, well, what else can you feel except wretched? We'd only been away from home a matter of weeks but already we were starting to miss it. Or at least miss its comforts and the licence it gave us to lock ourselves away from the world, weather and all.

Yet astonishingly, the following morning when we woke everything had changed beyond recognition. Overnight – and entirely contrary to what the weather forecasts were predicting – the rain had cleared, the clouds had dispersed and the sun was shining brightly. And no doubt it would probably have been smiling too if it could have done, like that creepy *Teletubbies'* sun with the baby face. From then on, it got warmer and warmer, and not just warm but hot, very hot indeed, a Mediterranean heat that burned you to a crisp in no time if you were stupid enough to stay in it for long without protection. It remained like that for months on end with barely a cloud in the sky.

We cruised down the River Thames in these dog days, which turned out to be one of the hottest summers of recent years. On occasions it was so torrid we couldn't function properly until the evening, when we ate on deck and sat there into the early hours basking in the cool air, gathering ourselves for the day ahead. On a boat, you're fully exposed to the sun: it hits you directly from above, and unless you're passing through woodland there's no respite from it, no shade anywhere. It hits you reflecting off the water, too; and if there's the barest suggestion of a breeze it aggravates the effects, drying out your skin so that at the end of the day your face feels like an overcooked slab of steak. There were days that were so hot that if we ventured out at all it was only to sit reeking of suntan lotion under umbrellas, sipping at chilled drinks until the ice in them melted. We'd watch iridescent blue damselflies playing mating games around the boat. We'd fan ourselves with the books we were pretending to read and wave languidly to other boats with crews more resolute than us and more determined not to interrupt their journeys.

Who'd live in England with this weather, wet and dismal one day, cloudless and sweltering the next? And yet who'd live anywhere else? I would hate to have to wake up in a climate like Quibdó in Colombia, said to be the wettest city in the world, where it rains every day for months on end. Or Mawsynram, which has rainfall ten times India's national average. Blimey, Manchester's bad enough. But equally, I wouldn't want it monotonously warm and sunny either. San Diego? LA? You can keep them as far as I'm concerned. The Canaries? Not a place to tweet home @bout in my opinion. Just imagine how tedious the weather forecasts must be. 'And today it's going to be sunny and warm … the same as it was yesterday, the same as it'll be tomorrow…'

This was the thing about that summer on the Thames. There was something unnatural about it, something implausible and slightly dubious. I puzzled long and hard over what that might be until it struck me that weather like this just wasn't English. There was something suspiciously foreign about it, like a hint of garlic in your chips. Travelling up the Great Ouse towards Ely and beyond was more my cup of tea. This was three years later, and it was the sort of summer I could deal with. Blue skies, yes; but lots of clouds, too, the fluffy ones like wads of cotton wool, each pure white but with a darker edge as if to remind you not to go out without an umbrella. Long periods of sunshine as well; but nothing too excessive, nothing too knackering. When the sun comes out in Britain you shouldn't have to go inside to shelter from it, you should be able to cast off as many clothes as you decently can and go out and enjoy it. That's the way we do things here. We work on the basis that if you don't get out and enjoy the benefits of a sunny day while you can, you probably won't see another until the far side of next spring.

Ely's a place worth travelling halfway around the world to see, let alone halfway across the country on a narrowboat. We kept returning to it during the time we spent on the Great Ouse, partly because moorings are limited and so tightly controlled we could only stay there in short bursts, but mainly because the place draws you back in ways it's easy to understand. It's an alluring city with charming narrow streets, red steeply angled tiled roofs and, of course, that spectacular cathedral, which, naturally, we had to visit as everyone who comes to Ely does. It was the Octagon or Lantern Tower, the lower of the cathedral's two towers, that interested us most – even me despite my ingrained antipathy to ecclesiastic architecture, not to mention my vertigo. There's something about that exquisitely designed tower that is so uplifting it would have atheists queuing for baptism. From below, it's spectacular enough. It seems to float high above the space created where the nave crosses the transept. Perched on top of internal arches that support a series of fan-vaulted ceilings, the central part of the tower rises higher yet. On each of its eight sides, above what appear to be tiny paintings representing the celestial throng, are stained-glass windows that in a certain light glow like a lantern, giving the tower its name and illuminating the figure of God the Almighty who sits in the centre of another vaulted dome above. Even an addled old sceptic like me couldn't remain immune to its grandeur.

But impressive though all this is, up in the tower itself it's even more awe-inspiring. We booked a tour that took us across the roof and into it by a side entrance. It was rebuilt in wood after the original stone Norman tower collapsed in 1322, when no one was going to trust the foundations a second time. The massive timber beams used were hewn from trees 250 years old when they were felled – so huge that it's said we couldn't build anything like this today because we haven't got trees big enough. But then (spoiler alert) just as I thought I couldn't be further impressed with Ely Cathedral, the tour leader suddenly threw open one of the boards around the narrow walkway along which we'd been shuffling. It wasn't just a board, it was a door, an enormous door. And on the other side of it – the side that faced into the cathedral – was one of those apparently 'tiny' paintings of the celestial host we'd seen from below. They weren't tiny at all, they just seemed like that because we'd looked at them from so far away. In fact they were huge. Em took a picture of me against them from the opposite side and they tower above me, a staggering 20–25ft (6–7.6m) high.

The tour guide beamed with pleasure. He was used to this sort of response from visitors. Indeed, the gusto with which he'd thrown open the door was designed to evoke it. It was theatre, pure theatre. However, what happened next was simply serendipity. Or maybe, literally, a godsend. For at that moment from within the depths of the cathedral below rose the voices of a heavenly choir. Well, the cathedral choir, at least. It must have been one of its regular practices. All the same, it was still heavenly.

Ely is built on a hill, the highest point of the Fens. At 85ft (25.9m), it's not exactly Ben Nevis, but from the cathedral roof you can see how that had once made it an island, the surrounding agricultural flatlands of today once a marshy quagmire, a muddy and dangerous swamp connected to the outside world by only a few causeways.

The city exudes the sense of a different, older England more than any other English city I know. And it does this without locking itself into the past as so many of these heritage venues do. It may seem odd to say it of somewhere lauded for its great age, but it's a very contemporary city too, remarkably so. Other places have followed modern fashion in encouraging the return of independent traders, markets and specialist food shops, which they lost years ago. Ely seems to have had them all along and it adds a reassuring continuity in the way the city feels. There's a fascinating antiques emporium where I bought some brasswork for the boat, for instance. There's a pork butcher selling some of the tastiest scotch eggs I've ever eaten. And there's an old-style market where one stall sells traditional baskets woven out of locally harvested rushes. All over the place, wherever you look, there seem to be idiosyncratic pubs and tea rooms, some of them so intimate it's like dropping into someone's living room.

Still, all this doesn't completely explain why Ely can get under your skin in the way it did with me and the way it does with many others, why months later some sudden recollection of it can flash into your mind, insistent and unprovoked. It might be a building, a view, or some vaguely recalled incident that happened there. Even now, I often find myself mentally retracing the short walk from the river through Jubilee Gardens and up past the site of the old castle, where you get an unrivalled view of the side of the cathedral nestled beside a meadow with sheep grazing on it as if it were a field in the middle of the countryside. Em and I did that walk on many occasions at all times of day, but I loved it most in the evening when you could smell the fragrance of bruised grass and hear the distant sound of evensong from the cathedral. That view moved me in a way so much of Ely did – though maybe this was just my threadbare soul responding unconsciously to the sanctity of the surroundings. Which would be odd really – and not only because I'm a dyed-in-the-wool secular cynic, but because although the cathedral is a sacred place, it's equally a symbol of conquest, subjugation and dominance.

It was built by the Normans, along with the nearby castle, only the mound of which exists today. This was the pattern of things for the invaders after the Conquest, when both were signs that they'd finally got these Anglo-Saxon bastards under their thumb and could now start screwing them for everything they'd got. The Normans had particular reasons for wanting to subjugate Ely, because it was where Hereward the Wake made his last stand after a long guerrilla war of resistance against their occupation. You don't hear much of Hereward the Wake nowadays. Years back, there was a kids' TV series based on him, which made him into a sort of outlaw along the lines of Robin Hood; and back in Victorian times he was a cult figure whose reputation was secured after Charles Kingsley of *Water Babies* and *Westward Ho!* fame wrote a novel about him, the subtitle of which was 'The Last of the English'. Now that's a difficult concept to get your head around isn't it, since it begs the question of what it is to be English. Like, is there some bloodstock from before the Conquest that precludes you from calling yourself English unless you share it? Like, is everyone since Hereward the Wake *not* English since we're all infected by the Normans now? Covid-1066, perhaps?

It's odd how we English adulate these fringe outsiders confronting European influence, whether it's Hereward the Wake in Ely, Boudicca leading the Celts in an uprising against the Roman invasion, or indeed, to some people, Nigel Farage sitting in the European Parliament raging against ... well, raging against the European Parliament. It's almost as if we need to build our national narrative around these self-appointed warriors for sovereignty who confront the flow of history regardless of the social cost of their resistance and in the face of what so often proves to be the hopelessness of their cause.

Ely's other favourite son, Oliver Cromwell, was made of sterner stuff. He lived in Ely for more than ten years and his house is on the city's tourist trail. Cromwell became Lord Protector of England, so much a king that he was eventually offered the throne – which at least he had the good grace to refuse since to have done otherwise would have been a travesty of decency. After all, he'd signed the previous king's death warrant and finished up as leader of one faction of a civil war, which like all civil wars had brought out the worst sort of savagery in the combatants. Forget the deeply held principles for which the two sides fought. Why not? They've been forgotten years ago by everyone else except academics in university history departments. The fact is that for beliefs that seem trivial to us today, some 100,000 died and probably as many again lost their lives as a result of the ensuing famine and disease. This was 3.6 per cent of the population, a greater percentage than died in the First World War. Make no mistake about it, the English Civil War was a bloody and savage period of our past and we wouldn't want another ever again.

But time sanitises history's worst horrors for contemporary consumption. Even the words used to describe events hide their awfulness. The words 'civil war' sound inoffensive in the context of something that happened so long ago. A bit like 'hanged, drawn and quartered'. Or 'plague'. It's only when you take time out to consider the reality of what the words describe that you understand the dreadfulness of them. That's why when I think about the Civil War I can't help thinking too that so much of human conflict is futile since whoever successfully challenges the establishment eventually becomes the establishment. It'll happen with Brexit as well, mark my words. You could say it already has.

Much as we both loved Ely, sometimes we had to get out of the place. It became too hot and muggy even on the river and sometimes too crowded, especially at weekends when the place filled with visitors piling into the bars and restaurants along the river frontage. There aren't that many mooring spaces in town, and in that it's a little like York, which doesn't go out of its way to encourage visitors by boat either because it gets so many visitors anyhow. In Ely, you only get to moor free for periods of 48 hours. Any longer and they have river rangers like traffic wardens who'll chase you for the £100 a day it costs to stay longer. £100! It's not cheap for a 24-hour stay anywhere barring, perhaps, the Grand Canal in Venice. In fact, it's so steep you might be forgiven for thinking it wasn't so much a charge but more a fine to discourage you from staying longer. But no, that would be entirely wrong. If it were a fine there would have to be legal processes associated with it. Like being able to defend yourself against it in a court, for example. But no, in Ely the £100 is a charge – though it is interesting that if you pay it within 14 days it reduces to £70. Just like a fine, in fact…

We couldn't be bothered with the hassle. We used to go upstream to the River Cam near Wicken Fen a couple of hours away, where you could get a drink at the nearby pub and spend the night on tranquil GOBA moorings. Thank God for GOBA, I say. GOBA is the Great Ouse Boating Association and my top tip for cruising the Great Ouse is to join before you get anywhere close because the EA, who oversee the river, have all but given up providing moorings and left it to this charitable members organisation to do the job for them. GOBA moorings are sited all along the river, and of course if you wanted you could take advantage of their facilities without joining; they won't send river rangers out to apprehend you, that's for sure. But surely you wouldn't be that much of a cheapskate, would you? A year's membership only costs a quarter of what you'd pay for a night's overstay in Ely.

Wicken Fen is a 600-acre (254-hectare) wetland nature reserve owned by the National Trust that you get to by turning off at the pub on to what are called the Cambridgeshire 'Lodes' – a term surviving from Late Middle English meaning watercourses. They were originally built by the Romans but are unnavigable for a boat as deep-draughted as *Justice* so what on earth made us try to navigate them I haven't the first idea. We were with friends who were visiting for a few days and we managed to negotiate the lock, which was the first hazard on this insane attempt to do the impossible. Then we stuck fast in the mud. It was immediately clear that this was as far as we were going to get and so we ran up the white flag, moored and had a pleasant lunch on deck before spending the next couple of hours reversing the 200 yards (182m) back through the mire to the lock we'd just come through. We must have been crazy. We *were* crazy. But if you're going to manhandle a 20-ton narrowboat from one end of the country to the other, it helps sometimes to be crazy.

The pub where you turn is called, somewhat charmingly, Five Miles From Anywhere No Hurry Inn, a name that, unlike the Dog in a Doublet, won't be shortlisted for awards for creativity any time soon, but that does tell you all you need to know about a place that is, indeed, right out in the sticks. The mooring opposite is delightful, and that night with our friends we brought our dining table out on to the wide towpath and ate al fresco in the balmy evening, watching great crested grebes diving as they fed. They're fascinating birds, and the trick with them after they've plunged underwater is seeing where they surface, since this can often be so far away it's as if they've disappeared.

You see great crested grebes from time to time on the waterways; they aren't rare. On the Great Ouse, however, there are so many of them that they're almost emblematic of the river. It's hard to believe these elegant birds were almost hunted to extinction by Victorian egg collectors and clothing manufacturers, who used their feathers for hats and their skin and the soft underpelt of their breast as a sort of fake fur. At one stage, it's estimated the birds were down to just 40 pairs in the UK and their plight was one of the main reasons the Royal Society for the Protection of Birds (RSPB) was founded in 1889. It makes me weep even to even think about it. Quite apart from their ornate head plumes, their leonine burnished mane and their stylish stiletto-sharp beaks, they have the most extraordinary courtship ritual involving much shrill clucking and head shaking that once seen is never forgotten. Later, when the chicks hatch from the floating platforms where they nest, they arrive looking like fluffy zebras, so unlike their parents that if I were a great crested grebe I'd have some serious questions of my mate about what she'd been getting up to. They *are* sweet, though. They travel on mum's back like cygnets sometimes do.

We cruised into Cambridge the following day and because of the good offices of some friends we managed to get a mooring on Midsummer Common in a space left vacant by the usual occupant, who'd gone off to a remote Scottish island as one of the contestants in a Channel Four reality documentary series. This is about as unusual a reason as you'll ever hear for copping a mooring space this convenient, but Em and I were grateful for it all the same – though I doubt the occupant of the space we borrowed was as happy about his foray into the world of television since the show was taken off the air after four episodes for lack of viewers.

Cattle still graze the common so it's not unusual on a boat to look out of your window here to see a huge rare-breed Red Poll cow looking back at you. It couldn't have been a better-sited mooring for getting into the centre of town, but its drawback was that it lay opposite a number of college rowing clubs, which were out practising every morning at ridiculous times. The river is narrow at this point, and though mercifully they keep the flotillas of summer punts away from this section, when the rowing crews were out they frequently passed so close to us they scuffed our hull. This we didn't mind too much. *Justice* is a tough old girl and can take a knock or two. But what did hack us off was their wash, which we could scarcely believe was caused by boats as light as a feather. One thing was for sure: we were never in danger of sleeping late. So much turbulence did they cause that some mornings we had to hang on to each other in bed for fear we'd get bounced out of it.

It goes without saying that Cambridge is as fascinating as you'd expect from such a renowned and ancient city. It's filled with illustrious libraries and galleries and venerable old colleges. But as our home port of Banbury is close to Oxford, we're used to illustrious libraries and galleries and venerable old colleges. In fact, it's fair to say that over the years we've had it up to the back teeth with them. Besides, like Oxford, Cambridge is a bear garden in the summer months. The pavements are packed with dozy sightseers sucking ice creams, noisy frat-house college kids over from the United States for summer school, or bands of overseas tourists gobbling like a raft of turkeys as they criss-cross on the paths, vying to take the best photograph. At lunchtime, Midsummer Common became a picnic park, and some evenings you couldn't walk along the towpath for hordes of entranced lovers arm in arm, blocking the way. We couldn't take it for long. We made a visit to the Pepys Library in Magdalene College to see the famous diaries, which was interesting and at least bearable because they restricted numbers. But hacking around the quadrangle at Queens' College was the last straw. We were shuffling along with hundreds of others around the outside while in the middle a select group, preening like peacocks, enjoyed the commodious conviviality of a wedding reception. At the centre of the small cluster was the newly appointed Secretary of State for Brexit, David Davis. I'm not certain but I think that was the same David Davis who was arguing during the referendum campaign that the British establishment was too entitled.

We turned back downstream and at Pope's Corner, the confluence of the Cam with the Great Ouse, we turned our tiller not towards Ely again, but in the other direction, up what's called The Old West towards St Ives, where the route beckoned us with banks thick with goldenrod and red campion. We were heading ultimately for Bedford, which would have to be the

287

end of our journey. Not only was summer petering out faster than we could keep track, but we'd heard from our tenants back in London that they were intending to vacate the house at the end of the contract. This unexpected bit of news had set us thinking for the first time in years about our future plans. Were we intending to keep on travelling as we had? Or was this some sort of augury of the end, a natural break that fate had decreed for us? Looked at one way, it did seem that way. The fact is, as things stand you can't go further than Bedford in a boat: it's a dead end, a natural full stop.

We pressed on, and towards St Ives we were astonished to come across a crew cutting rushes for what we discovered was the still-surviving craft of rush weaving. They were led by Felicity Irons, an affable woman whom we spent a while chatting with, us leaning on the tiller on the back deck and her balanced nonchalantly on a wobbling punt. She and her team must surely be the only surviving rush cutters in the country, harvesting the crop from flat-bottomed punts using traditional long-handled bill hooks and weaving it mainly into floor coverings. Known as medieval or apple matting, they grace all sorts of locations, from the Globe Theatre in London to New York's Metropolitan Museum of Art. Unsurprisingly, the National Trust is a big customer of hers as well. Felicity also makes high-end baskets and table mats, selling them worldwide through Ralph Lauren shops. Craft skills don't come cheap though, as I found when coincidentally I had bought one of her baskets in Ely a few days before as a souvenir. It was a tiny thing, small enough to fit in the palm of your hand, and it would embarrass me to tell you what I paid for it. But hand on heart, who would have thought this onetime staple of the Fenland economy still existed at all? And who would resent shelling out a few quid to encourage it?

We were reminded of another traditional Fenland industry when we berthed at St Ives and spotted an eel in the water near to the quay as we were tying up. It was a wondrous sighting since these once-common creatures, with their extraordinary life cycle, which starts in the Sargasso Sea 3,700 miles (5,955km) away off the coast of Bermuda, have been fished to the point at which they're now on the endangered species list. At one time, they were caught in huge numbers along the Great Ouse using traditional willow traps called hives. The Domesday Book records 52,000 of them being caught in one year, and at periods during the Middle Ages they were used as a local currency, with surrounding villages paying their taxes with them. In recent years, thank God, there has been considerable improvement in numbers with the invention of a new design of eel pass, which allows thousands to return to their traditional haunts in what had been described as the biggest migration since the 1970s.

Up until a couple of hundred years ago, St Ives was an important market centre and a bustling hub of river trade. The quayside – what is now called the Old Riverport – still has the feel of a harbour about it, though the many bawdy houses that always seem to be associated with boats and sailors have long since closed so that now the town has that easy-going, chilled ambience typical of English market towns in rural areas. We moored there for a couple of nights in the shadow of the town's splendid 15th-century six-arched bridge, which unusually incorporates a chapel halfway across it. Two of the bridge arches were blown up by Oliver Cromwell during the Civil War to construct a defensive drawbridge, and when these came to be replaced later they were rebuilt in a different style, with rounder apexes rather than sharper Gothic ones. The difference is obvious when it's pointed out – which is more than you can say for the road that leads off the bridge southwards away from the town. This is the old London Road, though unless you climb down to the meadow below, you'd hardly give it a second glance even if you were told it was something special. From underneath, however, you can see that it's a raised causeway laid on 55 brick arches to carry the road across the river floodplain, and in its own way it's as impressive as the bridge.

St Ives was a lovely place to be, but with the prospect of a possible return to London suddenly on the agenda, we'd got into that zone of boating where we were seeking complete isolation to work out what we were going to do. So, after stocking up with supplies, we moved up to Houghton Meadows a couple of miles upriver, a nature reserve that, when we arrived, was blooming with a carpet of blinding yellow buttercups and purple clover. We never did get the isolation we were craving, however, for this Site of Special Scientific Interest is a popular picnic spot, where the kids splash around on the river beaches. And who would begrudge them that? There are so many places on the waterways you'd describe as idyllic that the word quickly becomes meaningless. But Houghton Meadows really *is* idyllic and it's wonderful that local folk still have access to it.

A little further upriver is the impressively restored National Trust Houghton Mill, which is grinding flour again after a 30-year career as a youth hostel. We visited it as part of a delightful circular walk we did one day, ambling back to St Ives along one bank of the river and returning via the Ouse Valley Way on the other. En route, we took in stops for tea in a cafe with a river terrace in town, and a drink at the Axe and Compass in Hemingford Abbots, a picture-postcard village of beautifully maintained thatched cottages and more Neighbourhood Watch signs than I've seen in a long time.

We'd have enjoyed the walk more if it hadn't been for the niggling question about possibly going back to London. We'd got an email that morning from the estate agent. They wanted to know whether we wanted them to find us new tenants. Decisions were going to have to be made soon.

19

To Bedford and home

As we'd got closer to it, the warnings about Bedford from those on the river became more feverish. At Houghton Meadows, the skipper of a large gin-palace of a cruiser that moored next to us shook his head incredulously when we told him our plans. 'You need to be careful,' he said. 'They can be funny up there.'

I couldn't work out what he meant. Funny? Did they all wear harlequin suits and sport red noses? Were they all cracking bad jokes about the rest of us? Criticising the way we dressed? Or did he mean funny, as in strange. As in Royston Vasey and the *League of Gentlemen* strange? Were the people there 'local'? Were they people who wouldn't welcome outsiders? Cue spooky music.

In St Neots they told us it was unsafe to moor in Bedford. In Huntingdon they said it was downright dangerous. But for me, the last straw was some geezer outside The Anchor at Great Barford, where I stood surveying the 17 arches of the beautiful bridge, one of the most impressive on the whole river. He was bending my ear about all the horrors I'd face in Bedford, from street muggers to marauding gangs of vandals.

'You know it well then, do you?' I asked.

'Haven't visited for years,' he replied. 'Wild horses wouldn't drag me there.'

True, it was hard going by boat, but that was more down to the EA, who clearly hadn't spent any more time maintaining the river than they had the locks on it, which had been a pain all the way up, every one of them needing some sort of knack to get them to work. The river was shallow and it badly needed dredging, and as it got narrower the tree cover got denser for want of pruning until at last it was sweeping the flowers we kept on the roof into the water. Well, it was late in the year. The geraniums were getting a bit leggy. We had other more serious things than flowers to worry about.

Actually, when we finally reached Bedford and negotiated the tricky lock at what seems to be the end of the river, we suddenly found ourselves on a wide and elegant waterway bounded by fine balustraded buildings like the imposing Swan Hotel, which looked as if it was on standby as the location for a Jane Austen costume drama. Along the banks was a meticulously tended park, draped with decorative willows, and linked to the town by a strikingly modern bridge, the Butterfly Bridge, as it's known locally, which is not unlike the Millennium Bridge in London. As for those marauding gangs of vandals we were warned about. Well, we did see a few elderly people out for a constitutional, and a few mums with their kids enjoying the sunshine. The river was very busy with canoes and scullers, too, but I don't think any of them were out to mug us.

A little-known fact about Bedford is that it has a large Italian population – about 14,000 of the 100,000 who live there. They came in numbers after the war when there was a critical labour shortage in the brick-making industry, still a significant employer in these parts. Many couldn't stand the chill weather, or the chill reception, not to mention the conditions in which they were housed, which was frequently in former prisoner of war camps; but large numbers stayed, contributing not just to the local economy but also to Bedford's reputation as one of the best places in the country to get Italian food. We went to a pizzeria recommended by one of Em's former work colleagues who lived in the place. Trust me, Pizza Express it was not. It was midweek but the place was heaving with customers and as soon as we got our order we could see why. That pizza was remarkable, so delicious that it tasted of Italy, so authentic that it wouldn't have surprised me to hear it burst into an operatic aria.

'What do you think then?' I asked Em as I knocked back the remnants of the Valpolicella in my glass and topped up both of us ready for *that* conversation, the one we'd been promising each other for the past few days.

She knew what I was talking about; she'd obviously been considering the question a lot. 'The way I see it, we don't have much choice,' she said immediately. 'If we decide to keep renting the house then we're going to have to go back to London to see the estate agent and find new tenants. That's not going to happen overnight and already it's getting towards the end of summer...'

'But if we don't keep renting, what then? Are we going to keep travelling and leave the house unoccupied?'

'I don't think I'd be keen on that,' she admitted. 'I'd be too worried about something happening – a break-in, or a burst pipe. Besides, if the house was sitting empty I'd be inclined to go back to it this winter anyway.'

I took a bite of my pizza and knocked back another glug of wine. I could see the way this conversation was going. The truth is that though we were both loath to accept it, we'd made the decision. I have to admit, it made me feel sorrowful. There was too much of a sense of an ending about it for my liking, too much like breaking up with someone after a long relationship. 'Well, that does seem to settle it then, doesn't it?' I said at length. 'It looks to me that whichever way we cut it, we're leaving the waterways and going back home.'

For a moment or two Em didn't react. She looked down at her plate and then surveyed the restaurant distractedly. 'Four years.

It's been unforgettable,' she said finally, addressing the room so that I couldn't see her eyes, which I knew had teared up.

'It's been a long time,' I said, blinking back some tears of my own. 'I wouldn't have missed it for the world.'

We left Bedford the next morning on a grey and overcast day that smelled of autumn. Yes, there was a sense of ending about the decision we'd taken the previous night, but over the previous few weeks both of us could see the way things were going. Too much had happened that pointed that way and it couldn't all be blamed on the tenants. First, there was the side door on *Justice*, which we'd caught coming into a lock that had knocked a hinge and made it difficult to close. It was a trivial matter in the run of things, but it was a nuisance and it would need repairing, a job that would be insignificant back at our home moorings, but that was likely to be a pain in the neck on the move.

A couple of days later, we had another, more significant mishap when I was pulling the boat into the bank at an approach to another lock, and the fixing for our centre rope gave way. The weld holding it to the boat had fractured. This was an altogether more serious problem. When you're cruising on a narrowboat, the centre rope is critical, the one you depend on the most. It's the one you use to hold a boat waiting to enter a lock, the one you use in the lock to control it when the paddles are opened and it's getting tossed about from pillar to post. Of course, you can manage without it, but without it life gets difficult. These irritating breakages coming close together didn't stop us cruising but they did make us wonder if someone was telling us something.

Then there was my knee. My knee had never been right since wrenching it at the water point in Banbury at the very start of our travels. Over the years we'd been on the boat I'd had to go back to London from time to time for orthopaedic consultations, and eventually I'd been offered a replacement, which I'd had to refuse with some regret. What else could I have done? How could I have serious surgery, living as I was? How would it be possible for me to convalesce hauling a steel narrowboat around the waterways? Besides, by a regime of diet and exercises I'd unearthed on the net, I'd managed to effect some encouraging improvement. It wasn't that my knee didn't still trouble me, but it seemed to be strengthening and not hurting as much as it did. But I was deceiving myself. At St Neots, when we were coming through the lock, all the improvements I'd worked so hard and for so long on were reversed in one agonising moment when I felt something twist under my kneecap and I suddenly found myself on the ground writhing in agony, barely able to stand let alone walk. I took a taxi to a local surgery and a doctor gave me painkillers and ordered me back to bed to rest up for a few days. The idea was to try and take the weight off my leg but with my lifestyle he might as well have asked me to stop putting food in my stomach. Putting my feet up would have been unfeasible at the best of times. But this wasn't the best of times. It was a time when we were having problems with the lavatory...

Ah, yes, the lavatory. You didn't think you were going to read a book about the waterways without lavatories being mentioned at least once, did you? It has to be the Number One topic of discussion whenever boaters get together. It's what we talk about when you see us huddling in canalside pubs, what we're whispering about when you see us clustering conspiratorially on the towpath. It's unwholesome talk, this toilet stuff; civilians really shouldn't be party to it. But it's important to us boaters, a key part of our lives afloat.

Recently, there's been a growing use of composting toilets on boats, but most of us still use one of two other main systems, one more familiar than the other to those who live in houses in that you flush your lavatory and – hey presto! – the contents disappear.

Except this is a boat. They don't actually disappear anywhere. What they do is finish in a holding tank, which is generally positioned under your bed. This is neither an ideal location nor a nice idea. Neither does it make for a particularly attractive bouquet if the system malfunctions, as they sometimes can, especially in summer. The alternative is a more rudimentary system, a version of the old 'bucket and chuck it' method whereby you deposit your emissions into a cassette that you empty at disposal points located regularly along canals. We carry four of these cassettes, one in use and three as back-ups; but the trouble was they were all filled up and we weren't on the canals. We were on the Great Ouse, where the EA hasn't made adequate provision for sewage disposal.

We soon found out why.

'Just chuck it in the river,' one boater said to us without embarrassment. I couldn't believe what I was hearing. What? Throw it over the side? Where we'd seen kids splashing around in the water just a few days before?

'Yes, just chuck it. Everybody does. The Environment Agency knows,' said a man at a boatyard when we complained to him about the situation. I still couldn't believe that a government agency committed to upholding the highest environmental standards was party to allowing boats to dispose of their effluence into a river that passes so many illustrious and venerable cities. I mean, do the good burghers of Ely know this is happening? Do their eminences on the councils of St Ives, Bedford and St Neots actually care that this crap – literal crap – is floating past their beautifully maintained parks, which are such an attraction to residents and visitors alike?

We couldn't bring ourselves to do it. Instead, we'd instigated a rigorous regime of using the facilities in local pubs and cafes, a practice I had to adhere to despite my infirmity, which had reduced mobility to a three-legged shuffle with a walking stick.

At least deciding to return to London meant that we'd have to go back to Denver Sluice, where on the way through we'd noticed there was a rare disposal point. Not that this was much use when it came down to it. It was out of order and it had obviously been like that for months on end. That hadn't stopped people using it, however – if you can describe them pouring stuff over the floor in that way. What riles me is that it must have been boaters who did it. It *has* to have been.

That night, we capitulated to the inevitable, and as soon as darkness had fallen we emptied our cassettes into the water, where hopefully the tide shifted them eventually out into the Wash. I only hope the stuff didn't finish up next to any narrowboat beached on a crossing. It struck me that perhaps I'd misjudged the seals. Perhaps it wasn't them who stank so much.

You can move quite quickly on the waterways when you set your mind to it. It stands to reason. They were once industrial thoroughfares and people didn't hang around when they were transporting goods, materials or perishable agricultural produce. Time was money, then as much as now. Em and I didn't travel fast, we certainly didn't speed, but we took to rising early in the morning and travelling until last light, after which we'd eat and collapse into bed exhausted. We slipped back across the Middle Level and were soon back in Northampton, where, in one of those English idiosyncrasies that define us as a nation, the pronunciation of the River Nene changes from 'Neen', as in bean – which it is in the east – to 'Nen', as in pen – which it is in the west as the river moves into the Midlands. We took a break for a couple of days in the beguiling village of Elton, where we moored between an enormous derelict mill and an enormous bull, which persisted in disporting his tackle shamelessly every morning at the bathroom porthole. Em didn't know where to look; he was enormous and I couldn't look anywhere else.

Elton's a sublimely beautiful village of wide tree-lined grass verges and honeystone cottages with thatched roofs and long eaves that sweep down to the street. It also has a pub, the Crown Inn, which stands in its own courtyard shaded by an enormous chestnut tree. We went for a drink there one lunchtime and for no reason we could rationally think of a local farmer had brought a sow and her litter of piglets to show off. He sat outside in the sunshine at one of the wooden tables, a rotund, red-faced man straight out of central casting, a pint in front of him and a huge beaming smile on his face, while the piglets and their mother reclined in a pen next to him, gently snoring as they dozed. Elton's the sort of place you want to take American friends to show them that this sort of England really does exist outside of the major conurbations, though having cruised through both town and country in our decades of boating it seems that the stark contrast that there's always been between the two is more pronounced than ever now, as if each existed in a parallel universe, aware of each other but rarely engaging together.

We paused briefly, too, at Oundle, a small market town dominated by its venerable co-educational public school and still governed by the Worshipful Company of Grocers in the City of London, as it has been since its foundation in the 16th century. That seemed in a parallel universe, too. The place gives you the impression of an Oxbridge college so that anyone moving on to one of those universities would immediately feel comfortable. Its alumni include the playwright David Edgar and the feminist journalist Caroline Criado Perez, both of them talented people and both radicals in different ways, unafraid to challenge the status quo. But as someone from a dirt-poor working class family who still can't believe he managed to avoid the draft for a life as factory fodder or the dole, I can't help wondering how much easier it must surely be to fight the establishment when you're a part of it. I don't know, I really don't know. All I could think of was some of those no-hope estates we passed through in cities like Coventry, Liverpool and the old Manchester mill towns. The schools there look more like penal institutions than places of learning. What chance do people have in this country of ours when those who challenge how things are can only do it because they've benefitted from that system? How do you break a cycle like that when those few who succeed and manage to get to university are shamed for their accents, young women preyed on by posh boys who, according to recent reports, compete to seduce the poorest of them?

Em and I moored up a day or two later under the old castle mound at Fotheringhay. It's a haunting place, a sleepy hamlet with no more than a hundred or so inhabitants; yet it was once a place of extraordinary importance, its palatial castle the seat of the Yorkist faction who fought in the Wars of the Roses. This bit of floral flummery, which only came into common use in the 19th century, is, of course, a euphemism for another savage and brutal English civil war, which divided the country for the better part of 30 years. It culminated in the victory of Henry Tudor over Richard III at the Battle of Bosworth Field in 1485, after which Fotheringhay, the Yorkist stronghold, gradually fell into disrepair until it was barely used at all except as a place to confine high-status prisoners.

It's in that role that it's most famous, for a hundred years later – after shunting her around the country in various prisons for nearly 20 years – Queen Elizabeth I finally lost patience with her cousin Mary, Queen of Scots, who had designs on the English throne. Elizabeth dispatched her to Fotheringhay, where she was put on trial and eventually executed in the Great Hall. Afterwards, her body was stripped and her organs, including her heart, were buried somewhere inside the castle grounds, where presumably they still remain.

The Mary and Elizabeth story is surely one of the most compelling tales of British history, a sort of gripping soap opera that incorporates war, death, betrayal, kidnapping, rape and murder. The castle itself has long since been demolished – the castle mound now its only remaining feature. However, it's still a fitting memorial to the drama that happened there, the poignancy of which is so skillfully captured in Sandy Denny's moving song 'Fotheringay,' which imagines the final night before Mary's death.

Em and I walked to the top of the castle mound one evening after a warm day, when the long shadows of the dwindling sun were creeping across the fields burnished with the last embers of the day. We looked over the twisting river to a pasture that had only recently been cut and where long mounds of dampening grass lay in endless lines to the horizon melting into the treeline at the field edge. In the distance, we could see the remnants of corn fields cut to stubble, and beyond that a stratum of low cloud kissing the landscape like froth on a cappuccino kisses your lips. You could smell the freshly cut grass even so far away. Its scent seemed to blend with the smell of a thin mist that was beginning to rise from the water, a heady and unmistakable bouquet of the English countryside. It was silent, still, not a breath of wind in the air, not a bird moving in the sky. The day was gradually drawing to a close. Soon it would be dark. Soon we'd have to go back to the boat before it became too dangerous to negotiate the steep slope back.

People say they love England, but I never know what they mean by that when so many of them seem to know so little of it. When so many of them appear to know Siena better than Stafford, Benidorm better than Barnsley. Not that this prevents them from pontificating about England at the drop of a hat; I guess in these days of social media, folk feel more empowered to be more forthright about what they think, as if being born in a country endows them with some sort of instinctive knowledge about it without the need for any critical analysis. Yet most of us would have difficulty answering the questions about British traditions and customs that we expect immigrants to know in our citizenship test. And British culture, what's all that about then? *Corrie* and *EastEnders*? *The X Factor* and *Strictly*? I'd warrant most of us couldn't name one contemporary classical British composer, let alone a contemporary novelist, ballet dancer or opera singer. But this stuff is just elitist now, isn't it? It doesn't matter any more, right?

England isn't Fotheringhay, or the Lake District, or the Cornish coastline, Shropshire's Long Mynd or any other tourist spot for that matter. Yes, those places are a part of England and we should celebrate them as such. But there are other Englands, too, just as much the real England and just as important as well. Because all parts of the country, rich and poor, *are* equally important. Yet although we mouth this self-evident fact we don't seem to get it. I wonder if this is because most of us are myopic and can't see further than the ends of our noses. Like that guy posting on my timeline on Facebook recently, complaining that he'd met a Londoner who didn't know that Lancashire was a county. I couldn't help wondering if he knew that Waltham Forest and Havering were parts of London. And I couldn't help wondering how much he even knew of Lancashire. Would he know the Fylde, for instance? Would he know the Forest of Bowland or the old mill towns? *Really* know them, I mean. Or would wild horses not drag him to such places?

The sad truth is that most of us live in communities of similar people and we don't venture much beyond 20 or 30 miles (32–48.3km) of where we live. And on that basis, we make up our minds about the rest of the country. Which means we make up our minds based mainly on our prejudices, judging those who dwell on this small island of ours as cartoon images of the real.

301

Londoners are all wealthy bankers living in big houses. Mancs live in terraced streets and eat black pudding. Scousers are skiving layabouts. And all this is before we even get on to the racial stereotypes... Yes, we know the clichés. But do we realise how much we lean on them for our understanding of the world?

I'm sick to death of people accusing me of being unpatriotic because I welcome others from overseas to our land to share and contribute to our culture as those from overseas have done throughout history. I'm fed up of people accusing me of being less than English because I am proud of being a European, too. Frankly, I couldn't care less whether 'Land of Hope and Glory' is played at the Last Night of the Proms. I would just like it if people knew what the Proms were and how they'd come about, who'd composed the music and who'd written the lyrics.

But we're divided now in this country of ours, fractured down the middle by bad leadership based on flawed history. I have on my notice board in front of me as I write a collection of quotations from newspapers, magazines and the net, the common feature of which is how England excels. We have the best police in the world, the best legal system, the best television, the best health service, the best processes for beating infectious diseases. We have world-beating this, and world-beating that; we are the strongest, the biggest, the best, the most liberal. But it isn't true. And people would realise that if they just looked at their country with more appraising eyes. Or if they just looked at their country at all.

What we are is a small island off the north-west coast of Europe. And there's nothing wrong with that. As long as we can hang on to a few of our core values, such as empathy and decency, compromise in the face of disagreement, and respect for others at all times, then we've still time enough to build Jerusalem in this green and pleasant land.

However, if we can't learn how to get on with each other better, then I fear for the future. I can't help thinking about that famous quote from Yeats as he was meditating on the conflict in Ireland which led to the 1916 uprising and civil war:

'We had fed the heart on fantasies,
The heart's grown brutal from the fare,
More substance in our enmities
Than in our love'

Em and I left Fotheringhay the next morning. Soon, we were in Northampton where a flight of 17 narrow locks leads back to the Grand Union Canal and the main waterways system. Before long, we were in Banbury and shortly afterwards, back home in London.